A Grammar of Akɔɔse
A Northwest Bantu Language

SIL International and
The University of Texas at Arlington
Publications in Linguistics 143

Publications in Linguistics are published jointly by SIL Internatinal and the University od Texas Arlington. The series is a venue for works covering a broad range of topics in linguistics, especially the analytical treatment of minority languages from all parts of the world. While most volumes are authored by members of SIL, suitable works by others will also form part of the series.

Series Editors

Donald A. Burquest   Mary Ruth Wise
University of Texas at Arlington   SIL International

Volume Editors

Eugene E. Loos
Bonnie Brown

Production Staff

Judy Benjamin, Compositor
Barb Alber, Graphic Artist

A Grammar of Akɔɔse

A Northwest Bantu Language

Robert Hedinger

SIL International

and

The University of Texas at Arlington

© 2008 by SIL International
Library of Congress Catalog No: 2008935445
ISBN: 9781556712227
ISSN: 1040-0850

Printed in the United States of America

All rights reserved. No part of this publication may be reproduced, stored in a retrieval system, or transmitted in any form or by any means—electronic, mechanical, photocopy, record, or otherwise—without the express permission of the SIL International. However, short passages, generally understood to be within the limits of fair use, may be quoted without written permission.

Copies of this and other publications of the SIL International may be obtained from

International Academic Bookstore
SIL International
7500 W. Camp Wisdom Road
Dallas, TX 75236-5699

Voice: 972-708-7404
Fax: 972-708-7363
Email: academic_books@sil.org
Internet: http://www.ethnologue.com

Contents

Abbreviations and Symbols xii

1 Introduction and Outline of Phonology 1
   1.1 Introduction 1
   1.2 Outline of Phonology 3
      1.2.1 Consonants 4
      1.2.2 Vowels 5
      1.2.3 Syllable structure 5
      1.2.4 Assimilation and elision 6
      1.2.5 Tone 6
      1.2.6 Tone rules 7
      1.2.7 Alphabetical list of examples 8

2 The Noun 11
   2.1 Noun classes 11
   2.2 Noun genders 12
      2.2.1 Examples of count nouns by gender 13
      2.2.2 Examples of non-count nouns by gender 15
   2.3 Agreement or noun class concord 16
      2.3.1 Agreement within the noun phrase 16

		2.3.2	Agreement between subject and verb	16
		2.3.3	Agreement across clauses	16
		2.3.4	Exceptions	17
		2.3.5	Summary tables of noun class and concord prefixes	19
	2.4		Internal structure of the noun	22
		2.4.1	Noun prefixes	22
		2.4.2	Nouns derived from verbs	23
		2.4.3	The class/gender changing personifier suffix -ɛ	26
		2.4.4	Names, vocatives, and titles/terms of address	26
		2.4.5	Numeral nouns	28
		2.4.6	Reduplication in nouns	28
	2.5		Diminutive nouns	29
	2.6		Negative nouns	30
	2.7		Compound nouns	30
3	**The Noun Phrase**			**33**
	3.1		Introduction	33
	3.2		Structure of the noun phrase	33
	3.3		Noun modifiers	34
		3.3.1	Demonstratives	34
		3.3.2	The emphatic pronoun	39
		3.3.3	Possessives	42
		3.3.4	Property concepts	44
		3.3.5	Numerals	50
		3.3.6	Relative clauses	57
	3.4		Other elements of the noun phrase	59
		3.4.1	Appositions	59
		3.4.2	Emphatic particles	59
		3.4.3	Quantifier	60
		3.4.4	Intensifier	60
		3.4.5	Modifiers as noun phrase heads	61
	3.5		Negation and the noun phrase	61
	3.6		The associative noun phrase	62
		3.6.1	The associative marker (AM)	62
		3.6.2	Tone in the associative noun phrase	64
		3.6.3	Agreement in embedded AssNPs	65
		3.6.4	Relationships expressed by the AssNP	65
	3.7		Possessive noun phrase	70

Contents

3.8 Coordinate noun phrase ... 70
- 3.8.1 With *ne* ... 71
- 3.8.2 With *bɔ́* ... 72
- 3.8.3 With *káa* ... 73

3.9 Prepositional phrases ... 74
- 3.9.1 Prepositional phrases expressing location ... 74
- 3.9.2 Prepositional phrases with post-nominal element ... 75
- 3.9.3 Prepositional phrases with "complex prepositions" ... 76
- 3.9.4 Prepositional phrases with *ne* ... 77
- 3.9.5 Other prepositional phrases ... 78

3.10 Question phrase ... 80
3.11 Pronouns ... 80
- 3.11.1 Personal pronouns ... 80
- 3.11.2 Class pronouns ... 81
- 3.11.3 Compound pronouns ... 81

4 The Verb ... 83

4.1 Introduction ... 83
4.2 The infinitive ... 84
4.3 Subject markers ... 85
4.4 Verb stems ... 86
- 4.4.1 Verb roots ... 86
- 4.4.2 Root tones ... 86
- 4.4.3 Derivational affixes or verbal extensions ... 86
- 4.4.4 Vowel initial extensions ... 87
- 4.4.5 Consonant initial extensions ... 88
- 4.4.6 -V(C) extensions illustrated ... 89
- 4.4.7 -CVC extensions illustrated ... 92

4.5 Extensions and valency changes ... 96
- 4.5.1 Valency increasing *-ed* 'causative' ... 97
- 4.5.2 The *-ɛn* extension ... 97
- 4.5.3 Valency increasing *-e* 'applicative' ... 99

4.6 Tense, aspect, negation and dependent forms ... 100
- 4.6.1 Tense and aspect ... 100
- 4.6.2 Verb negation ... 101
- 4.6.3 Dependent verb forms ... 102
- 4.6.4 Distribution of dependent verb forms ... 104
- 4.6.5 The infinitive forms of the verbs illustrated ... 107

	4.6.6 Major verb tenses	109
	4.6.7 Minor verb tenses	134
	4.7 Verb moods	145
	4.7.1 Imperative perfective	145
	4.7.2 Imperative imperfective	146
	4.7.3 Hortative perfective	146
	4.7.4 Hortative imperfective	147
	4.7.5 Imperative and hortative negative	148
	4.7.6 Negative prohibitive	149
5	**The Verb Phrase**	**151**
	5.1 Introduction	151
	5.2 The simple verb phrase	152
	5.3 The serial verb phrase	152
	5.4 The split verb phrase	153
	5.5 Phrasal verbs	154
	5.6 Infinitives and the verb phrase	155
	5.6.1 Verb-verb infinitives	155
	5.6.2 Verb-object infinitives	156
	5.7 Echo verbs	157
	5.8 Intensification	157
	5.9 Auxiliary verbs	157
	5.9.1 Distributional subclasses	158
	5.9.2 Semantic subclasses	158
	5.9.3 Auxiliary verbs illustrated	162
6	**The Clause and Clause Constituents**	**165**
	6.1 Non-verbal clauses	165
	6.2 Verbal clauses	167
	6.2.1 Non-active clauses with copular verb -bé/-dé 'to be'	168
	6.2.2 Non-active clauses with copular verb -wóŋ 'to have'	171
	6.3 Active clauses	172
	6.3.1 Intransitive clauses	172
	6.3.2 Transitive clauses	173
	6.3.3 Ditransitive clauses	174
	6.3.4 Tritransitive clauses	175
	6.3.5 Clauses with locational complements	175

Contents

- 6.3.6 Verbs with a clause as object (complement clauses, predicate complements) 175
- 6.4 Oblique phrases 176
  - 6.4.1 Instrument phrases 176
  - 6.4.2 Accompaniment phrases 177
  - 6.4.3 Time phrases 177
  - 6.4.4 Locational phrases 180
  - 6.4.5 Manner phrases 184
  - 6.4.6 Other oblique phrases 186
- 6.5 Subject repetition for emphasis 186

7 Sentence Modifications 189

- 7.1 Introduction 189
- 7.2 Questions 191
  - 7.2.1 Yes/no questions 191
  - 7.2.2 Content questions 193
  - 7.2.3 Leading questions 198
  - 7.2.4 Tag questions 198
  - 7.2.5 Indirect questions 199
  - 7.2.6 Questions expressing doubt 199
- 7.3 Topicalisation 199
  - 7.3.1 The topic marker 200
- 7.4 Relative clauses 202
  - 7.4.1 Structure 202
  - 7.4.2 Constituents relativised 203
- 7.5 Fronting 210
- 7.6 Vocatives and politeness adverbs 211

8 Complex Sentences 213

- 8.1 Analytic causatives 213
- 8.2 Reported speech 214
  - 8.2.1 Speech margin 214
  - 8.2.2 Reporting particle 215
  - 8.2.3 Direct, indirect and semidirect speech 218
  - 8.2.4 Verbs of speech, perception and cognition 221
  - 8.2.5 Content clauses illustrated 222
  - 8.2.6 Intention 224
- 8.3 Indirect questions 224

8.4		Sentence pro-form 224
8.5		Other clause combinations 225
	8.5.1	And-coordination 225
	8.5.2	Or-coordination 225
	8.5.3	But-coordination 226
	8.5.4	Temporal sequence 227
	8.5.5	Prior action 227
	8.5.6	Beginning and end points 228
	8.5.7	Purpose 229
	8.5.8	Reason and cause 231
	8.5.9	Result 232
	8.5.10	Means 233
	8.5.11	Concessive 234
	8.5.12	Contra-expectation 235
	8.5.13	Circumstantial 235
	8.5.14	Conditional 236
8.6		Comparative clauses 238
8.7		Summary list of conjunctions 238

9 Negation 241

9.1		Clause negation 241
	9.1.1	Verbal clauses 241
	9.1.2	The verb 'to be' 242
9.2		Non-verbal clauses 243
9.3		Lexical negation 243
9.4		Miscellaneous negative items 243

Appendix A 245

Lexical Notes and Special Word Forms 245

A.1.	Numerals 245
	Numerals used for counting 245
	Numerals used in a noun phrase 246
A.2.	Ideophones 248
A.3.	Exclamations 250
A.4.	Loanwords 250
	From English 250
	From Douala 251

Contents   xi

    From German.. 251
    From Efik 252
    From French 252
    From Portuguese 252
  A.5.   Seasons 252
  A.6.   Kinship terms 252
  A.7.   Colour terms 254

Appendix B.. 255

Swadesh 100 Comparative Wordlists 255

Appendix C 261

Text 261

Bibliography 287
    General works 287
    Works written in Akɔɔse 290

Index 293

Abbreviations and Symbols

↓	tonal downstep	AssNP	associative noun phrase
=	marks clitics	AUX	auxiliary verb
-	marks affixes	Ben	benefactive
0	gap in relative clause	C	consonant
1	noun class 1	CAUS	causative extension
2	noun class 2	cl	class
3	noun class 3	clit	clitic
3,4, etc.	noun class 3,4, etc.	COM	comitative
1pl	1st person plural	comp	complementiser
1sg	1st person singular	conj	conjunction
2pl	2nd person plural	cons	consecutive aspect
2sg	2nd person singular	cp	concord prefix
3pl	3rd person plural	dem	demonstrative
3sg	3rd person singular	dev	developmental marker
acc	accompaniment extension	DEP	dependent
add	additive post clitic	DIST	distal form of demonstrative
adj	adjective		
adv	adverb	DO	direct object
AdvP	adverbial phrase	DS	downstep
am	associative marker	ED	-ed extension
ana	anaphoric	EMPH	emphatic
app	applicative extension	EN	-ɛn extension
asp	aspect marker	EXCL	exclamation

Abbreviations and Symbols

excl.	exclusive	NP	noun phrase
EXT	unspecific extension	np	(in glosses) noun prefix
far.dist	far distal demonstrative	num	numeral
fem, fem.	feminine	o	(in glosses) non-subject dependent clause
fut	future tense prefix		
G	glide		
H	high tone	o	object
⁺H	downstepped high tone	par	particle
hort	hortative suffix	past	past tense affix
I	independent clause, independent verb form	perf	perfect aspect suffix
		pers	personifier suffix
ideo	ideophone	pfx	prefix
IMP	imperative suffix	PL, pl	plural
impf	imperfective aspect suffix	POSS	possessive
		pp	prepositional phrase
incl.	inclusive	prep	preposition
inf	infinitive marker (=class 5)	prior	prior form of the verb
		pro	pronoun
Inst	instrument	PRO-S	pro-form for sentence
inst	instrument extension	prox	proximal demonstrative
InstP	instrument phrase		
INT	intensifier	q	question marker
IO	indirect object	QADV	question adverb
ITER	iterative	QPRO	question pronoun
itr.	intransitive	QW	question word
L	low tone	RC	relative clause
Loc	location	REC	reciprocal extension
loc	locative prefix	refl	reflexive
LocP	locative phrase	REFL.DEM	reflexive demonstrative
log	logophoric		
Man	manner	rel	relative pronoun
ManP	manner phrase	rp	reporting particle
masc, masc.	masculine	s	(in glosses) subject dependent clause
MOD	modifier		
N	noun, nasal	S	subject, sentence
n1,2,3	noun of class 1,2,3 etc.	]S	sentence
n1/2	noun of gender 1/2	sb.	somebody
NC	nominal complement	sf	non-specific verbal suffix
neg	negative prefix		
neut	neutral form	SFX	suffix

SG, sg	singular	TemP	temporal phrase
sm	subject marker	TIT	title
sp.	species	TNS	tense marker
st.	something	top	topicalisation marker
Sub	subject	tr.	transitive
SUBS	subsequent form of the verb	V	verb, vowel
		voc	vocative
T	tone	VP	verb phrase

1

Introduction and Outline of Phonology

1.1 Introduction

This description of the grammar of *Akɔɔse* is intended for a wide audience, both linguists and non-linguists, speakers and non-speakers alike. I have therefore tried to use non-technical language as much as possible while at the same time giving a linguistically sound description of the facts of the language.[1]

The Bakossi people live in the Tombel and Bangem subdivisions of the South West Province of the Republic of Cameroon (see map). There are approximately 100,000 speakers. They trace their origin to a certain ancestor called Ngoe who lived on Mwaneguba mountain. Traditionally the Bakossi lived from hunting and subsistence farming. Today coffee and cocoa, as well as cocoyam and plaintain, are important cash crops. Many people have gained higher-level education and are now employed in various fields such as education, medicine, administration, etc.

---

[1] I am indebted to many people without whose help and insights I would never have been able to write this grammar: Joseph A. Epang, of Ndom; Godfred Elong Roggy Metuge and Martin Ebage Mesumbe, both of Nyasoso; S. N. Ejedepang-Koge, of Ndom; Rev. Nelson Ndando, also of Nyasoso; Rev. David Ngole, of Tombel; Ngalame Hipolite, of Mekom; and Nkwelle Joseph, of Ngomboku.

Bakossi is the anglicised form of the name used widely for the language, the people and the area. Native speakers refer to the language as *akɔ́ɔ́sē*, the area as *ekɔ́ɔ́sē* and the speakers as *bekɔ́ɔ́sē* (sg: *nkɔ́ɔ́sē*). I will use *Akɔɔse* without the tone-marking for the rest of this grammar.

Other names such as Kɔssi, Nkōssi and other variations are found in the literature (Hedinger 1987:28). *Akɔɔse* is spoken by a number of clans, the names of some of which have appeared as language names in the literature. These include Nninong and Elung.

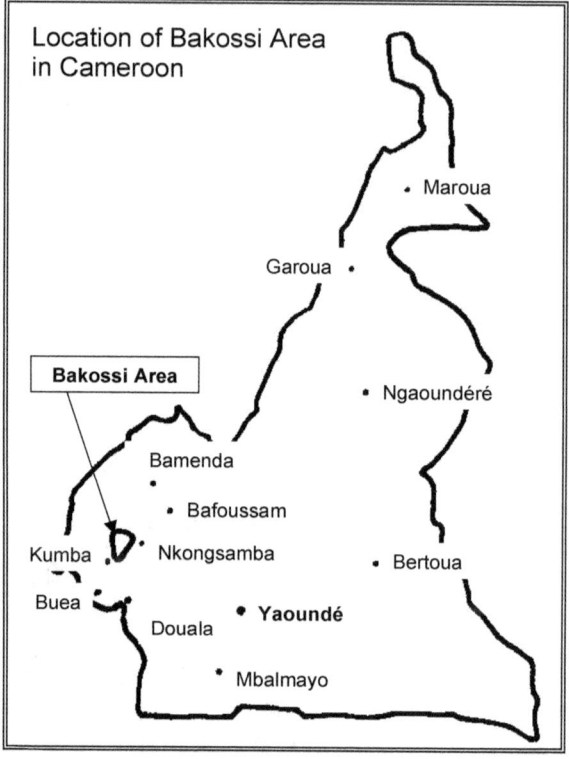

Location of Bakossi Area in Cameroon

Akɔɔse is a Northwest Bantu A language belonging to the Manenguba cluster which is part of the Lundu-Balong group (A10), Ngoe sub-group (Gordon 2005:56). Guthrie (1967–71.I:30) classified it as A.15. (See also Maho 2003:641.)

The earliest wordlists of closely related languages on record go back to the early 1800s (Kilham 1828, Clarke 1848, Koelle 1854). The first people to study Akɔɔse were Basedow (Dorsch 1910/11:241) and Dorsch. The latter published a grammar and vocabulary (Dorsch 1910/11, 1911/13, 1915). Others who took an interest in the language and focussed on various aspects of the language and culture are Ittmann (1930, 1936), Angenot et al. (1973), Wamunshiya (1973), Alobwede (1982), Enang (n.d. and 1994) and Ngome (n.d.). More recently several speakers of Akɔɔse have written linguistic theses at Yaoundé and Buea Universities on aspects of Akɔɔse, e.g. Alobwede d'Epie (1982), Apuge (1997), Ekanjume (1998, 2006), Ebong (1999), Palle (2000).

Akɔɔse is an SVO language. It has a typical Bantu noun class concord system (see chapter 2) with agreement in noun class within the noun phrase and subject-verb agreement marked on the verb.

Akɔɔse has several dialects. A commonly made distinction is between Upper and Lower Bakossi with the former being spoken in the north and the latter in the south. There is also a western dialect spoken in the villages around Nyandong. In the north the Nninong, Elung and Ngemengoe clans speak the most distinctive dialects. Differences among dialects are vowel and consonant differences, differences in words and differences in noun class prefixes (see Hedinger 1987 and appendix B).

Akɔɔse is the language of the home and village. With non-Bakossi people, Pidgin English or English is used. English is the language used in the schools. In the churches a mixture of languages is used including Akɔɔse, Duala, Pidgin English and English. Duala was the church language in some churches but has been rapidly losing ground over the last four decades.

Many Bakossi people live in towns around the country, and there is a sizeable community in the USA and other countries. Many do not transmit the language to their children, with the result that many growing up in town do not speak Akɔɔse. There is also a recent trend in the Tombel area for parents to speak Pidgin English rather than Akɔɔse to their children. (See also Hatfield et al. 1991).

1.2 Outline of Phonology

This section gives a brief outline of the main elements of the phonology of Akɔɔse. A fuller description was presented in Hedinger and Hedinger (1977).

The transcription used is broadly the one used in the orthography. The orthographic symbols which are different from the International Phonetic Alphabet (IPA) have the equivalents shown in (1).

(1) | IPA | Transcription |
|---|---|
| tʃ | **ch** |
| dʒ | **j** |
| ʔ | **'** |
| ᵐb | **mb** |
| ⁿd | **nd** |
| ŋg | **ng** |
| ⁿz | **nz** |
| ɲ | **ny** |
| j | **y** |

1.2.1 Consonants

There are twenty-one consonant phonemes in Akɔɔse, given in (2) in orthographic form.

(2)   The consonant phonemes

p	t	ch	k	ʼ
b	d	(j)	g	
mb	nd		ng	
	nz			
	s		h	
m	n	ny	ŋ	
	l	y	w	

The /ch/ phoneme has an allophone [j], in other words, there is no voicing contrast between [ch] and [j]. Some speakers tend to write *j* instead of *ch*. The /d/, when occurring between vowels, is often pronounced as a flapped [r]. [r], as well as [f] and [v], occurs in borrowed words and ideophones but these are not distinctive sounds in the phonological system of the language.

Only the consonants in (3) can occur in root-initial position; /g/, /ŋ/ and /ʼ/ do not.

(3)   Consonants in initial postition

p	t	ch	k
b	d	(j)	
mb	nd		ng
	nz		
	s		h
m	n	ny	
	l	y	w

No verb root begins with a prenasalised consonant (/mb/, /nd/, /nz/, /ng/), and only the consonants in (4) can occur in syllable-final or word-final position.

1.2 Outline of Phonology

(4) Consonants in final position

b	d	g	ʼ
m	n	ŋ	
	l		

The glottal stop only occurs in grammatical morphemes (noun class prefix, aspect marker, additive marker, developmental marker). The voicing distinction between stops is neutralised in syllable-final position. In prepause position /b/, /d/ and /g/ are devoiced and unreleased.

1.2.2 Vowels

There are eight short and ten long vowels.

(5) The short vowels

i		u
e		o
ɛ	ə	ɔ
	a	

(6) The long vowels

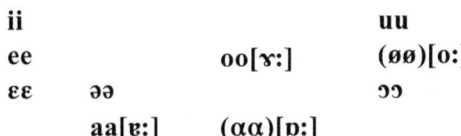

The two long vowels in parentheses are the result of the deletion of the velar consonants /g/ and /ŋ/ after /o/ and /a/. Because the contexts in which they occur is very restricted, it is debatable whether these vowels should be written in the practical orthography. At the time of writing they are not used in the orthography. They are used here, however, and in the verb section for purposes of exposition.

1.2.3 Syllable structure

Akɔɔse has the syllable types in (7).

(7) Syllable types

    CV   CGV
    CVC   CGVC

    CVV   CGVV
    CVVC   CGVVC

    V   VC   N

The G represents the vowel glides or semivowels /y/ and /w/. VV represents long vowels. The first eight types can be reduced to the following type: C(G)V(V)(C). Syllable types in the last row appear exclusively as affixes.

1.2.4 Assimilation and elision

Nasals assimilate to the point of articulation of the following consonant. /h/ and /w/ behave like the velars /g/ and /k/ in that preceding nasals become velar. Final /ŋ/ frequently disappears when followed by a vowel-initial word (8). Similarly, the glottal stop frequently elides when it occurs between vowels (9). Also vowels across word boundaries frequently assimilate or elide (10).

(8) asoŋ á nzyɔg   >   asoó nzyɔg   'elephant tusk
                                             (lit. tooth of elephant)'

(9) awobɛ' byěm   >   awobe byěm   'she washes thing'

(10) mwǎ ekɛn   >   mwěkɛn   'small insect'
    baá e'kɛn   >   baá'kɛn   'small insects'
    aláá á mbɔ́té   >   aláá mbɔ́té   'pressing iron
                                                 (lit. stone of shirt)'

1.2.5 Tone

There are two tone levels: high and low. There is also a phenomenon of DOWNSTEP which lowers the level of high tones in relation to the preceding high tones. High and low tones can combine into falling and rising contour tones. Examples (11) and (12) give the tone inventory of Akɔɔse.

1.2 Outline of Phonology

(11) | Level tones | Abbreviation | Transcription | | | |
|---|---|---|---|---|---|
| High | H | é | éé | | |
| Low | L | e | ee | | |
| downstepped-High | ꜜH | ē | ēē | or | ꜜé ꜜéé |

(12) | Contour tones | | | | | |
|---|---|---|---|---|---|
| High-Low | HL | ê | êe | | |
| Low-High | LH | ě | eé | | |
| High-downstepped-High | HꜜH | - | éē | or | éꜜé |
| Low-High-Low | LHL | - | ěe | | |

LHL is found on a few words like *hǐin* 'many', and *bwǎam* 'much, well'.

Every syllable is associated with one of these level or contour tones. Many pairs of nouns and verbs as well as function words are only distinguished by tone, as shown in (13).

(13) | | | | | |
|---|---|---|---|---|
| **edíb** | 'river' | **melám** | 'traps' |
| **edib** | 'lake' | **melâm** | 'liquor' |
| **nyén** | 'see' | **léb** | 'give advice' |
| **nyen** | 'lift' | **leb** | 'mourn' |
| **sé** | 'we' | **né** | 'then' |
| **se** | 'right' | **ne** | 'and, with' |

Also, there are several grammatical distinctions in the verb (tense/aspect, negation) that are only distinguished by tone. Tone marking in the practical orthography is therefore important. It is still not clear, however, what the most optimal system of marking tone will be.

1.2.6 Tone rules

Several tone rules operate both in the formation of words and across word boundaries. The most common ones are listed below.

Automatic downstep occurs when successive H tones are separated by intervening L tones creating a terracing effect.

Non-automatic downstep results from the loss of a low tone between two high tones resulting in the second H tone being at a lower level than the immediately preceding H. Example (14) shows how the H tone on the second syllable of *edíb* 'river' becomes a downstepped H when the original L tone of the first syllable is lost due to elision in the formation of 'at the river'.

(14) á + edíb   > édīb   'at the river'
      LOC   water

Tone simplification occurs when a HL contour simplifies to a H before a L tone or when an LH contour simplifies to an L tone before an H tone, as seen in (15).

(15) pǐm + chɔ́   > pim chɔ́   'throw it away!'
      throw it

Tone replacement occurs in a number of specific grammatical contexts. An L tone is replaced by an H tone between two H tones in the associative NP and in some verb-object contexts. More specifically, the L prefix tone of nouns with a following high stem tone is replaced by an H tone when preceded by an associative marker with an H tone (16a) or by a verb ending in an H tone (16b). Example (16) shows how the L prefix tone on the first syllable of *mendib* 'water' is replaced by an H tone and no downstep results.

(16) a. epíd + é + mendíb   > epíd é méndíb   'water bottle'
          bottle of water

      b. mwé + mendíb   > mwé méndíb   'drink the water!'
          drink   water

1.2.7 Alphabetical list of examples

A list of words illustrating the vowel and consonant phonemes is given in (17). The two extra long vowels are included for illustrative purposes even though they are not included in the writing system.

1.2 Outline of Phonology

(17) Examples of vowels and consonants

a	abad	'cloth'
aa	nyaá	'tear!'
αα	nyάά	'lick!'
b	bad	'people'
ch	chii	'today'
d	dĭn	'name'
e	nsém	'palm leaf'
ee	mbeé	'pot'
ɛ	kwĕl	'cut!'
ɛɛ	ngwɛɛ	'peacemaking'
ə	yŏl	'body'
əə	epəə́	'peelings'
f	fâm	'farm'
g	asóg	'end'
h	hŏm	'place'
i	edíb	'river'
ii	nsii	'sand'
k	kém	'monkey'
l	la'n	'ladder'
m	e'mii	'finger'
mb	mbód	'goat'
n	nén	'this'
nd	ndáb	'house'
ny	nyam	'animal'
nz	nzab	'soup'
ŋ	asoŋ	'tooth'
ng	ngab	'money'
o	nló	'head'
oo	bóó	'abandon!'
øø	bǿǿ	'care for!'
ɔ	ehɔ́b	'voice, speech'
ɔɔ	kɔɔ	'snail'
p	pó	'mouse'
r	radio	'radio'
s	sé	'we'
t	tâl	'chest'

u	kúb	'fowl'
uu	muú	'fire'
v	aviôn	'aeroplane'
w	wɛ	'you'
y	yə̆l	'body'
'	e'nɔn	'bird'

2
The Noun

2.1 Noun classes

Like all Bantu languages Akɔɔse has noun classes. That is, the nouns are divided into different groups based on the noun prefixes and the agreement between these nouns and the modifiers in the noun phrase. Although today it is not possible to see why the nouns in a class are grouped together, historically this grouping had a semantic basis where humans, animals, liquids, long objects, etc., were put in separate groups. Traces of this are still present in that nouns referring to humans are in classes 1/2, paired body parts are found in classes 7/6, animals are found in classes 9/10, liquids in class 6, etc.

The system for numbering the noun classes commonly used by Bantuists (Welmers 1973:163) is used in this grammar. The singular and the plural in each class are numbered separately; the singulars usually have odd numbers, while the plurals have even numbers. Akɔɔse has classes 1 to 10, 13, 14 and 19, plus traces of the locative classes 16 and 17 (Hedinger 1980 and 1983).

2.2 Noun genders

The combination of singular and plural classes are referred to as GENDERS. Below are some examples of typical genders. These are all count nouns that have a singular and a plural form.

(18) Gender 1/2 class 1 **nchîb** 'thief'   **mod** 'person'
                 class 2 **bechîb** 'thieves' **bad** 'persons'

     Gender 5/6 class 5 **abad** 'cloth'   **dúu** 'nose'
                 class 6 **mebad** 'cloths' **múu** 'noses'

     Gender 7/8 class 7 **echem** 'tongue'   **chyaá** 'leaf'
                 class 8 **e'chem** 'tongues' **byaá** 'leaves'

Non-count nouns that refer, for example, to masses, liquids and abstract concepts, have only one form. These are referred to as single-class genders.

(19) Gender 1   class 1   **ndɔ́léé**   'pneumonia'
     Gender 3   class 3   **mwĕntud**   'smoke'
     Gender 6   class 6   **mekíí**   'blood'
                          meləŋ   'leprosy'
     Gender 14 class 14 **e'bíi**   'knowledge'
                          e'kɔ́mkɔ́m 'tiredness'
                          e'yəg   'redness'

Approximately eighty percent of the nouns are found in double-class genders and the remaining twenty percent in single-class genders. Figures 2.1 and 2.2 illustrate which classes combine to form the different genders and which classes exist as single-class genders.

2.2 Noun genders

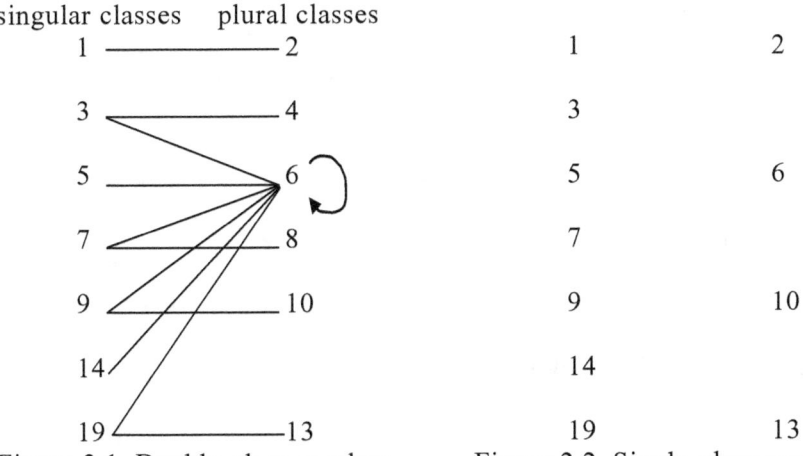

Figure 2.1. Double-class genders   Figure 2.2. Single-class genders

In figure 2.1 the lines indicate singular-plural pairings. The most frequent combinations of classes into genders are 1/2, 3/4, 5/6, 7/8 and 9/10, with some seventy-five percent of the nouns occurring in these five double-class genders. Figure 2.2 indicates which classes contain nouns which don't have a singular-plural distinction. There are some count nouns where both the singular and the plural noun belongs to class six (6/6) hence the circular arrow in figure 2.1.

2.2.1 Examples of count nouns by gender

Examples of nouns which have a singular and plural form are given in (20). They are therefore considered double-class genders.

(20) a. Gender 1/2   **nlem**   **belem**   'wizard(s)'
                    moonyoŋ   **baányoŋ**   'human being(s)'
                    nlagɛɛ   **benlagɛɛ**   'large antelope(s)'

   b. Gender 3/4   **mwě**   **myě** or **mwě**   'year(s)'
                    mwɛd   **myɛd** or **mwɛd** 'prong(s)'
                    njág   **njág**   'handle(s)'

   c. Gender 3/6   **nwoŋ**   **menwoŋ**   'joint(s)'
      (only one example has been found in this gender)

d.	Gender 5/6	dĭn	mĭn	'name(s)'
		abaa	mebaa	'liver(s)'
		dyɛnɛ	medyɛné or mwɛnɛ	'mirror(s)'
e.	Gender 6/6	mɔɔ	mɔ́ɔ	'headband(s)'
		melonge	melongé	'bucket(s)'
f.	Gender 7/6	ehɔ́b	mehɔ́b	'voice(s)'
		etud	metud	'raffia palm(s)'
		etúu	metúu	'ear(s)'
g.	Gender 7/8	chŏŋ	bŏŋ	'hoe(s)'
		chŏm	byĕm	'thing(s)'
		elóm	e'lóm	'cave(s)'
h.	Gender 9/10	nyam	nyam	'animal(s)'
		seb	seb	'squirrel(s)'
		nguu	nguu	'pig(s)'
i.	Gender 9/6	nde	mende	'gift(s)'

Two other nouns also found in gender 9/6 have alternative plurals in the more typical class 10. The plural in class 6 (21a) is clearly a more recent formation for these nouns.

(21)	a.	Gender 9/10~6	ndáb	ndáb or mendáb	'house(s)'
			nzii	nzii or menzii	'path(s)'
	b.	Gender 14/6	e'lám	melám	'trap(s)'
			bwɛl	mɛl	'tree(s)'
			e'mii	memii	'finger(s)'
	c.	Gender 19/13	hyɛ	lĕ	'pangolin(s)'
			hyɔ́b	lɔ́b	'kind of hawk(s)'
			hii	lií	'camwood(s)'

Only three nouns are found in gender 19/13 and they have alternative plural forms in gender 19/6 where the class 6 prefix *me-* is prefixed to the singular form of the noun.

2.2 Noun genders

(22) Gender 19/6 hyɛ̌   mehyɛ̌   'pangolin(s)'
                   hyɔ́b   mehyɔ́b   'kind of hawk(s)'
                   hii   mehií   'camwood(s)'

2.2.2 Examples of non-count nouns by gender

Non-count nouns have only one form with either a singular or a plural prefix and therefore belong to single-class genders; they are exemplified in (23).

(23) a. Gender 1   mbwɛmbwɛ   'morning'
                   ngɔ́mé   'Ngome (male name)'

   b. Gender 2   bejəŋléné   'wasting of time'
      (only one noun has been found in this gender)

   c. Gender 3   mog   'soot'
                  nkwě   'salt'

   d. Gender 5   akɔ́ɔ́sē   'Bakossi language'
                  akií   'being an in-law'

   e. Gender 6   mǒl   'oil'
                  mekií   'blood'
                  melě   'oath'

   f. Gender 7   epame   'stubbornness'
                  chǔ   'death ceremony'

   g. Gender 9   nyam   'meat'
                  ngɔn   'moon'
                  píd   'thirst'

   h. Gender 10   ngɔn   'groundnuts'
                  nyɔl   'sawdust'

   i. Gender 13   lɔɔ   'aughter'
      (only one noun has been found in this gender)

   j. Gender 14   e'bíi   'knowledge'
                  bǒŋ   'brain'

k. Gender 19   **hyǎg**   'clay'

2.3 Agreement or noun class concord

As is typical in Bantu languages, Akɔɔse has noun class concord or agreement between the head noun of the noun phrase and the noun modifiers, between the subject and the verb in sentence-initial clauses, as well as between the subject and the verb in subsequent clauses which share the same subject.

2.3.1 Agreement within the noun phrase

The following noun phrase modifiers agree with the head noun: demonstratives, possessives, some numerals, adjectives, the associative marker, the pronouns, the relative pronoun, and the words for 'all' and 'other'. In (24) the noun is singular and has a class 1 prefix. All the modifiers have class 1 prefixes agreeing with the head noun.

(24) POSS   N   NUM   REL   Verb
    awí   **mwaád**   **a'só**   **awé**   **a-nsóg**   'his first wife, who was fat'
    1.his   1.wife   1.first   1.which   1-PAST.fat

2.3.2 Agreement between subject and verb

Verbs have an obligatory subject agreement marker. This marker agrees in noun class with the subject noun phrase, whether it is present in the same clause, in a previous clause or implied. In (25) the verb agreement marker is of the same class (cl.2) as the head noun in the subject noun phrase.

(25) S   V   O
    [**ábé**   **bǎn**]   [**bé-kal-e**]   [**me-tóm**]   'those children tell lies'
    2.those   2.children   2-tell-IMPF   6-lies

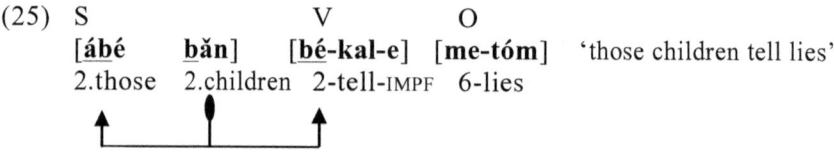

2.3.3 Agreement across clauses

In discourse, one participant is normally the subject of several clauses in a larger unit such as a sentence, paragraph, section, etc. Each verb agrees in noun class with its antecedent subject noun phrase. In the following example,

2.3 Agreement or noun class concord

the black symbols indicate different antecedent nouns while the corresponding white symbols indicate agreement with the noun in that noun class.

(26) ...Esélɛ....
    ...1.duiker....

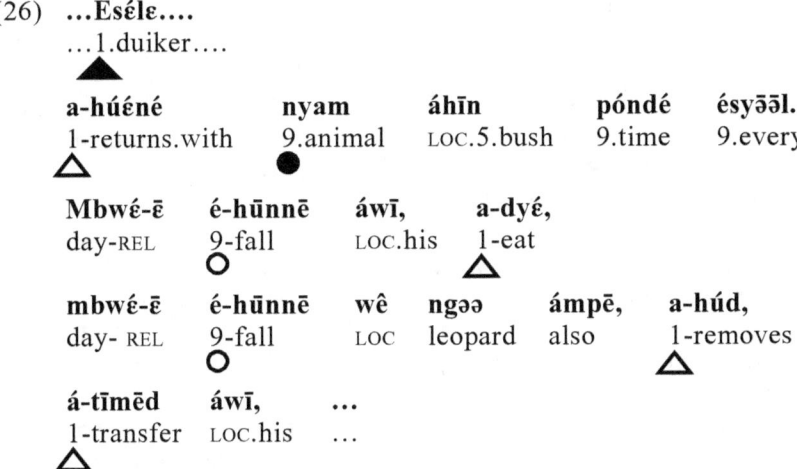

a-húéné   nyam   áhīn   póndé   ésyɔ̄ɔ̄l.
1-returns.with 9.animal LOC.5.bush   9.time   9.every

Mbwé-ē   é-hūnnē   áwī,   a-dyé,
day-REL   9-fall   LOC.his   1-eat

mbwé-ē   é-hūnnē   wê   ngəə   ámpē,   a-húd,
day-REL   9-fall   LOC   leopard   also   1-removes

á-tīmēd   áwī,   ...
1-transfer LOC.his   ...

'Duiker comes back with animals every time. The day it falls into his (trap), he eats, the day it falls into leopard's, he takes it out and transfers it to his (trap)...'

There is also agreement of object pronouns with noun phrases in clauses that precede them. In (27) the pronoun *chɔ́* agrees in noun class with the head of the object noun *ehid* 'bone' in the first clause.

(27) A-tédé   ehid   é   nyam,
     1-take.pref 7.bone   7.am   9.animal

     á-kɛɛné   chɔ́   áhîn   tê.
     1-take.PREF 7.PRO   LOC.5.bush   in

'He took the animal bone and took it to the forest.'

2.3.4 Exceptions

There are some exceptions to the general rules of agreement with another principle overriding the general one.

In the associative construction in which two nouns are associated with each other, the first noun (N₁) is *grammatically* the head and therefore determines the class of the associative marker, as well as the concord of any verbs of which the head noun is subject. However, in some cases the second noun (N_2) is *semantically* the head noun and N_1 the modifier. When this is the case there is tension between whether the agreement should be between N_1 or N_2 and any following verbs. This is illustrated with (28).

(28)   AssNP   NP   S   S
[[[nhɔn   ḿ   mod]   nhɔ́g] ḿ-bédé].   [a-wóŋ   bebaád   híin].
3.rich   3.AM   1.person   3.one 3-was   1-have   2.women   many
● ○ ▲ ○ ○ △

'There was a rich man. He had many wives.'

In the associative noun phrase *nhɔn* is the grammatical head and agreement within the first sentence is in class 3. However, *mod* is the semantic head being modified by the first noun *nhɔn*. The subject marker of the next (and subsequent) clause(s) agree(s) in noun class with the semantic head of the AssNP.

Another exception involves the kinship terms *nyaŋ* and *sáŋ* which belong to the generally non-human class 9. This can be seen from the agreement of the possessives in (29) and (30) marked with round symbols. However, agreement in the noun phrase with the relative clause in (29) and between subject and verb in (30) is in class 1, the class that is used for human referents.

(29)   Noun   Relative clause
[echém   nyaŋ   [awé   a-chyáá   me]]
9.my   9.mother   1.REL   1-bear.PERF   me
○ ●▲ △ △

'my mother who bore me'

(30)   Subject   Verb
[[echem   sáŋ]   a-lɔ́gnédé   me   kálag   pɔ́g]
9.my   9.father   1-left.with.PERF   me   9.book   9.one
○ ●▲ △

'My father left me one book.'

Another exception is the possessive in locational phrases. In (31) the possessive agrees in noun class with the head noun it modifies. However, when the same noun phrase expresses location, the possessive is replaced with the locative possessive which takes class 5 agreement (32).

2.3 Agreement or noun class concord

(31) **echem ndáb**   'my house'
     9.my   9.house

(32) **áwem ndáb**   'to/at my house'
     LOC.my 9.house

When this locational phrase is the subject of a sentence, agreement is determined by the class of the possessive and not by the head noun; compare (33) with (34).

(33) **[áwem ndáb] á-bóó**   'in my house it is good'
     LOC.my 9.house 5-good.PERF

(34) **[echem ndáb] e-bóó**   'my house is good'
     9.my   9.house 9-good.PERF

2.3.5 Summary tables of noun class and concord prefixes

Table 2.1 gives a summary of the noun prefixes and the agreement prefixes or concord markers are given in table 2.2. It should be noted that there is partial overlap between some noun classes. For example, classes 1, 3 and 4 have nasal noun prefixes. The nouns for classes 9 and 10 cannot be distinguished on the basis of the noun prefixes only. Many nouns in classes 8 and 14 cannot be distinguished except for the fact that 14 is a singular class and 8 a plural class.

When it comes to concord, classes 3 and 4 are identical,[1] and partially identical with class 6. The concords of classes 5 and 13 are identical, as are the ones for classes 7 and 10, as well as 8, 14 and 19. Sometimes the noun prefixes help distinguish these classes, and sometimes it is the fact that one is a singular and the other a plural that keeps these classes distinct. However, it is clear that there is a process of gradual levelling of the noun classes. It should also be noted that, as is typical for Bantu languages, classes 1 and 9 agreement elements have low tone whereas all the other classes have high tone.

I have chosen to follow the system used for numbering the noun classes in Bantu languages to make comparison with other languages easier. However, with a strictly synchronic description one could argue for an

---

[1] Actually, in the past there was a concord distinction between classes 3 and 4, as can be seen from the material in Dorsch 1910/11:250ff.

eight rather than a thirteen class system. This could be schematised as follows (see figure 2.1):

Table 2.1. Noun prefixes

Class	/__ C	/__ V
1	N-, Ø-	m-, mw-, w-
2	be-	b-
3	N-	mpw-, mw-, m-
4	N-	mpw-/mpy-, mw-/my-, m-
5	a-	d-, dy-, (h-)
6	me-	m-, my-
7	e-	chw-, chy-, ch-
8	e'-	b-, by-
9	Ø-*	ny-†
10	Ø-	ny-
14	e'-	bw-, b-
19		hy-, h-
13		l-

*The Nninong dialect in Upper Bakossi has an interesting example of gender 9/10: *mbwê, mbyé* 'dog(s)', probably formed by analogy on gender 3/4. This would have to be analysed as *mbw-/mby-* rather than as zero prefixes.

†If the *ny-* is interpreted as part of the stem then all nouns in classes 9 and 10 will have Ø prefix and be limited to consonant-initial stems.

2.3 Agreement or noun class concord

Table 2.2. Noun class concord elements

	POSS REL DEM ANA	DEM pre	DEM post	EMPH DEM+ REFL	PRO	NUM SG	NUM PL	all	big, small, which	AM- SM-	AM+ SM+	other	new
1	aw-	an-	↓n-	mw-	m-	N-			a-	a-	a-	a-	a-	e-
2	áb-	áb-	b´-	b-	b-	be-	bé-	be↓-	bé-	bé-	bé-	be↓-	be↓-
3	ḿm-	ḿm-	m´-	m-	m-	N-		Ń↓-	Ń-	Ń-	mé-	me↓-	me↓-
4	ḿm-	ḿm-	m´-	m-	m-	N-	Ń-	N↓-	Ń-	Ń-	mé-	mé↓-	me↓-
5	ád-	ád-	d´-	d-	d-	a-		a↓-	á-	á-	dé-	de↓-	de↓-
6	ḿm-	ḿm-	m´-	m-	m-	me-	mé-	me↓-	mé-	mé-	mé-	me↓-	me↓-
7	éch-	éch-	ch´-	ch-	ch-	e-		é↓-	é-	é-	é-	é↓-	é↓-
8	áb-*	áb-	b´-	b-	b-	e'-	é'-	é'↓-	é'-	é'-	bé-	be↓-	be↓-
9	en-	en-	n´-	ch-	ch-	Ø		e-	e-	e-	e-	e-	e-
10	éch-	éch-	↓ch-	ch-	ch-	e-	é-	e↓-	é-	é-	é-	é↓-	e↓-
14	áb-	áb-	b´-	b-	b-	e'-		é'↓-	é'-	é'-	bé-	be↓-	be↓-
19	áb-	áb-	b´-	b-	b-	e'-		é'↓-	é'-	é'-	bé-	bé↓-	be↓-
13	ád-	ád-	d´-	d-	d-	a-	á-	a↓-	á-	á-	dé-	dé↓-	de↓-

*The *áb-* prefixes in classes 8, 14 and 19 appear as *é'b-* in some dialects; this clearly reflects an older stage of the noun class system.

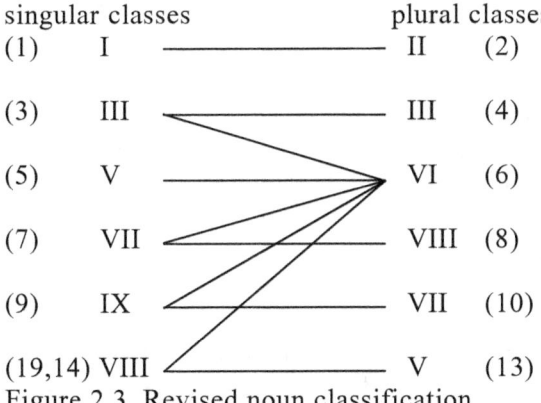

Figure 2.3. Revised noun classification

In this system classes III, V, VII and VIII can be singular or plural (the Bantu numbers are given in brackets). I and IX are singular only and II and VI are plurals only.

One could envisage that eventually classes 2, 8, 14 and 19 (II and VIII) would merge into one class, as well as classes 3, 4 and 6 (III and VI) in another class, giving just six classes with only 1 (I) and 9 (IX) singular and the remaining four serving both as singular and plural classes.

2.4 Internal structure of the noun

Akɔɔse nouns typically consist of a prefix and a stem. The majority of nouns (approximately fifty-five percent) have two syllables—a prefix plus a monosyllabic root or a disyllabic root with a null prefix. Approximately thirty percent have three syllables, twelve percent are monosyllabic, and the remaining ones have four or five syllables. The prototypical noun consists of a noun class prefix plus a noun root, as shown in (35).

(35) **n-** + **chóm** > **nchóm**   'male, husband'
      be- + **chóm** > **bechóm** 'males, husbands'

2.4.1 Noun prefixes

The noun prefixes vary depending on the class/gender to which the noun belongs as well as on whether it is attached to a noun stem which begins with a vowel or one which begins with a consonant.

Table 2.3. Noun prefixes

Class	/__ C	/__ V	Class	/__ C	/__ V
1	N-, Ø-	m-, mw-, w-	2	be-	b-
3	N-	mpw-, mw-, m-	4	N-	mpw-/mpy-, mw-/my-, m-
5	a-	d-, dy-, (h-)	6	me-	m-, my-
7	e-	chw-, chy-, ch-	8	e'-	b-, by-
9	Ø-	ny-	10	Ø-	ny-
14	e'-	bw-, b-			
19		hy-, h-	13		l-

The most common prefixes are the ones before C-initial stems; V-initial stems are more rare. The distribution of the pre-V variants is not predictable, specific roots preferring one or the other.

In class 4 the prefixes with /y/ are the original forms which are being replaced by the corresponding /w/ forms used in class 3.

There is one word in class 5 (*hŏm* 'place') that has an *h-* prefix. This is a relic from an old class 16 prefix.

2.4 Internal structure of the noun

In class 9 many nouns have an apparent *N*- prefix. This has been reanalysed as part of the noun stem with the nasal being the pre-nasalisation part of the initial C (see chapter 1).

Double prefixes

Some nouns appear to have two prefixes for the same class.

(36) **m-mw-aád** 'woman (cl.1)'   **be-b-aád**   'women (cl.2)'

In gender 9/10 singular and plural forms are not distinguished on the noun. Some of these nouns take the class 6 plural prefix to make an explicit plural form.

(37) **ndáb**   'house (cl.9)'   **ndáb / me-ndáb** 'houses (cl.10/6)'

In gender 19/13, which has very few words, the plural for some nouns seems to be moving to class 6 by adding the plural prefix to the full singular form.

(38) **hyɔ́ɔ́b**   'buzzard (cl.19)'   **lɔ́ɔ́b / mehyɔ́ɔ́b** 'buzzards (cl.13/6)'

2.4.2 Nouns derived from verbs

2.4.2.1 Agentive nouns

Some nouns are derived from action verbs by adding the class 1 prefix *n-* (and class 2 *be-* prefix for the plural). The resulting noun is used to refer to the one doing the action implied by the verb.

(39) **chíb**   'to steal' > **n-chîb**   'thief (cl.1)'
     be-chîb   'thieves (cl.2)'

     chog   'to play' > **n-chog**   'player (cl.1)'
     wóŋ   'to have' > **n-wóó**   'owner (cl.1)'

2.4.2.2 Action nouns

The following is a noun with zero prefix in class 9 derived from a verb root.

(40) **yag**   'to circumcise' > **yag**   'circumcision (cl.9)'

2.4.2.3 Abstract nouns with e'- prefix

There is a group of nouns which refer to abstract qualities and are derived from verbs. They all have the prefix *e'-* and are considered part of class 14. Since class 8 is identical to class 14 in all respects (except that 8 is usually plural and 14 singular) class assignment is somewhat arbitrary for these nouns.

(41) bíí   'to know'   > e'-bíi   'knowledge (cl.14)'
     yəg   'to be red' > e'-yəg   'redness (cl.14)'

2.4.2.4 Infinitives or verbal nouns

Infinitives are formed by the addition of the class 5 prefix *a-* to any verb stem. These are used as infinitives and verbal nouns.

(42) chog   'to play'   > a-chog   'to play, playing (cl.5)'
     wóŋ   'to have'   > a-wóŋ   'to have, having (cl.5)'

The agreement in (43) demonstrates that the verbal noun belongs to class 5.

(43) adyé   á   chóm   'eating of things'
     5.eat   5.AM   7.thing

     adyɛ   á   e'wóngé   'staying in marriage'
     5.stay   5.AM   14.marriage

A common linking device in Akɔɔse is to use the infinitive form of the verb as a kind of resumptive form in connection with a relative clause.

(44) ahún   áde   á-húné
     5.fall   5.REL   5-fall.PREF

     'Falling down, he...'

There is also an infinitive form where the *á-* prefix has a high tone. This is used in purpose clauses (see sections 4.6.5 and 8.5.7).

2.4 Internal structure of the noun

2.4.2.5 Verb stem with -ag

Some nouns consist of a verb stem plus the old imperfective marker -*ag*.[2] The tone on this "suffix" varies from noun to noun.

(45) kab 'to share' > **n-kabâg** 'sharing (cl.3)'
     lɛled 'to greet' > **me-lɛlag** 'greeting (cl.6)'

2.4.2.6 Verb stem with -ɛn

The following noun stem appears to consist of a verb root plus the instrumental extension -*ɛn*.

(46) **-hyɔ́ɔ** 'to sweep' > **ehyɔ́ɔn** 'broom (cl.7)'

2.4.2.7 Undefined "suffixes"

There are many nouns that appear to be derived from verb roots. They have a suffix following the root but some of the suffixes have no independent meaning or function. Compare the examples in (47) which are derived from the verb *hín* 'to be black'. The first one has the suffix -*de* but this has no meaning or separate existence. The second noun has the suffix -*tén* which exists as a verbal extension with a variety of meanings (see section 4.4.7.9).

(47) **hín** 'to be black' > **ehínde** 'blackness (cl.7)'
                          > **ehíntén** 'darkness (cl.7)'

2.4.2.8 Noun stems with locative suffix sé

Nouns like *nkŏŋsé* 'world' and *moosé/baásé* 'ancestor(s)' end in *sé*. These are fixed forms consisting of a noun stem plus the locative particle *sé* 'down' (see sections 3.9.2 and 6.4.4.2). These might be derived from associative constructions consisting of the noun *nkoŋ* 'town' + *ń* + *sé*, and *mod/bad* 'person/people' + *a* + *sé*, respectively.

---

[2] See sections 4.6.1 and 4.6.6.3 for the form of the imperfective marker.

2.4.3 The class/gender changing personifier suffix -ε

In class 1 (gender 1 and 1/2) many nouns are found which end in εε. This appears to be the result of the coalescence of the stem final vowel with the personifier suffix -ε. When one considers the prefixes of these nouns it is clear that they come from other classes. In other words, the addition of the -ε suffix changes class membership from the original class of those nouns to class 1 (and 2). The nouns in (48) now all belong to class 1. The class from which they have come, as suggested by the form of the prefix, is indicated parentheses:

(48) nheetɛɛ 'kind of bird' (cl.1<3?) from ??
    ahíndɛɛ 'black monkey' (cl.1<5) from hín 'to be black'
    médulɛɛ 'tug of war' (cl.1<6) from dul 'to pull'
    ebéndɛɛ 'sour guava' (cl.1<7) from bɛn 'to be sour'
    enyindɛɛ 'sweet guava' (cl.1<7) from nyin 'to be sweet'
    bɔ́léé 'kind of dance' (cl.1<14?) from ??

Variant forms of this "ending" are əə, αα and oo. These are the result of the -ε merging with the stem vowel in some cases following the elision of ŋ.

(49) ngəə 'leopard' (cl.1<9) from ngo 'leopard (cl.9)'
    sáá 'father' (cl.1<9) from sáŋ 'father (cl.9)'
    nkoo 'keeper' (cl.1) from koŋ 'to keep'
    nkɔ̌kəə 'grass sp.' (cl.1<3) from ??

In folk tales where animals frequently are the main participants, the -ε suffix is added to animal names thus endowing them with human characteristics.

The examples in (49) seem to be fixed, however, the process seems to be somewhat productive, as in (50).

(50) kúlɛ 'Tortoise' (cl.1<9) from kûl 'tortoise (cl.9)'

2.4.4 Names, vocatives, and titles/terms of address

Personal names are characterised by the personifier suffix -ε. The same rules of ŋ elision and vowel coalescence apply as above (see section 2.4.3). Personal names belong to class 1 and take class 1 agreement concord.

2.4 Internal structure of the noun

(51) **Sibɛ** (masc.)
    Sénzeɛ (fem.)
    Kɔmé (masc.)
    Mélóó (fem.)
    Písáá (masc./fem.)

Vocatives are expressions used to address or call a person. This is usually done with names. There are two forms in which names are used to address a person: the name with a vocative prefix or simply the name.

In the first form of the following examples, i.e. vocative plus name, the -ɛ suffix is dropped showing the stem-final C (52), final V (53) or final ŋ (54).

(52) VOC+name   Name
    á Ngɔm   **Ngɔmé**   (masc.)
    á Dyɔn   **Dyɔné**   (fem.)

(53) **á Kɔle**   **Kɔléɛ**   (fem.)
    á Mesámbe   **Mesámbeɛ**   (fem.)

(54) **á Bwaŋ**   **Bwaα**   (masc.)
    á Toŋ   **Toó**   (fem.)

The vocative marker coalesces with the vowel in vowel-initial names (55).

(55) VOC+name   Name
    Ésem   **Esemɛ**   (masc.)
    Á'chal   **E'chalé**   (masc.)
    Abán   **Abánɛ**   (fem.)
    Alóŋ   **Alóó**   (masc.)

Notice that the tone of the vocative marker is the opposite of the first tone of the stem in the first two examples of (55). (Other tone polarisation rules are found in verb derivations, see Hedinger 1985a:15–16).

In (56) several titles that can be used for direct address are listed. The first three can also be used to refer to a person not being directly addressed. The last is used only for direct address.

(56)   sé   'father, Mr.'   sé Ebáge   'Mr. Ebage'
       mwê   'friend'   mwê Ngəə   'friend Leopard'
       lo   'Mr.'   lo Kúlɛ   'Mr. Tortoise'
       amwéē   'friend'

2.4.5 Numeral nouns

Akɔɔse has a set of nouns derived from the first five[3] numerals. They are used to refer to seed pods which contain one, two, three, etc. nuts. All the examples in (48) have their singular in class 1 and plural in class 2.

(57)   épɔkélé   1/2   (póg 'one')   'seed pod with one seed'
       ébɛé   1/2   (é'bɛ 'two')   'seed pod with two seeds'
       élaáné   1/2   (é'láán 'three')   'seed pod with three seeds'
       énííné   1/2   (é'niin 'four')   'seed pod with four seeds'
       étaané   1/2   (é'táan 'five')   'seed pod with five seeds'

2.4.6 Reduplication in nouns

Although there does not appear to be a productive process of reduplication (though see section 2.6 on negative nouns), it is clear that there are many nouns that have undergone reduplication.

(58)   choóchoŋ   'saviour'   see choŋ   'to get well, survive'
       símesim   'shrub sp.'   see sím   'rub in medicine'
       hííhyɔ̄gɛ   'mud wasp'   see hyəg   'clay'
       mŏlmólɛ   'yellow coloured' see mŏl   'oil'
       nsoosoo   'spear grass'   see soŋ   'to spear'
       ntótód   'stinging ant'
       ndándáá   'argument'
       nkɔ̌kɔ̄ə   'kind of grass'
       nkunékūne   'old cocoyams'
       tintinɛ   'star'
       pípín   'cockroach'
       pípíí   'behind'
       ewɔmwɔm   'laziness'
       epagpag   'tiredness'
       emwedmwed   'lightning'

---

[3]More research needs to be done to see if there are any such nouns for six, seven, etc. and how they are formed.

(59) **méngoŋméngoŋ** 'forest fruit'
    mbwɛmbwɛ 'morning'
    mbúmbú 'ash'
    mbódɛ́mbódɛ 'kind of tree'

These examples have atypical noun structures and are best explained as resulting from reduplication. As this is not a productive process, no attempt is made here to describe the details. Whereas the nouns in (58) are partially reduplicated, the nouns in (59) are completely reduplicated.

The noun in (60) is derived from *soŋ* 'to spear', apparently via reduplication of the verb root. However, this noun might have its origin in a verb-object reduction derived from *nsoo* 'one who spears' plus *asonge* 'hunt'.

(60) **nsoosonge** 'hunter'

2.5 Diminutive nouns

Some nouns can be preceded by the diminutive marker *mwǎ* (pl: *baá*). It appears to be related to *mwǎn* 'child' and functions like a noun as shown by the fact that the resulting expression takes noun class concord for class 1/2. In this respect it parallels the associative construction from which it might be derived (see section 3.6).

(61) **mwǎ pāa** 'small knife' (**páá** 'machete')
    mwǎ nsɔn 'small amount of work'
    mwǎ mǐm 'a little wine'
    mwǎ sɔ̄pe 'some soap'

(62) **mwěkɛn** 'small insect' (**ekɛn** 'insect')
    baá'kɛn 'small insects' (**e'kɛn** 'insects')

(63) **baá mélín métáan** 'some five stems, or five little stems'
    little stems five

In (62) typical vowel elision between the two words has taken place.

2.6 Negative nouns

Akɔɔse has a small set of negative nouns. These are derived from the basic noun by reduplication but taking on the opposite meaning. This applies only to the singular forms.

(64)   **mod**   'person'   **modmod**   'nobody, neither'
       chŏm   'thing'   **chŏmchom**   'nothing'
       dyam   'thing, affair'   **dyamdyam** 'nothing'
       hŏm   'place'   **hŏmhom**   'nowhere'

Note that the tone is simplified in that the high part of the LH tone is dropped at the end of the reduplicated form.

There is one item (65) which is inherently negative.

(65)   **mbéed**   'never'

Compare this with (66):

(66)   **bɔɔb**   'now (adv.)'
       e'bɔɔb   'now (noun)'
       saké bɔɔb 'not now'

2.7 Compound nouns

Akɔɔse has many "compound nouns". Many of these are names of animals, birds, etc. Though they are clearly composed of more than one lexical item, from a semantic perspective they form single concepts. There is a problem in that there seems to be a gradation from what is clearly a compound to what is clearly an associative noun phrase (see section 3.6). Compounds themselves may originate from the associative NP[4] resulting in different degrees of transparency. For this reason it is not always clear when to consider an expression as a compound noun and when as an associative NP.

The clearest indication that an item is a compound and not an associative noun phrase is when it ends with the suffix -ε (see section 2.4.3), which is true of all of the compound nouns in (67). They all refer to single concepts but clearly contain more than one root. Some of the roots are recognisable as having a separate meaning, but the meaning of the whole cannot be derived

---

[4]This is supported by the fact that in many cases it is clear that whole words rather than roots are juxtaposed.

2.7 Compound nouns

from the parts. The identifiable roots are indicated in parentheses. Some of the compounds in (67) contain a nominalised verb as the first part.

(67)
ekwɛlmbwéɛ	1	'kind of poison'		
kaanyamɛ	1	'chickenpox'		
kidecháde	1	'kind of oath'		
mbwéngemɛ	1/2	'kind of cricket'	(**mbwé** 'dog')	
ngaabobɛ	1/2	'spider'	(**ngaŋ** 'divination')	
mbódekɛnɛ	1	'grasshopper'	(**mbód** 'goat', **ekɛn** 'insect')	
mélongembɛlɛɛ	1	'nickname of duiker'		
boókúné	1	'palm-nut vulture'		
edyěnjemɛ	1/2	'kind of fish'	(**dyɛ** 'stay')	
dekalengɔmɛ	1	'so-and-so'	(**de** 'we' (incl.), **kal** 'tell')	
edogmengɔné	1	'dusk'	(**dog** 'deceive', **ngɔn** 'moon')	
mpɛmĭnɛ	1/2	'crazy person'	(**pɛ** 'reach', **mĭn** 'madness')	
ekobmetuné	1	'persevering person'	(**kob** 'welcome', **metunɛ́** 'suffering')	
ndyɛndyadɛ	1	'sparrow'	(**dyɛ** 'stay', **dyad** 'compound')	
edyébaábɛ	1/2	'MacKinnon's shrike'	(**dyé** 'eat', **baáb** 'friends')	
e'sélnyamɛ	1	'duiker'	(**e'sél** 'duiker', **nyam** 'animal')	
elâmmelámɛ	1	'trapper'	(**lâm** 'trap (v)', **melám** 'traps')	
ekuuehógé	1/2	'man on stilts'	(**ekuu** 'leg', **ehóg** 'one')	
ésɛmekwɛé	1	'snake'	(**sɛ** 'not be', **mekuu** 'feet')	

Some items in (68) clearly contain two roots and refer to single concepts but lack the -ɛ suffix.

(68)
esambwɔg	7	'sandbank'	
echogelechǒ	7/8	'kind of plant'	
mbódébód	3/4	'wasp'	(**mbód** 'goat')
ngubakoó	1/2	'swallow'	
akúlɛɛmbínze	1/2	'hunchback'	(**mbínze** ??)
ebéchǔ	7	'kind of caterpillar'	
ebelékwáŋ	7	'wizard place'	
e'búúbwóg	14	'fear'	

The first root in the items in (69) is *chyaá* 'leaf'. The item as a whole, however, constitutes a single concept.

(69) **chyeékóm** 7/8 'kind of leaf' (**chyaá** 'leaf')
chyĕngwaa, byăngwaa 7/8 'kind of leaf' (**chyaá** 'leaf',
ngwaá 'partridge')

In (70) the second root is clearly identifiable as a separate lexical item.

(70) **mwɛnchóm, baachóm** 1/2 'man, male' (**nchóm** 'male')
eloonyam 7 'powerful animal' (**nyam** 'animal')
mbolkáb 9/10 'bush buck' (**káb** 'antelope')
ebóténgule, e'bóténgule 7/8 'lizard' (**ngule** 'lizard')
ebwéngo 7/8 'golden cat' (**ngo** 'leopard')
echinéngwaá 1/2 'kind of plant' (**ngwaá** 'partridge')

In (71) the first part is a noun derived from a verb of which the second noun is the object. These are more transparent than other compounds. However, they are clearly compounds in that in the plural the expected associative marker linking N1 and N2 is absent (see section 3.6). Example (72) is very similar to (71) except that the class 2 associative marker *bé* is present.

(71) **nlámmelám, belámmelám** 1/2 'trapper' (**nlám** 'trapper',
melám 'traps')
nsoóbwɔg 1/2 'carver of mortars' (**nsoó** 'carver',
bwɔg 'mortar')
(72) **mbaá mbɔ̄tē, bebaa bé mbɔ́té** 1/2 'tailor' (**mbaá** 'sewer',
mbɔ́té 'shirt')

The lexical items in (73) refer to single concepts but appear to be full associative NPs with the associative marker present. Due to elision the associative marker is absorbed by adjacent nouns in some cases.

(73) **aláámbɔ́té < aláá á mbɔ́té** 5/6 'pressing iron' (**aláá** 'stone',
mbɔ́té 'shirt')
echóg é médíb, e'chóg bé médíb 7/8 'well' (**echóg** 'hole',
medíb 'water')
atɔ́nɛɛ kém < atɔ́nɛɛ a kém,
bɛtɔ́nɛɛ bé kém 1/2 'mona monkey' (**atɔ́n** 'spot',
kém 'monkey')

3
The Noun Phrase

3.1 Introduction

For the purpose of this description I distinguish the following noun phrase types: the standard noun phrase (3.2), the associative noun phrase (3.6), the possessive noun phrase (3.7) and the coordinate noun phrase (3.8). I also deal with prepositional phrases in this chapter (3.9).

3.2 Structure of the noun phrase

The noun is the head of the noun phrase (NP). It can be modified by a number of optional constituents or modifiers. Most of these follow the head noun with the exception of the demonstrative and the possessive which may precede or follow the head noun. All the modifiers belong to closed classes. Property concepts are expressed via adjectives (3.3.4.1), via nouns in an associative NP (3.3.4.2) and via verbs (3.3.4.3) in a relative clause.

The formula in (74) gives a summary of the types of modifiers and their relative order in the NP.

(74)

$$\text{NP} \rightarrow \left(\begin{Bmatrix} \text{Dem} \\ \text{Poss} \end{Bmatrix} \right) \text{N (Adj) (NumP)} \left(\begin{Bmatrix} \text{Dem} \\ \text{Poss} \\ \text{-mpée} \\ \text{-ĕdɛ} \end{Bmatrix} \right) \text{(-ĕn (pɛn)) (-syəə́l) (Rel Clause)}$$

No NP has been found with all these constituents present.

Only one demonstrative (Dem) or possessive (Poss) can be present, either preceding or following the head noun. The position before the head noun is the unmarked position.

Each constituent agrees in noun class with the head noun[1] (see section 3.3).

Following the noun is first a very small class of adjectives (3.3.4.1), which may be followed by a numeral phrase (see 3.3.5). The next three constituents are *-mpée* 'other' (3.3.4.1), *-ĕn (pɛn)* 'himself/themselves (only)' (3.3.2) and *-syəə́l* 'all' (3.3.4.1). As these can co-occur they are considered single members[2] of separate distribution classes.

There is also the modifier *-ĕdɛ* 'particular' (3.3.1.3) which follows the head noun. It is not yet clear what other constituents *-ĕdɛ* can occur with.

An optional relative clause comes as the last element of the NP (3.3.6).

There are a few noun modifiers that do not take agreement marking. They are not included in the above formula and will be listed in sections 3.4.2 and 3.4.3.

3.3 Noun modifiers

I will now present the different noun modifiers in turn. Because many of these vary according to noun class, their forms will be presented in the form of tables.

3.3.1 Demonstratives

Akɔɔse demonstratives distinguish three degrees of distance: proximal, distal and far-distal. A fourth form expresses a notion similar to "aforementioned." Compare the following noun phrases.

---

[1] Exceptions are the numerals six to nine, which are invariable, and ten, which is structurally a noun.

[2] Each of these have several forms depending on the noun class of the head noun.

3.3 Noun modifiers

(75) **ábén**   **bebaád**   'these women'
these.proximal   women

ábé   **bebaád**   'those woman'
those.distal   women

ábíníí   **bebaád**   'those women over there'
those.far.distal   women

bebaád   **bědɛ**   'the women talked about'
women   those.aforementioned

Each of these forms has variants for the different noun classes as well as pre- and post-nominal forms. This results in a rich inventory of different forms presented in the next sub-sections.

3.3.1.1 Pre-nominal demonstratives

The unmarked position for demonstratives is before the noun (76)–(77). In that position they have the form as in table 3.1. The pre-nominal demonstratives can stand alone without a head noun (see (78)).

The pre-nominal demonstrative has three stems: *-én* 'this/these (proximal)', *-e* 'that/those (distal)', *-íníí* 'that/those over there (far-distal)' to which the noun class concord element is prefixed. No tone has been assigned to the stem *-e* because it carries the same tone as the prefix, that is, a low tone in classes 1 and 9, but a high or falling tone in the other classes (see table 3.2 for falling tones).

Table 3.1. Pre-nominal demonstratives

Class	'this/these'	'that/those'	'that/those(far)'
1	anén	ane	aníníí
2	ábén	ábé	ábíníí
3	ḿmén	ḿmé	ḿmíníí
4	ḿmén	ḿmé	ḿmíníí
5	ádén	ádé	ádíníí
6	ḿmén	ḿmé	ḿmíníí
7	échén	éché	échíníí
8	ábén	ábé	ábíníí
9	enén	ene	eníníí
10	échén	éché	échíníí
14	ábén	ábé	ábíníí
19	ábén	ábé	ábíníí
13	ádén	ádé	ádíníí

Some examples follow:

(76) a. ádén   abad
    5.this   5.cloth

   b. ádé   abad
    5.that   5.cloth

   c. ádíníí   abad
    5.that.over.there   5.cloth

(77) a. ḿmén   myɛsú
    4.these   4.forks

   b. ḿmé   ndim
    4.those   4.corpses

   c. ḿmíníí   nsii
    4.those.over.there   4.files

(78) **Anén a-dyâg aníníí, aníníí-'ɛ a-dyâg anén.**
   1.PROX 1-eat.IMPF 1.FAR.DIST 1.FAR.DIST-ADD 1-eat.IMPF 1.PROX
   '(Riddle:) This one eats that one, and that one eats this one.'

3.3 Noun modifiers

3.3.1.2 Post-nominal demonstratives

The post-nominal demonstratives have the same deictic meanings as pre-nominal ones indicating the spatial relation to the speaker. The stem is also the same. They differ in that they have a reduced prefix, as shown in table 3.2, and always follow the noun. This appears to be the marked order, but the reason for this is not yet understood. Compare the examples in (79) where the pronoun in (a) is in pre-nominal position and in (b) in post-nominal position.

(79) a. **enén kúb**   'this hen'

   b. **kúb ⁺nén**   'this hen'

Table 3.2. Post-nominal demonstratives

Class	'this/these'	'that/those'	'that/those(far)'
1	⁺nén	ne	⁺níníí
2	bén	bê	bíníí
3	mén	mê	míníí
4	mén	mê	míníí
5	dén	dê	díníí
6	mén	mê	míníí
7	chén	chê	chíníí
8	bén	bê	bíníí
9	⁺nén	ne	⁺níníí
10	chén	chê	chíníí
14	bén	bê	bíníí
19	bén	bê	bíníí
13	dén	dê	díníí

It should be noted that ⁺*nén* and ⁺*níníí* when following a high tone are downstepped as, for example, in *kúb* ⁺*nén*. This is best explained by saying that they have a preceding floating low tone `*nén*, `*níníí*. Similarly, the falling tones come from a floating H tone before the distal root: *bé-* + *-e* > *bê*.

The post-nominal demonstratives cannot stand on their own as head of an NP.

3.3.1.3 *The anaphoric demonstrative*

There are two other pronouns which are related in form. One is pre-nominal (*-edé*, table 3.3), the other post-nominal (*-ĕdɛ*, table 3.4). These pronouns differ tonally, segmentally, and in the agreement prefix set (*aw-* etc. versus *mw-* etc.) they take. They are treated together under a single heading because they have a similar function: they both are used to refer back to already mentioned participants or circumstances.

Table 3.3. The anaphoric demonstrative pronoun (pre-nominal)

Class	'that'	Class	'that'
1	awedé	2	á⁺bédé
3	ḿ⁺médé	4	ḿ⁺médé
5	á⁺dédé	6	ḿ⁺médé
7	é⁺chédé	8	á⁺bédé
9	echedé	10	é⁺chédé
14	á⁺bédé		
19	á⁺bédé	13	á⁺dédé

(80) **Echedé póndé échê ndáb é-kwē ásē wuuuu.**
     9.that 9.time 10.those 10.houses 10-fall down IDEO
     'At that particular time those houses fell down boooomm.'

(81) **Awedé mod-ɛ ne-e?**
     that man-SF DEM-Q
     'Is that that particular man?'

The anaphoric demonstrative *-ĕdɛ* below is used to refer to a participant previously referred to.

3.3 Noun modifiers

Table 3.4. The anaphoric demonstrative pronoun (post-nominal)

Class	'that'	Class	'that'
1	**mwĕdɛ**	2	**bĕdɛ**
3	**mĕdɛ**	4	**mĕdɛ**
5	**dĕdɛ**	6	**mĕdɛ**
7	**chĕdɛ**	8	**bĕdɛ**
9	**chĕdɛ**	10	**chĕdɛ**
14	**bĕdɛ**		
19	**bĕdɛ**	13	**dĕdɛ**

(82) Mod <u>mwĕdɛ</u>   a-nkĕ   á   ahín.
person that.aforementioned he-went LOC forest
'The man (already talked about) went to the bush.'

3.3.1.4 Other demonstratives

The demonstratives in (83) have also been observed. They look similar in form to the ones presented above. However, further exploration is needed to see whether they are a complete set, whether they differ in function, whether they are dialect variants, etc.

(83) awed
ábed
áded
éched

The end part of *áned* 'so, it' is similar in form as well. It is used anaphorically to refer back to speech content.

(84) Aá,   á   nyaŋ,   néngāne é-hɔ́bé,   mĕ-hīd   áned.
3SG.RP VOC 9.mother as   O.2SG-say.PERF 1SG.FUT-follow it
'She said, mother, as you said, I will follow it (your instructions).'

3.3.2 The emphatic pronoun

The pronoun *-ĕn* 'himself, herself, etc.' is not a reflexive pronoun to indicate an action carried out by the subject on itself but rather to emphasise the noun which it follows. For how reflexive actions are expressed see section 6.3.2.1.

There is an emphatic pronoun for each noun class and person. The ones for the noun classes are given first (table 3.5), followed by the ones for persons (table 3.6). It should be noted that there is overlap between the two sets in that the class 1 and 2 forms are also the forms for third-person singular and third-person plural, respectively.

Table 3.5. The emphatic pronoun for classes

Class	'....self'	Class	'....self'
1	**mwěn**	2	**běn**
3	**měn**	4	**měn**
5	**děn**	6	**měn**
7	**chěn**	8	**běn**
9	**chěn**	10	**chěn**
14	**běn**		
19	**běn**	13	**děn**

(85) **ábé**   **bad**   **běn**
 2.DEM 2.people 2.themselves
 'those people themselves'

(86) **mod**   **mwěn**
 1.person 1.himself
 'the man himself'

In addition to the forms required by the different noun classes above there are forms for first-, second- and third-person singular and plural. As indicated above the third-person singular is the same as *mwěn* for class 1 above and the third-person plural *běn* is the same as for class 2 above.

Table 3.6. The emphatic pronoun for persons

Person	First	Second	Third	
Singular	**mměn**	**mmǒŋ**	**mwěn**	class 1
	'myself'	'yourself'	'himself'	
Plural	**(sé) běn**	**(nyí) běn**	**(bɔ́) běn**	class 2
	'ourselves'	'yourselves'	'themselves'	

3.3 Noun modifiers

Note that for the plural there is only one form *běn*. In order to distinguish between the persons, *běn* may be preceded by the pronoun for the corresponding person, as indicated in the table.

The main difference between these two sets is that the ones for classes typically occur with a noun, whereas the ones for persons do not. That is, they stand alone as an NP (87) or they modify a pronoun (88).

(87) Awem nsón ne mměn sê-nké áhīn.
    my   friend and myself we-went to.bush
    'My friend and I myself went to the bush.'

(88) mɔ́ mwěn
    'she herself'

3.3.2.1 The exclusive adverb

The reflexive demonstrative can itself be modified by the adverb *pɛn* to give a more restricted meaning. It is invariant and does not agree with its head.

(89) mwěn   pɛn
    himself only
    'he only'

(90) Běn   pɛn bé-dé á   ndāb te.
    themselves only they-be LOC house in
    'They alone are in the house.'

This is the most frequent use of this adverb. However, it also can occur with nouns (91)[3] or with both a noun and an emphatic pronoun (92).

(91) nsɔ́n pɛn
    work only
    'only work'

(92) tááse chěn pɛn
    starch itself only
    'only the starch itself'

---

[3] Because it has such a restricted use, it is questionable whether it should be analysed as an element of the NP, of a very restricted DemP or both.

3.3.3 Possessives

Akɔɔse has several ways of expressing possession, an important one being possessive pronouns. (For other ways of expressing possession, see section 3.7.) Possessive pronouns normally precede the noun they modify, as in (93) and (94).

(93) **awi   mwǎn**
     1.his 1.child
     'his child'

(94) **échêm   nguu   ésyɔ̄l**
     10.my   10.pig 10.all
     'all my pigs'

They may also follow the head noun.

(95) **ne   nsii   ḿmem**
     and   3.file 3.my
     'and my file'

This is less common than the position preceding the head noun. More research is needed to determine the significance of the two positions.

There are six possessive stems, as shown in table 3.7.

Table 3.7. The possessive pronoun stems

	singular	plural
first person	-em	-ɛd
second person	-oŋ	-ɛn
third person	-i	-ab

These combine with the noun class agreement prefixes to produce the forms in table 3.8.

3.3 Noun modifiers

Table 3.8. The possessive pronouns

	Person Class	1SG 'my'	2SG 'your'	3SG 'his/her'	1PL 'our'	2PL 'your'	3PL 'their'
Possessed	1	awɛm	awoŋ	awi	awɛd	awɛn	awab
	2	ábɛm	áboŋ	ábi	ábɛd	ábɛn	ábab
	3	ḿmɛm	ḿmoŋ	ḿmi	ḿmɛd	ḿmɛn	ḿmab
	4	ḿmɛm	ḿmoŋ	ḿmi	ḿmɛd	ḿmɛn	ḿmab
	5	ádɛm	ádoŋ	ádi	ádɛd	ádɛn	ádab
	6	ḿmɛm	ḿmoŋ	ḿmi	ḿmɛd	ḿmɛn	ḿmab
	7	échɛm	échoŋ	échi	échɛd	échɛn	échab
	8	ábɛm	áboŋ	ábi	ábɛd	ábɛn	ábab
	9	echɛm	echoŋ	echi	echɛd	echɛn	echab
	10	échɛm	échoŋ	échi	échɛd	échɛn	échab
	14	ábɛm	áboŋ	ábi	ábɛd	ábɛn	ábab
	19	ábɛm	áboŋ	ábi	ábɛd	ábɛn	ábab
	13	ádɛm	ádoŋ	ádi	ádɛd	ádɛn	ádab
	LOC	áwɛm	áwoŋ	áwi	áwɛd	áwɛn	áwab

The possessive stems in table 3.8 are listed with a low tone. The stem tone varies according to the tonal contexts. It may be low, falling, high (on all but the first-person singular forms) or rising (only on the plural forms).

It should be noted that there is a possessive pronoun to indicate location (last line of table 3.8). This can be glossed as 'at my, at your', etc. The locative possessive pronoun replaces any of the others in the case where a possessed NP indicates a location. Compare (96) with (97), repeated from section 2.3.4.

(96) **echem ndáb**
9.my 9.house
'my house'

(97) **áwem ndáb**
LOC.my 9.house
'to/at my house'

Historically, the locative possessive prefix *áw-* appears to come from proto-Bantu class 17, of which there are only traces in Akɔɔse.

In Akɔɔse there is no class 17 concord; class 5 is used for all locative concord.

There is another way of forming possessives which is used in some dialects. It appears that it consists of the relative pronoun plus the personal pronoun.

(98)   **toŋ**   echesé
      9.room   9.REL.we
      'our room'

(99)   **Échenyí**   ekɔyé   chén   é-bémé   áte.
      7.REL.your 7.hatred 7.this 7-has.lasted into
      'Your hatred has lasted a long time.'

3.3.4   Property concepts

Concepts which in European languages are typically expressed by adjectives (e.g. good, black, tall, deep) are in Akɔɔse expressed mainly by either verbs or nouns. This is evident by the fact that they have either verb or noun morphology. These will be described in sections 3.3.4.2 and 3.3.4.3.

There are, however, three words in Akɔɔse, which can be called adjectives proper. They are *-mbáá* 'big', *-sad* 'small' and *-ekɔ́ɔ́lé* 'new'. They follow the noun they modify and have neither verbal nor nominal morphology, but agree in class with the head noun. They can only be used attributively, not predicatively.

(100) **ndáb**   ekɔ́ɔ́lé
       9.house   9.new
       'a new house'

(101) **mwǎn**   asad
       1.child 1.small
       'a small child'

3.3.4.1 Adjectives

In this section we present the three adjectives mentioned above plus three other noun modifiers which share morphological characteristics with them but belong to different semantic and distributional sub-classes (102).

3.3 Noun modifiers

(102) -mbáá   'big'
     -sad   'small'
     -ekóólé 'new'
     -mpée 'other'
     -syəə́l 'all'
     -héé   'which?'

The adjectives *-mpée* 'other' and *-syəə́l* 'all', which could also be considered determiners, can co-occur with the first three in the same NP; *-héé* 'which?' is a question adjective. The stem *-syəə́l* is also found with final *n* instead of *l*: *-syəə́n* depending on speaker or dialect. These adjectives follow the noun and are always used as noun modifiers, not as nominal complements. The agreement prefix is added to the six stems giving the forms in table 3.9.

Table 3.9. The adjectives

Class	-mbáá 'big'	-sad 'small'	-kóólé 'new'	-mpée 'other'	-syəə́l 'all'	-héé 'which?'
1	ambáá	asad	ekóólé*	ampée	asyəə́l	ahéé
2	bémbáá	bésad	bé⁺kóólé	bé⁺mpée	bé⁺syəə́l	béhéé
3	ḿbáá	ńsad	mé⁺kóólé	mé⁺mpée	ń⁺syəə́l	ŋ́héé
4	ḿbáá	ńsad	mé⁺kóólé	mé⁺mpée	ń⁺syəə́l	ŋ́héé
5	ámbáá	ásad	dé⁺kóólé	dé⁺mpée	á⁺syəə́l	áhéé
6	mémbáá	mésad	mé⁺kóólé	mé⁺mpée	mé⁺syəə́l	méhéé
7	émbáá	ésad	é⁺kóólé	é⁺mpée	é⁺syəə́l	éhéé
8	é'mbáá	é'sad	bé⁺kóólé	bé⁺mpée	é'⁺syəə́l	é'héé
9	embáá	esad	ekóólé	empée	esyəə́l	ehéé
10	émbáá	ésad	é⁺kóólé	é⁺mpée	é⁺syəə́l	éhéé
14	é'mbáá	é'sad	bé⁺kóólé	bé⁺mpée	é'⁺syəə́l	é'héé
19	é'mbáá	é'sad	bé⁺kóólé	bé⁺mpée	é'⁺syəə́l	é'héé
13	ámbáá	ásad	dé⁺kóólé	dé⁺mpée	á⁺syəə́l	áhéé

*It is not clear why the agreement prefix here should be *e-* rather than *a-*.

One could ask why these (except *-héé*) are not considered to be the second noun in an associative construction where the prefix is interpreted as the associative marker (see section 3.6). The following are arguments against this alternative.

First, in associative constructions there is typically no downstep following the H toned AM as there is a tone rule that raises L tones to H preventing

DS from appearing. So, if the forms here were part of an associative NP with the structure (N₁) + AM + N₂ there would not be a downstep.

Second, these stems do not exist as nouns in their own right in other contexts.

(103) ne   e'kɔ́mkɔ́m   bê   é'⁺syɔ́ɔ́l
with 14.tiredness 14.DEM 14.all
'with all that tiredness'

(104) Bě   me   sabé   ampée.
give me 1.orange 1.other
'Give me another orange.'

(105) bad   béhéé
2.people 2.which
'which people'

All except the question adjective have reduplicated forms which make them more emphatic.

(106) nkalaŋ   mé⁺mpé⁺pée
3-story 3-other
'yet another story'

(107) mwǎnyaŋ   mmwaád   asasadɛ
1.sibling 1.female 1.small
'small sister'

3.3.4.2 *Property concepts expressed by nouns*

When property concepts are expressed via nouns, Akɔɔse uses the associative noun phrase, in which two nouns are linked. The noun expressing the quality is typically in the second position (108) but may be in the first position (109)–(110). This choice is determined by the adjectival noun chosen.

(108) e'lám   bé   e'só
14.trap 14.AM 14.face
'the first trap'

3.3 Noun modifiers

(109) **njun   ḿ   mod**
      3.old 3.AM   1.person
      'old person'

(110) **bejun bé   bad**
      2.old 2.AM   2.person
      'old people'

Here is a list of nouns that express such qualities.

(111) **abuu**   'much, many'
      e'béb   'wickedness'
      e'bén   'sourness'
      ebéd   'useless'
      e'boŋ   'goodness'
      nhɔn   'richness'
      ntógétóké 'poverty'

3.3.4.3 Property concepts expressed by verbs

Many property concepts are expressed by verbs. This includes the three primary colour terms white, red and black. In order to modify a head noun with a verbal structure, a relative clause is used.

(112) **e'popé**   [**ábe**   **é'-hín-é**]
      8.eyelash   8.REL   8-black-PREF
      'black eyelashes'

(113) **ebongé**   [**éche**   **é-púb-ɛ'**]
      7.thread   7.REL   7-white-IMPF
      'white thread'

These verbs can, of course, all be used predicatively to make a statement about a nominal subject. Note that there is no copular verb involved. Also note the verbal morphology (subject agreement prefix and aspect suffix).

(114) **Mesáá   mé-hín-é.**
      6-plum   6-black-PREF
      'The plums are black.'

(115) **E'sɛd   é'   ndáb   é'-púb-ɛ'.**
8.wall   8.AM   9.house   8-white-IMPF
'The walls of the house are white.'

(116) **A-yəg-e   nê   muú.**
1-red-IMPF   as   fire
'He is red like fire.'

Here are a few verbs that encode properties.

(117) **boŋ**   'be good'
 bíi   'be soft'
 buu   'be much'
 cho   'be bitter'
 lɛl áte[4] 'be difficult'
 sɔb   'be wet'
 tún   'be blunt'
 wɔm   'be lazy'

For some concepts there is both a noun and a verb form (compare (118) with (109)).

(118) **Ane   mod   a-chun-é.**
1.DEM   1.person   1-old-PERF
'That person is old.'

3.3.4.4 Comparatives

Different structures are used for making comparisons depending on whether a quality is expressed by a verb or a noun. When comparing entities which are equal in respect to some quality then the verb expressing that quality is used plus a prepositional phrase with the preposition *nég* 'like'.

(119) **A-kɔ́l-é nég ane mwǎn.**
1-big-PERF   like 1.that 1.child
'He is as big as that child.'

When the quality is expressed by nouns, an equational clause with the verb 'to be' plus a prepositional phrase with the preposition *nég* 'like' is used.

---
[4] For the *áte* see section, 5.5 "Phrasal verbs."

3.3 Noun modifiers

(120) **A-dé   mbéb   nέε   mbwé.**
  1-be   bad   like   9.dog
  'He is bad like a dog.'

(121) **E'yəg   ábī   é'-díē   nέε   e'yəg   é'   mbin.**
  14.redness   14.his   14-be   like   14.redness   14.AM   9.deer
  'He is red like a deer.'

When comparing entities which are unequal with respect to some quality, the verb expressing that quality is used plus a prepositional phrase with the preposition *tóma* 'more than'.

(122) **A-kəl-é   tóma   mə́.**
  1-big-PERF   more.than   him
  'He is bigger than him.'

If the quality is expressed in a noun, then there are two structures: one with the verb 'to be' plus the prepositional phrase containing *tóma* 'more than' (123)–(125) and the other with the verb *-tóm* 'surpass' plus the noun of quality (125).

(123) **A-dé   ngíne   tóma   nzyə́g.**
  '1-be   9.power   more.than   9.elephant
  'He is stronger than an elephant.'

(124) **Nkumbé   ń-dé   ngíne   tóma   mod   asyəə́n   á   nkoŋsé.**
  3.gun   3-be   9.power   more.than   1.person   1.all   LOC   world
  'The gun is stronger than any person in the world.'

(125) **Bad   bé-tóm-é   wε   ngíne.**
  2.people   2-surpass-PERF   you   9.power
  'The people are more powerful than you.'

3.3.4.5 Superlatives

Superlatives are expressed by comparative structures plus a prepositional phrase with a noun modified by the word 'all' (126) or by the verb *-tómtén* 'surpass' plus the quality verb in the infinitive (127).

(126) **A-kə́l-é   tóma   bad   bésyə́ə́l.**
  1-big-PERF more.than 2.people 2.all
  'He is the biggest. He is bigger than everbody.'

(127) **Ekág   chê   é-dé   hyɛn   ábē   é'-tómtén-é   aboŋ.**
  7.ekag 7.TOP 7-be 19.mushroom 19.REL 19-surpass-PERF INF.good
  'Ekag is the best mushroom.'

3.3.5 Numerals

Akɔɔse has a decimal numeral system with numbers one to nine, ten, hundred, thousand and million being basic numbers. Numerals are used for counting and as modifiers of nouns in NPs to quantify them. There are cardinal and ordinal numerals as well as some nouns derived from numerals. As noun modifiers numerals always follow the noun. They can also stand on their own when the noun is understood.

3.3.5.1 Cardinal numerals

As noun modifiers numerals always follow the head noun.

(128) **é'ked   é'bɛ**
  8.riddles 8.two
  'two riddles'

  sú   saámbé
  10.day   seven
  'seven days'

Numerals one to five (129) take a different prefix according to the class of the noun they modify. Numerals six to nine are invariant (130). The higher numerals (131) are structurally nouns and have singular and plural forms.

(129) **-hə́g** or **pə́g** 'one, some'
  -bɛ   'two'
  -láán   'three'
  -niin   'four'
  -táan   'five'

3.3 Noun modifiers

(130) **ntóób**   'six'
   saámbé   'seven'
   waam   'eight'
   abog   'nine'

(131) **dyôm**   'ten (5/6)'
   mbwókɛl   'hundred (9/10)'
   ekólé   'thousand (7/8)'
   edun   'million (7/8)'

Typically, one would expect the numeral one to be used with singular nouns and the numerals two to nine with plurals. However, in Akɔɔse the numeral one can be used both with singular and plural nouns. In the latter case the meaning is 'some' (132).

(132) **bad behóg** 'some people'

Table 3.10. The numeral 'one' -hóg, póg

Class	'one'	Class	'some'
1	nhóg	2	behóg
3	nhóg	4	nhóg
5	ahóg	6	mehóg
7	ehóg	8	e'hóg
9	póg	10	ehóg
14	e'hóg		
19	e'hóg	13	ahóg

It should be noted that all the prefixes for this numeral have low tone. In class 9 the numeral one has no prefix and the initial stem consonant is p instead of h.[5]

The numeral one is commonly used like an indefinite article to introduce a noun into the discourse (133).

(133) **mod   nhóg**
   1.person   1.one
   'a man, a certain man'

---

[5] Historically, there is a relationsip between p and h in that the latter derives from the former (see Hedinger 1987:61, 119–122).

hŏm   ahóg
5.place 5.one
'a place, a certain place'

The numerals two to five and and the numeral question word 'how many?' are found only with the plural classes. They all have a high tone on the prefix.

Table 3.11. The numerals 'two' to 'five' and 'how many?'

Class	prefix	-bɛ 'two'	-láán 'three'	-niin 'four'	-táan 'five'	-tɔ́ŋ 'how many?'
2	bé-	bébɛ	béláán	béniin	bétáan	bétɔ́ŋ
4	ń-	ḿbɛ	ńláán	ńniin	ńtáan	ńtɔ́ŋ
6	mé-	mébɛ	méláán	méniin	métáan	métɔ́ŋ
8	é'-	é'bɛ	é'láán	é'niin	é'táan	é'tɔ́ŋ
10	é-	ébɛ	éláán	éniin	étáan	étɔ́ŋ
13	á-	ábɛ	áláán	ániin	átáan	átɔ́ŋ

Numerals used for counting

When counting in Akɔɔse, the numerals one to five take the class 7 and 8 prefixes. There is no specific noun in mind. So, 7/8 looks like the default. This may be because the generic term *chŏm* 'thing' belongs to this gender.

(134) 1 ehóg   (cl.7)   6   ntóób
      2 é'bɛ   (cl.8)   7   saámbé
      3 é'láán   (cl.8)   8   waam
      4 é'niin   (cl.8)   9   abog
      5 é'táan   (cl.8)   10 dyôm   (cl.5)

Numerals eleven to nineteen consist of *dyôm* 'ten' plus a digit linked by *ne* 'and/with'.

3.3 Noun modifiers

(135) 11 **dyôm ne ehɔ́g**
     12 **dyôm ne é'bɛ**
     13 **dyôm ne é'láán**
     14 **dyôm ne é'niin**
     15 **dyôm ne é'táan**
     16 **dyôm ne ntóób**
     17 **dyôm ne saámbé**
     18 **dyôm ne waam**
     19 **dyôm ne abog**

The numerals from twenty to ninety are based on the plural form *môm* 'tens' of the numeral *dyôm* 'ten' plus the numerals two to nine which agree with *môm* in class 6. Numerals two to five have the class 6 prefix. Numerals seven to nine are linked with the associative marker for class 6. Apart from these combinations, *môm* does not exist.

(136) 10 **dyôm** cl.5
     20 **móōbɛ < môm mébɛ** cl.6
     30 **móo méláán** cl.6
     40 **móo méniin** cl.6
     50 **móo métáan** cl.6
     60 **móo mé ntóób** cl.6
     70 **móo mé saámbé** cl.6
     80 **móo mé waam** cl.6
     90 **móo mé abog** cl.6

The digits are added to the tens with the conjunction *ne* as follows. The numerals one to six agree in class with the larger numeral, twenty in this case.

(137) 21 **móóbɛ ne nhɔ́g** cl.6
     22 **móóbɛ ne mébɛ** cl.6
     23 **móóbɛ ne méláán** cl.6
     24 **móóbɛ ne méniin** cl.6
     25 **móóbɛ ne métáan** cl.6
     26 **móóbɛ ne ntóób**
     27 **móóbɛ ne saámbé**
     28 **móóbɛ ne waam**
     29 **móóbɛ ne abog**

The numerals based on the number *mbwɔ́kɛl* 'hundred' are given in (138). In the first five, the unit numbers agree in class with *mbwɔ́kɛl*. Just like any class 9/10 nouns, this numeral does not display a singular/plural distinction, but the singular/plural distinction comes out in the agreement. The unit numbers from six to nine are simply placed after the head numeral.

(138) 100 mbwɔ́kɛl (pɔ́g)   cl.9
      200 mbwɔ́kɛl ébɛ   cl.10
      300 mbwɔ́kɛl éláán   cl.10
      400 mbwɔ́kɛl éniin   cl.10
      500 mbwɔ́kɛl étáan   cl.10
      600 mbwɔ́kɛl ntóób
      700 mbwɔ́kɛl saámbé
      800 mbwɔ́kɛl waam
      900 mbwɔ́kɛl abog

The numerals based on *ekɔ́lé* 'thousand' are formed like the ones above except that agreement is in class 7/8.

(139) 1,000 ekɔ́lé (ehɔ́g)   cl.7
      2,000 e'kɔ́lé é'bɛ   cl.8
      3,000 e'kɔ́lé é'láán   cl.8
      4,000 e'kɔ́lé é'niin   cl.8
      5,000 e'kɔ́lé é'táan   cl.8
      6,000 e'kɔ́lé ntóób
      7,000 e'kɔ́lé saámbé
      8,000 e'kɔ́lé waam
      9,000 e'kɔ́lé abog

There is a numeral for million. Ejedepang (1986:340), however, says that not many people know it.

(140) 1,000,000 edun (ehɔ́g)   cl.7
      2,000,000 e'dun é'bɛ   cl.8
                 etc.

Zero

There is no word for zero. But the idea can be expressed with the expression in (141) which literally means 'not even one'.

(141) ké   ehɔ́g/pɔ́g
      not.even   one

3.3 Noun modifiers

Larger numerals as noun modifiers

As can be seen from the above examples, several structures are used to form numerals: simple juxtaposition with or without agreement (e.g. *e'kálé é'táan* '5,000' cl.8 and *e'kálé ntóób* '6,000'), the associative construction (e.g. *móo mé ntóób* '60' cl.6) and the prepositional phrase with *ne* (*móóbɛ ne nhɔ́g* '21').

There is some variation in the way larger numbers are formed when a noun phrase head is present. For example, when a plural noun is expected a singular noun may be found (compare (142) with (143)).

(142) **mod**   **dyôm**
      1.person   ten
      'ten people'

(143) **bad**   **dyôm**
      2.persons   ten
      'ten people'

These are equivalent in meaning.

The position of the head noun can occur in two different places. In (144) it is in the typical head noun position with the numeral after it. In (145) it appears as N_2 with the numeral ten as the N_1 of an associative construction.

(144) **bad**   **móo**   **mé**   **abog**   **ne**   **abog**
      2.people   6.ten   6.AM   nine   and   nine
      'ninety-nine people'

(145) **móo**   **mé**   **bad**   **abog**   **ne**   **abog**
      6.ten   6.AM   2.people   nine   and   nine
      'ninety-nine people'

In the longer example given in (146) *bad* 'people' is the entity being counted. It occurs twice, once with the hundreds and once with the tens. Agreement is with the head numeral (cl.10 and cl.6) except for the last numeral which agrees in noun class (cl.2) with *bad*.

(146) **mbwɔ́kɛl** é **bad** ébɛ **ne móo mé bad mébɛ**
     10.hundred 10.AM 2.people 10.two and 6.tens 6.AM 2.people 6.two
     ne béláán
     and 2.three
     'two hundred and twenty-three people'

It should be noted that when the noun for the things counted is present, the numeral after *ne* agrees with that noun. For more examples see appendix A.

3.3.5.2 *Ordinal numerals*

Ordinal numerals are formed syntactically rather than by a derivational process. For "first", an expression based on the word *e'só* 'face, front' is used (147). For all the other numbers a syntactic structure involving a relative clause is used (148) and (149).

(147) **mod** **a'só** < a + **e'só**
     1.person 1.first 1.AM 4.face
     'the first person'

(148) **mod** **awě** **a-lónténé** **é'bɛ**
     1.person 1.REL 1-fill.PERF 8.two
     'the second person'

(149) **mod** **awě** **a-lónténé** **é'láán**
     1.person 1.REL 1-fill.PERF 8.three
     'the third person'

The ordinal numeral for first agrees in class with its head noun resulting in the following forms:

3.3 Noun modifiers 57

Table 3.12. The ordinal numeral -'só 'first'

Class	'first'	Class	'first'
1	a'só	2	bé'só
3	mé'só	4	mé'só
5	dé'só	6	mé'só
7	é'só	8	é'só
9	e'só	10	é'só
14	bé'só		
19	bé'só	13	dé'só

These clearly come from the combination of the associative marker (AM) plus -'só 'face' in the associative noun phrase. However, they are now probably best considered to be fixed expressions.

3.3.6 Relative clauses

Relative clauses are frequently used as noun modifiers and usually come after other modifiers. They follow the noun and are linked by the relative pronoun which agrees in class with the head noun.

(150) **dyam** [**áde á-láng-é mɔ́**]
 5.thing 5.REL 1-tell-PREF 1.him
 'the thing he told him'

(151) **mod nhɔ́g** [**awe bé-chɔ́g-é bán ngɔ́lɛ**]
 1.person 1.one 1.REL 2-call-PREF COMP Ngolle
 'a man called Ngolle'

3.3.6.1 Relative pronouns

The forms of the relative pronouns for each class are given in table 3.13.

Table 3.13. The relative pronouns

Class	'which'	Class	'which'
1	awe	2	ábe
3	ḿme	4	ḿme
5	áde	6	ḿme
7	éche	8	ábe
9	eche	10	éche
14	ábe		
19	ábe	13	áde

The tone on the relative pronoun stem -e varies according to the tonal context.

These relative pronouns can also be used to link two nouns in a possessive or associative relationship where the second noun possesses or is in some way associated with the first (see also section 3.7).

(152) **mwǎn   awě   Akumé**
       1.child 1.REL Akume
       'the child of Akume'

       e'mii   ábe   kém
       14.finger 14.REL 9.monkey
       'the monkey's finger'

3.3.6.2 Reduced relative pronouns

There is a reduced form of the relative pronoun in the form of a clitic -ɛ́ɛ̄ attached to the head noun. This is frequently used with the nouns for place, time and thing.

(153) **hǒm**   'place'   →   **hom-ɛ́ɛ̄**
       póndé 'time'   →   **póndé-ɛ́ɛ̄**
       chǒm   'thing'   →   **chom-ɛ́ɛ̄**
       dyam   'matter' →   **dyam-ɛ́ɛ̄**
       epun   'day'   →   **epun-ɛ́ɛ̄**
       mbwɛ   'day'   →   **mbwé-ɛ́ɛ̄**

When the cliticised form of the relative pronoun is used there is no other modifier between it and the noun it is attached to, as in (154)–(156).

(154) **A-kií hom[-ɛ̄ɛ̄ éché nyóod é-díí].**
1-went 5.place-REL 10.DEM 10.bee 10-are
'He went to the place where the bees were.'

(155) **A-hwéné chom[-ɛ̄ɛ̄ mmwaád mwěn á-kóó adəŋ].**
1-returned.with 7.thing-REL 1.woman 1.herself 1-really.PERF INF.like
'He returned with what the woman herself really liked.'

(156) **mbwɛ́ [-ɛ̄ɛ̄ á-pɛ́ɛ́né ḿmé mɔné wê kúlɛ]**
3.day-REL 1-take.PERF 3.that 3.money to 1.tortoise
'the day he took the money to tortoise'

For more details on relative clauses see section 7.4.

3.4 Other elements of the noun phrase

3.4.1 Appositions

Noun phrases can be added after a noun as an apposition. Examples (157) and (158) show descriptive phrases and nicknames used in apposition to the head noun.

(157) **e'sélɛ, mod a mwáne**
Duiker person of tricks
'Duiker, the trickster'

(158) **e'sélenyamɛ, mod a mwane, mélongembɛlɛɛ**
duiker.animal person of tricks (nickname)
'Duiker, the trickster, (nickname)'

3.4.2 Emphatic particles

There are two particles that can precede nouns: *ké* and *ken*. Both of these are often translated as 'even'.

(159) **ké ndyééd**
even food
'food (emphatic)'

ké dyad démpēpēe
even town other
'the other town (emphatic)'

(160) **ken ekə́lé é mbə́té**
     even 1,000 of shirts
     'thousands of shirts (emphatic)'

3.4.3 Quantifier

There is a quantifier *té* meaning 'each'. It occurs with singular nouns. It is invariant, that is, it does not agree in noun class with the head noun.

(161) **mod té**
     person each
     'each person'

     búmɔ̄ mod té
     he+he person each
     'the two of them' or 'each of them'

     Bə́ mod té a-nkě aboŋsɛn.
     2.they 1.person each 1-went INF.prepare
     'Each one went to prepare.'

3.4.4 Intensifier

At first sight *nyě* in (162) looks like an intensifier, intensifying what appears to be an adjective. This is certainly the case semantically. Structurally, however, each word is a noun linked to another noun via the associative marker *a*. The latter has fused with the vowel of the preceding noun.

(162) **nyě sánkala ntyə́g**
     1.huge.AM 1.huge.AM 3.box
     'a very huge box'

     benyě bé sánkala bé ntyə́g bébɛ
     2.huge 2.AM 1.huge 2.AM 4.box 2.two
     'two very huge boxes'

The conclusion is that there is no separate class of intensifiers. These functions are expressed through nouns in associative constructions.

3.5 Negation and the noun phrase

3.4.5 Modifiers as noun phrase heads

The following noun modifiers can stand as noun phrase heads when the noun is understood from the context: possessives, demonstratives and numerals. In (163)–(164) the underlined modifiers without head nouns fill object and subject positions typically filled by noun phrases.

(163) **mbíí** .... **á-laténnɛ** <u>**échī**</u>
 10.palm.nuts ... he-puts.together 10.his
 'palm nuts...he puts them together with his own'

(164) <u>**Ḿmíníí**</u> ń-húú hén, <u>**ḿmén-nɛ**</u> ń-húú hén,
 3.DEM.FAR.DIST 3-comes here 3.DEM.PROX-ADD 3-comes here
 ḿ-bomtén áte.
 3-meet into
 'That one comes here, this one too comes here, they meet up.'

(165) Nzé <u>**nhɔ́g**</u> ě-sɛ, nsɔ́n mé-kaké bwâm.
 if 1.one 1.NEG-be 3.work 3.NEG-go well
 'If one is missing, the work doesn't go well.'

In (164) and (165) the verb agrees in noun class with the respective subject which in turn takes its class from an understood noun. In (166) the determiner 'another' is the head of the object NP.

(166) **Bé-chélé** <u>**ampée.**</u>
 2-call.PERF 1.another
 'They called another one.'

3.5 Negation and the noun phrase

Akɔɔse has no phrasal negation like 'no money' in 'he has no money'. However, there is a kind of negative focus to deny an alternative by the use of *haké/saké* (167)–(168). This negative particle, which has two variants, precedes the phrase it modifies.

(167) a. **haké** mod asyəəl
 not 1.person 1.all
 'not every person'

b. Haké   bwĕm   é'syɔ̄ɔ̄n   é'-kíne   epun   ehɔ́g.
    not   14.thing 14.all   14-dry.IMPF   7.day   7.one
    'Not all things dry in one day.'

(168) Saké   me   n-wóó   enén   ndáb.
       not   1SG   1SG-have.PERF   9.DEM.PROX   9.house
       'It is not me who owns the this house.'

In fact this marker can be used to deny any phrase, including prepositional and adverbial phrases.

(169) Saké   á   dĭd   bé-chogɛé.
       not   LOC   5.eye   2-play.IMPF.SF
       'It is not in the eye that they are playing.'

3.6 The associative noun phrase

The associative noun phrase is a very frequently used construction in Akɔɔse. It consists of two nouns linked with the associative marker (AM). The associative marker agrees in noun class with the first noun (N_1).

(170) esɔg   é   kém
       7.group   7.AM   10.monkey
       'group of monkeys'

The structure of the associative NP can be represented as in (171).

(171) N_1 + AM + N_2

3.6.1 The associative marker (AM)

The AM takes a different form according to the class of N_1. In some classes there are two different forms depending on whether N_2 has a prefix (V-, CV-, N-) or not. The markers are as in table 3.14. They are identical in form to those of the subject markers of the verb (4.3) and adjective prefixes (3.3.4.1).

3.6 The associative noun phrase

Table 3.14. The associative markers

Class	/__	/__ Pfx	Class	/__	/__ Pfx
1	a	a	2	bé	bé
3	Ń	mé	4	Ń	mé
5	á	dé	6	mé	mé
7	é	é	8	é'	bé
9	e	e	10	é	é
14	é'	bé			
19	é'	bé	13	á	dé

The markers on the left occur before non-prefixed nouns (172), the ones on the right before nouns with prefixes (173). The homorganic nasal in class 9/10 is considered to be part of the noun stem (although historically it probably was a separate class prefix). This is supported by the fact that nouns with initial homorganic nasals take the AM for prefixless nouns (174).

(172) e'del   é'   kaké
      14.weight 14.AM   9.cocoa
      'the weight of the cocoa'

(173) e'del   bé   e-béné
      14.weight 14.AM   7-zinc
      'the weight of the corrugated iron'

(174) e'séd   é'   ndáb
      8.wall   8.AM   9.house
      'the walls of the house'

The associative marker frequently merges with the preceding (175) or the following noun (176).

(175) e'del   é'   kaké   →   [e'děl' kaké]
      14.weight 14.AM   9.cocoa
      'the weight of the cocoa'

      n-lóŋ   a   ndáb   →   [nlóó ꜜndáb]
      1-build   1.AM   9.house
      'builder'

(176) e'del   bé   e-béné   →   [e'del bébéné]
      14.weight   14.AM   7-zinc
      'the weight of the corrugated iron'

Syntactically, N_1 is the head of the associative NP since it controls the noun class agreement. N_1 is not, however, always the semantic head. See the qualifier-head noun phrase in (177).

(177) **mbîd**   **ń**   **nyam**
      3.rawness   3.AM   9.meat
      'raw meat'

N_1 (*mbîd* 'rawness') is the syntactic head (cl.3) controlling the agreement with the AM. Semantically, though, N_2 (*nyam* 'meat') is the head of the phrase and the first noun has a modifying function. This is a common structure where N_1 indicates colour, quantity, size, quality, etc.

3.6.2 Tone in the associative noun phrase

There is a tone replacement rule that characterises the associative NP. This is a tone replacement rule that is restricted to the AssNP and one or two other contexts.

A low tone on the prefix of N_2 is replaced by a high tone under the following conditions: the AM has a H tone and the first stem tone also is H (L → H / H __ H). This rule replaces the phonological rule (L → ꜜ / H __ H) which normally applies to a L tone between two Hs causing downstep.

```
              H         L H              H H H
(178) epíd    é         mendíb    →      epíd é méndíb
      7.bottle 7.AM     6.water
```

Since all AMs have a H tone except for those in classes 1 and 9, this tone change is observed after the AM of most classes.

Other tone changes follow the typical tone rules across word boundaries. However, there is an unusual phenomenon that needs further study. Nouns in gender 9/10 are only distinguished for singular/plural on the AM. When the AM elides, tone contours appear on N_1. In the plural (180) this is as expected with the L tone of N_1 combining with the H tone of the

3.6 The associative noun phrase

AM. However, in the singular (179) an H tone appears on N_1 resulting in a falling tone.[6]

(179) **mbum   e   ngun** > **mbúm e ngun** > **mbûm ngun**
9.grain   9.AM   9.corn
'grain of corn'

(180) **mbum   é   ngun** > **mbŭm ngun**
10.grain 10.AM 9.corn
'grains of corn'

3.6.3 Agreement in embedded AssNPs

An associative NP can be embedded in another associative NP (N_1 AM N_2 AM N_3). Agreement of the second AM may then be with the first (181) or the second noun (182).

```
       [[                              ]              ]
```
(181) **échem   esóŋ   é   mod   é   Mwăkɔ́le**
7.my   7.short   7.AM   1.person 7.AM   Mwakole
'my short man of Mwakole'

```
       [      [                     ]]
```
(182) **ahín   á   chɔl   é   mbwé**
5.pus   5.AM   7.boil 7.AM 9.dog
'pus from a dog's boil'

Example (181) has the structure [[Noun AM Noun] AM Noun] and (182) has the structure [Noun AM [Noun AM Noun]].

3.6.4 Relationships expressed by the AssNP

There is a wide variety of semantic relationships expressed by the associative noun phrase. This section gives a survey of these relationships.

I have already stated that many compound nouns appear to be derived from the associative NP. It is, in fact, not easy to draw a clear line between the two construction types. It is therefore not suprising that the same relationships can be found in compound nouns as in associative constructions, especially when there is a reasonably transparent relationship between the two elements. Some

---

[6] Further work needs to be done to determine whether there is a stem-final floating H tone that only appears in this context and, if so, which nouns do have this tone.

of the examples listed below may therefore better be listed under compound nouns. This ambiguity can be attributed to the fact that there is a historical lexicalisation process involving a transition from a fully transparent associative NP to a fused compound noun with the result that different expressions may be at different stages in this historical process.

3.6.4.1 Head-modifier

In (183) the second noun modifies the first noun with a property concept. N_1 is both the syntactic and grammatical head. Some of the phrases are given with the elided AM.

(183) **mbɔ́té e bwǎam**   shirt of good   'a fine shirt'
      ekáá é tɔnɛ   arm of nail   'pincers'
      esisǒŋ nkááĺe   elephant grass of whiteman 'Indian bamboo'
      mod atóg   man of poverty   'a poor man'
      ekɔbted é asóg   hook of last   'the last hook'

3.6.4.2 Modifier-head

In (184) N_1 is grammatically the head but is modifying the N_2, making N_2 the semantic head.

(184) **esóŋ é mod**   shortness of man   'a short man'
      posom e mod   largeness of man   'a large man'
      mbîd ń nyam   rawness of meat   'raw meat'
      melemlem mé mbɔ́té   sameness of shirt   'the same shirt'
      mbinde é mekan   dirt of thing   'dirty things'
      ndəngél e nguu   bigness of pig   'a big pig'

3.6.4.3 Part-whole relationship

The following express a part-whole relationship with the first noun being a part of the second.

(185) **mbɔl ń kúb**   'neck of the hen'
      mesó mé abad   'hem of the cloth'
      etúú é ndáb   'foundation of the house'
      eséd é ndáb   'wall of the house'
      ebom é ndáb   'crest of the house'
      alín á mangolɛ   'stem of the mango tree'

3.6.4.4 *Agent-object*

In (186) N_1 is the agent and N_2 the object or result of the action implied by N_1. Each N_1 here belongs to class 1/2 and is derived from a verb stem.

(186)   **nwobé**   **ᶥbyém**   'washerman'
        1.wash   8.things

       mbaá   **ᶥmbɔ́té**   'tailor'
        1.sew   10.shirt

       nkóbé   **ᶥsúu**   'fisherman'
        1.catch   10.fish

       nlám   **melám**   'trapper'
        1.trap   6.traps

       nkəɔ́   **ngəŋ**   'barber'
        1.shave   9.haircut

In these the AM obviously has merged with the preceding noun. The downstep results from the displaced L tone of the class 1 AM. Compare the singular and plural for cook in (187) where there is a downstep in the singular (cl.1) but not in the plural (cl.2). The high tone on the AM for class 1 is probably due to spreading of the last high tone of N_1.

(187)   **nchám**   é   **ᶥndyéd**   'cooks'
        1.cook   1.AM   9.food

       bechám   bé   **ndyéd**   'cooks'
        2.cook   2.AM   9.food

3.6.4.5 *Quantification*

In the examples in (188) the first noun indicates some kind of quantity of the second noun.

(188) **pún e nyam**   'piece of meat'
       atû á nyam   'share/piece of meat'
       mwǎmpīn ḿ póndé   'short time'
       etɔd é bad   'group of people'
       ngúse é bad   'some people'

3.6.4.6 Action-object

The following have a noun derived from a verb as N_1, and N_2 is the inherent object of that verb. The overall expression refers to an activity.

(189) **nsal**   **ḿ**   **mod**   **áte**   'postmortem, autopsy'
        3.cut   3.AM   1.person   inside

        apim   **dé**   **ekúú**   'disposal of bad luck'
        5.throw   5.AM   7.ill.luck
        achog   **á**   **bɔ́ɔl**   'football game'
        5.play   5.AM   9.ball

3.6.4.7 Specific-generic

In (190) the first noun is specific, the second noun generic and sometimes seemingly redundant. However, this is quite a common way of expressing things.

(190) **ngo nyamɛ**   leopard animal   'leopard'
       ebóté ngule   male-lizard lizard   'male lizard'
       nsɔg ń kém   monkey (sp.) monkey   'monkey (sp.)'
       epále é mbód   he-goat goat   'billy goat'
       etombɛɛ asáá   fat plum plum   'fat plum'
       mbǒn ehɔ́b   insult talk   'insult'

3.6.4.8 Container-contents

In (191) the first noun is the name for a container and the second for a liquid or semi-liquid.

3.6 The associative noun phrase

(191) **epíd é méndíb** bottle of water   'water bottle'
      mbâm mǐm   big jug of wine   'big wine jug'
      kúmbe e mǐm   bowl of wine   'bowl for wine'
      pɔ́ke e mesɛn chamber pot of urine   'chamber pot'
      etənge é méndíb jar of water   'water storage jar'
      ekě echuu   honeycomb of honey   'honeycomb'
      ekwém é kaké tin of cocoa   'cocoa tin'

3.6.4.9 Object-purpose

In (192) the first noun is an object which is used for the purpose of acting on or achieving N_2.

(192) **aláá ndóŋ**   stone of pepper   'grinding stone (for pepper)'
      aláá mbɔ́té   stone of shirt   'pressing iron'
      menyónge mé esoŋ rubber of purging   'tube for purging'
      akoó kaké   spear of cocoa   'knife for cutting cocoa'
      menyân mé kaké platform of cocoa   'platform for drying cocoa'
      etud é mbuu   raffia palm of thatch 'palm for thatching'
      etud é mwɛ   raffia palm of drink   'palm for wine'

3.6.4.10 Product-material

In the associative noun phrases in (193) N_2 indicates the material from which N_1 is made.

(193) **anɔŋ dé mebámbé** bed of planks   'wooden bed'
      mbeé hyəg   pot of clay   'clay pot'
      akad dé ményónge bundle of rubber   'rubber ball'
      nkɔɔd ń ngúbé   rope of banana fibre   'rope from banana stem'
      lan étud   ladder of raffia palm   'ladder (made from raffia palm)'
      kondé a ngob é nyam chair of skin of animal 'leather armchair'

There are probably other relationships not covered here, but the above examples show the range of semantic relations that are expressed by this construction.

3.7 Possessive noun phrase

In addition to the construction involving a possessive pronoun (see section 3.3.3) there are two structures to express possession involving nouns. In the first the possessor comes first in the structure as in (194).

(194) PossNP → Name NP

In this case the first noun is always a proper name. The NP consists of a posssessive pronoun (see table 3.8) plus the possessed noun.

(195) **Nzumé áwi mwǎn**
  Nzume his child
  'Nzume's child'

In the second PossNP the possessor comes last and is linked to the possessed noun with a relative pronoun (see table 3.13). This PossNP has the structure Noun + REL + Noun. This structure is very similar to the associative NP. Instead of the associative marker (AM), the relative pronoun is used as the link element. The relative pronoun agrees in noun class with N_1. This structure is typically used with names and kinship terms (196). It is also used as a more marked structure instead of the associative NP (197).

(196) **mwǎn awe Akumé**
  1.child 1.REL Akume
  'the child of Akume'

  baányaŋ ábe kə̂ŋ
  2.brother 2.REL 9.chief
  'the brothers of the chief'

(197) **e'mii ábe kém**
  14.finger 14.REL 9.monkey
  'the monkey's fingers'

3.8 Coordinate noun phrase

In the coordinate NP two or more NPs are linked with one of the three coordinating conjunctions *ne*, *bə́* or *káa*. The conjunction *ne* is the general

3.8 Coordinate noun phrase

one; *bɔ́* has the same function but is used with a human referent; *káa* is used to link alternatives.

3.8.1 With *ne*

This is identical in form to the preposition *ne* (see section 3.9.4) but has a different function here. When there is a list of three or more different items, then the conjunction may only occur between the last two (199).

(198) **mekáá ne mekuu**   'hands and feet'

(199) **ngo ngii ne ewake**   'leopard, lion and chimpanzee'

The conjunction *ne* is also used in the formation of numerals (200) (also see section 3.3.5.1).

(200) **dyôm   ne   bébɛ**
      ten   and   two
      'twelve'

Sometimes, to indicate "a lot of (something)" the construction: N_1 + *ne* + N_1 is used. Examples are given in (201) and (202) with the latter showing that not only prototypical nouns, but also a verb in its infinitival form can be used in this construction.

(201) **meloŋ ne meloŋ** place and place   'lots of places, place after place'
      nkute ne nkute sack and sack   'lots of sacks'
      mě ne mě   junction and junction 'lots of junctions'
      metɔ́n ne metɔ́n spots and spots   'full of spots'

(202) **akəg ne akəg**   trying and trying   'a lot of trying'

Duration and repetition is in focus in (203) and "different kinds" in (204).

(203) **mwě ne mwɛ**   year and year   'year after year'
      ngíndé ne ngíndé long time and long time   'for a long time'
      kɔ́ŋ ne kɔ́ŋ   until and until   'until at last'
      e'soŋ ne e'soŋ   piece and piece   'piece by piece'

(204) **nyaa ne nyaa**   kinds and kinds   'different kinds'
     kân ne kân   kinds and kinds   'many kinds of'

In (205) the position of entities in relation to each other is expressed.

(205) **mbíd ne mbíd**   back and back   'back to back, side by side'

The structure in (206) the emphatic demonstrative *bĕn* is repeated and used with verbs in the plural to make it reciprocal.

(206) **Bĕn   ne   bĕn   bé-wan-e   nzum.**
      2.selves and/with 2.selves 2-fight-IMPF 9.fight
      'They fight with each other.'

The structure in (207) is used to express a repeated action; *nê* is the comparative preposition. In (208) the noun is repeated to indicate a continuous process. Note that here the conjunction is obligatory between all the items.

(207) **nê   ne   nê   ne   nê**
      like.that   and   like.that   and   like.that
      'like that again and again'

(208) **Á-kún-εέ e'chɔ́ ne   e'chɔ́ ne   e'chɔ́.**
      1-sleep-IMPF.SF sleep and sleep and sleep
      'He sleeps and sleeps and sleeps.'

3.8.2 With *bɔ́*

This conjunction is identical in form to the third-person plural pronoun from which it probably is derived. It is used here, however, to link names and nouns referring to humans.

(209) **mod bɔ́ mwaád**   'man and wife'

When the word in the second position has the class 1 personifier suffix *-ε*, this suffix is dropped.

(210) **María bɔ́ Yosêb**   'Mary and Joseph'   from: **Yosébε**
      kúlε bɔ́ mbyε   'Tortoise and Eagle' from: **mbyεε**

3.8 Coordinate noun phrase

A very common use of *bɔ́* is as a kind of portmanteau for third-person singular plus the conjunction "and" as in (211).

(211) **bɔ́**   **awi**   **mwaád**   'he and his wife'
      they   his   wife

   bɔ́   **María**   'he and Mary'
   they   Mary

From (212) it is clear that the same is done with the first- and second-person plural.

(212) **sé**   **anén**   **nkáálé**   'I and this white man'
      we   this   white.man

   sé   **mwǎnyaŋ**   'I and my brother/sister'
   we   sibling

   nyí   **píinyɔ̌**   'you and viper'
   you.PL   viper

Compare this also with the pronoun *súmə̄* 'I and him/her (lit. we-(s)he)' (see section 3.11.3).

3.8.3 With *káa*

There is a disjunctive conjunction which is used to link phrases and sentences: *káa* 'or'.
In the following examples, noun phrases, verbs, locative phrases and positive/negative verbs are linked with this conjunction.

(213) **bekáálé**   **káa**   **bad**   **ábe**   **bé-hínɛ'**
      2.whites   or   2.people   2.REL   2-are.black
      'white or black people'

(214) **Bé-chámé**   **sóo**   **ngun**   **káa**   **bé-nyáŋ.**
      2.FUT-cook   us   corn   or   2-fry
      'They will cook corn or fry for us.'

(215) **A-kélle   mɔ́   hê   káa   á   kɔ̂bɔ̂d   te.**
      1-hang   it   there   or   LOC   cupboard   in
      'He hangs it there or in the cupboard.'

(216) **Ké   mě-chěm   mɔ́   káa   mě-chemmé...**
      whether   I.FUT-recognise   him   or   I.FUT.NEG-recognise.SF
      'Whether I will recognise him or not...'

3.9 Prepositional phrases

Prepositional phrases have the structure in (217) consisting of a preposition and a noun phrase.

(217) PP → P NP

There are the prepositions listed in (218).

(218) **á**   'general location'
  wê /wɛ   'specific location, where'
  ne   'with (and)'
  bootya   'from, beginning with'
  ngáne   'as, like'
  nɛ́ɛ   'as, like'
  tóma   'more than'
  áyɔle   'because of'
  tɔ́ngɛne   'because of'
  kɔ́ŋne   'until, even'

Several of these can also function as conjunctions (see chapter 8).

3.9.1 Prepositional phrases expressing location

The preposition *á* is the prototypical and perhaps the oldest preposition. It is cliticised to the following noun and often merges with vocalic prefixes. It is mainly used to express general location, without indicating specific location.

(219) **á nsəl**   <   á + nsəl   'in/from the mouth'
     ábum   <   á + abum   'in/on the stomach'
     ésukúle   <   á + esukúle   'in/at/from school'
     á'⁺wóngé   <   á + e'wóngé   'in marriage'

3.9 Prepositional phrases 75

This preposition is also used for temporal concepts as, for example, days of the week, as in the following expressions.

(220) á ⁺sɔ́ɔnde   'on Sunday'
     á ⁺sáteré   'on Saturday'

The preposition wê is used for specific location for human or animate objects and frequently with verbs of movement.

(221) wê ane mwǎn   'to that child'
     wê mwê   'to the friend'
     wê ngaabobɛ   'to Spider'

This preposition is also used as a locative adverb (see section 6.4.4.2).

3.9.2 Prepositional phrases with post-nominal element

Since the locational preposition *á* is very general, the following three particles (222) are used in final position to make a more specific spatial distinction. These adverbs probably are historically derived from nouns.

(222) te   'in, into'
     sé   'under'
     mîn   'on top'

In order to handle this, the phrase structure given above needs to be expanded as in (223) by adding an optional adverb.

(223) PP → P NP (Adv)

(224) á ⁺ndáb te   'in/into the house'
     á dyad têˆ   'in town'

     á ⁺díi sé   'under the palm tree'
     ékob sé   'under the door'

     á bwɛl mîn   'on the tree'
     ékone mîn   'on the hill'

Note that the tone on *te* changes depending on the tonal environment. It is falling when the preceding tone is low, but low when the preceding tone is high.

3.9.3 Prepositional phrases with "complex prepositions"

There is another prepositional phrase type containing elements which further specify locational concepts. Structurally it consists of an associative noun phrase preceded by the locative marker *á*. The first noun in the AssNP specifies the location of the second noun. The second noun is semantically the main noun. This structure can be represented with the following flat structure: LOC + N AM N. The associative marker agrees in noun class with the inherent class of the first noun.

(225) á   nkəg   ń   dǔ   'beside the fireplace'
      LOC   3.side   3.AM   fireplace

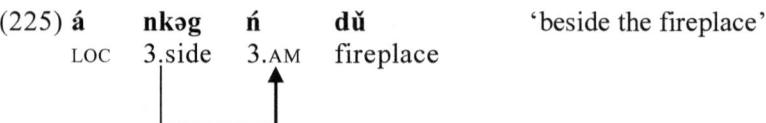

Such phrases have the internal structure in (226).

(226)

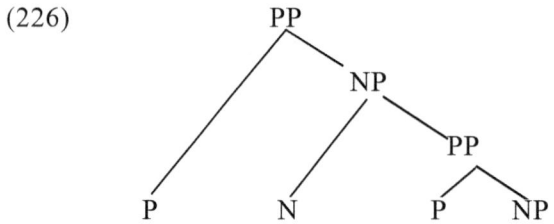

The words which give more precise locational information found in these structures are displayed in table 3.15. Some are derived from nouns referring to body parts like 'face', 'back', 'side', but for others it has not been possible to determine the source item.

Table 3.15. Locational expressions with source noun and class

á⁺'só	'in front'	from	e'só	cl.14	'face'
á mbíd	'behind'	from	mbíd	cl.9	'back (of person)'
á nkəg	'beside'	from	nkəg	cl.3	'side (of person)'
á ⁺tîntê	'in the middle'	from	tínte	cl.9	'space in middle of house'
á⁺kéb	'at the side'	from	akéb	cl.5	'side'
á ⁺nlééd	'in the middle'	from	nlééd	cl.3	'?'
á ⁺pípíí	'behind'	from	pípíí	cl.9	'?'
á⁺bédé	'behind'	from	abédé	cl.5	'?'

3.9 Prepositional phrases

A few examples are given in (227). Notice that the associative marker agrees in noun class with the first noun.

(227) á⁺'só   é'   ndáb   'in front of the house'
      LOC.14.face 14.AM   9.house

      á⁺béédé   á   ndáb   'behind the house'
      LOC.5.???   5.AM   9.house

      á   nkəg   ń   nzag   'at the side of the farm'
      LOC   3.side   3.AM   9.farm

3.9.4 Prepositional phrases with *ne*

Another common preposition is *ne*. It can be glossed as 'with'. It is used in oblique phrases[7] expressing instrument and accompaniment, as well as in coordinate NPs (see section 3.8) where it means 'and'.

3.9.4.1 Instrument

The instrument is an oblique referring to the thing with which an action is carried out.

(228) **ne páá**   'with the cutlass'
      ne ngíne   'with strength/power'
      ne mendíb mékɔ̄ɔ̄lē   'with new/fresh water'

3.9.4.2 Comitative

The comitative is an oblique phrase expressing a participant that accompanies the agent or object.

(229) Bé-dé   hê   ne   mwǎn.
      2-are   there   with   1.child
      'They are there with the child.'

      mbaaŋgé   échē   bad   bé-dyédé   ne   nzab
      10.cocoyam   10.which   2.people   2-eat.PERF   with   9.soup
      'cocoyam which the people ate with soup'

---

[7]Clause adjuncts without a grammatical relation to the verb, i.e. some element of the clause which is not the subject or direct or indirect object.

3.9.5 Other prepositional phrases

There are several other prepositions. These will be discussed in turn.

3.9.5.1 bootya 'from', (lit. beginning with)

The preposition *bootya* 'from' indicates a beginning point, either in time (230) or space (231). It appears to be related to the verb *-booted* 'begin'.

(230) **bootya échê epun**   'from that day'
       bootya epun é'só   'from the first day'

(231) **bootya á Lɔbɛɛ**   'from Lobe'
       bootya échê esóŋ é hóm   'from that part of the place'

3.9.5.2 kə́ŋne 'until'

The preposition *kə́ŋne* 'until' is used to indicate a duration of an action up to an end point in time.

(232) **kə́ŋne chii**   'until today'
       kə́ŋne bɔɔb   'until now'
       kə́ŋne ngə́ŋ ntóób   'until six o'clock'

This preposition consists of two parts, *kə́ŋ* and *ne*. The first part is similar to the conjunction *kə́ə́ŋ* 'until' (see section 8.5.6) and the second has the same form as the preposition/conjunction *ne* 'with/and'. *kə́ŋne* and *kə́nne* are individual/dialectal variants.

3.9.5.3 kə́ə́ŋ se 'all the way to'

In (233) the combination *kə́ə́ŋ* and *se* indicates the final endpoint of a spatial relation. It is added in front of a prepositional phrase beginning with *á*.

(233) **kə́ə́ŋ se á nkáálé**   'right to the white man' i.e. 'to the western world'

For *kə́ə́ŋ* see also the conjunction *kə́ə́ŋ* 'until'. The *se* is an emphatic particle also used in the verb phrase (see section 5.3).

3.9 Prepositional phrases

3.9.5.4 nɛ́ɛ 'as, like'

The preposition *nɛ́ɛ* is used to make comparisons.

(234) nɛ́ɛ páá   'like a cutlass'
      nɛ́ɛ aláá á ndóŋ   'as a grind stone (lit. as stone of pepper)'
      nɛ́ɛ ntâŋ   'as a slave'

It is also used as a conjunction (see section 8.5.8).

3.9.5.5 tóma 'more than'

The preposition *tóma* is used in comparative and superlative sentences. It appears to be derived from the verb *-tóm* 'to pass by, surpass'.

(235) tóma ádōŋ   'more than yours'
      tóma chii   'more than today'
      tóma nyóod   'more than the bee'
      tóma mod esyəə́l   'more than all people'

3.9.5.6 áyɔ̄le 'because'

The preposition *áyɔ̄le* gives the cause or reason for the action expressed in the clause in which it functions.

(236) áyɔ̄le ehuhu é nlém   'because of his foolishness'
      áyɔ̄le nsɔ́n   'because of work'

There is another preposition *tə́ngene* 'because', with the same meaning that has not been found in my corpus of texts but seems to be used in other parts of the Bakossi area.

The preposition *áyɔ̄le* appears to be derived from the noun *yŏl* 'body' with the locative preposition *á* prefixed to it plus a final vowel, while *tə́ngene* seems to be derived from the auxiliary verb *-tə́ngen* 'must'.

3.9.5.7 étōmɛé 'except, only'

The word *étōmɛé* is a verbal form and there is a question whether it should be considered a preposition. It is the perfect negative form of the verb *-tóm* 'pass' meaning literally 'it doesn't pass'.

(237) **Mod ampée e-sóle-'ĕ etág é wááb áte étōmɛé**
person other 3SG.NEG-enter-DEV rafter of friend into except
mwaád mwěn pɛn.
wife herself alone
'Nobody entered the rafter of the other, only the woman herself.'

3.10 Question phrase

A question phrase is formed by the question word *nzé* 'who, what' followed by a noun with the clitic *-é* suffixed to it. The tones on the noun are raised to high.

(238) **nzé chómé** 'which thing?' < **chŏm** 'thing'
    nzé módé 'which person?' < **mod** 'person'
    nzé pólé 'which story?' < **póle** 'talk'

3.11 Pronouns

Pronouns are forms that stand in for nouns or noun phrases. Akɔɔse distinguishes the following categories in the pronouns: person, number and noun class. There are simple and compound pronouns, topicalised and non-topicalised pronouns. (For the obligatory subject markers prefixed to the verb, see section 4.3.)

3.11.1 Personal pronouns

Table 3.16 presents the personal pronouns. The main categories distinguished are person and number.

Table 3.16. Personal pronouns

Person	Singular		Plural	
	Simple	Topicalised	Simple	Topicalised
1	me	meé	sé	séē̄
2	wɛ	weé	nyí	nyéē̄
3	mə́	mə̂	bə́	bə̂

Subject pronouns are always emphatic since the verb is already marked with a subject marker. (For subject agreement prefixes (subject markers) see table 4.2.)

3.11 Pronouns

(239) **boŋ**　me　n-lángé　wɛ
　　　but　1SG　1SG-tell.PERF　2SG
　　　'but I told you'

Object pronouns follow the verb and are non-emphatic.

When pronouns are left-dislocated for the purpose of topicalisation then the longer topicalised forms are used.

(240) **Meé**　n-lángé　wɛ.
　　　1SG.TOP　1SG-tell.PERF　2SG
　　　'It is I who told you.'

The third-person forms are also the forms for class 1 (singular) and class 2 (plural). Because of this overlap of categories I sometimes gloss them for person and number (3SG, 3PL), and sometimes for noun class (1, 2) in the examples in this grammar.

3.11.2 Class pronouns

In table 3.17 the pronouns for noun classes 1–19 are given. As indicated above, the third-person forms are also the class 1 and 2 forms and are therefore included in both this table and in table 3.16.

Table 3.17. Pronouns for classes 1–19

	Singular			Plural	
Class	Simple	Topicalised	Class	Simple	Topicalised
1	mə́	mə̂	2	bə́	bə̂
3	mə́	mə̂	4	mə́	mə̂
5	də́	də̂	6	mə́	mə̂
7	chə́	chə̂	8	bə́	bə̂
9	chə́	chə̂	10	chə́	chə̂
14	bə́	bə			
19	də́	bə̂	13	də́	də̂

3.11.3 Compound pronouns

Like many other languages in the geographic area, Akɔɔse has sets of compound pronouns consisting of two simple pronouns. There are two sets, one of dual pronouns referring to two people, and another set referring to more than two people. Note that the first element of both the dual and the plural pronouns comes from a plural form. The second element comes from a singular form in the dual pronouns and from a plural form in the compound plural ones. Compare (241) with table 3.16.

(241) **nyúᵼmɔ́**   <   **nyí + ? + mɔ́**   'dual: you and he/she'
      2PL + 3SG
      nyáᵼbɔ̂   <   **nyí + ? + bɔ́**   'plural: you and them'
      2PL + 3PL

These compound forms appear to be fixed now as can be seen from the irregularities. The dual forms appear to have a rounded back vowel link element and the plural ones a low central vowel. The first-person (1+1) forms are the most irregular ones.

Below are the dual pronouns (242) and the plural (243).

(242) **sóo**   'we/us two, I and you (sg) (inclusive)'   (1+2)SG
      súᵼmɔ́   'we/us two, I and he (exclusive)'   (1+3)SG
      nyúᵼmɔ́   'you two, you and he'   (2+3)SG
      búᵼmɔ́   'those two, he and he'   (3+3)SG

(243) **syá(ᵼné)**   'we/us, I/we and you (pl) (inclusive)'   (1+2)PL
      syáᵼbɔ̂   'we/us, I/we and they (exclusive)'   (1+3)PL
      nyáᵼbɔ́   'you pl, you and they'   (2+3)PL
      bɔ́ᵼbɔ̂   'they, he/they and they'   (3+3)PL

4
The Verb

4.1 Introduction

Akɔɔse has a typical Bantu verb structure (Meeussen 1967) which can be described as agglutinative. Historically there was a lot of fusion of affixes, however, making Akɔɔse more fusional than many other Bantu languages. The morphophonemics of Akɔɔse has been described in Hedinger (1985a and 1992), the details of which will not be repeated here.

There are several important differences between Akɔɔse and typical Bantu verb systems:

Akɔɔse does not have object concord prefixes in the verb; only one verbal extension can be present in a verb stem; Akɔɔse does not have the typical final vowel found in many Bantu languages.

The verb structure can be summarised as consisting of the following possible elements (the numbers in the final row refer to the sections in which more details can be found):

Table 4.1. The internal structure of the verb

Tone	Person/ concord prefix	Tense prefix	Neg. prefix	Stem Root	Extension	Aspect suffix	Tense suffix	Suffix	Tone
H	a-	N-	e-	wóg	-e	-ɛ'	-aa	-'ɛ	H
HL	bé-	a-		pim	-ed	-é			L
...				...	...				
4.6	4.3	4.6	4.6	4.4.1–2	4.4.3	4.6	4.6	4.6	4.6

The initial tone is realised on the person/concord prefix (subject marker) and the final tone on the last element. The minimum length of a verb is a stem plus a final tone in the imperative (244). In every other case there has to be a person/concord prefix and a stem as the minimum (245).

(244) **bwǎŋ** < bwəŋ + H 'scoop up! (imperative)'

(245) **bé-bwəŋ** < bé-bwəŋ 'they scoop up (neutral)'

Example (246) is a verb with a maximal expansion. To the right of the arrow are given the underlying morphemes (see Hedinger 1985a) which make up the actual verb form on the left.

(246)   tone PERS NEG root EXT ASP tense tone
é-wɔ́mtaá < H- a- e- wɔ́m -ed -ɛ' -aa -H
'he wasn't having (it) planed'

In the following section I start by presenting the verb infinitive. I then present the person/class prefixes, the stem (root and extensions), as well as the various tense/aspect/mood forms.

4.2 The infinitive

There are two tonally distinct forms of the infinitive, used in different contexts. Both take the *a*-prefix (class 5 nominal prefix). One has a Low tone, the other a High tone on the prefix.

(247) **apém**   'to carry'
       á↓pém   'to carry'

The infinitive with the low tone prefix is used as the second verb in the split verb phrase (see section 5.4). The infinitive with the high tone prefix[1] is used in purpose clauses (see section 5.6).

4.3 Subject markers

Every finite verb (except a second singular imperative) obligatorily has a subject marker, either to mark the verb for person or for agreement with the noun class of the subject NP. The subject markers are as in table 4.2.

Table 4.2. Subject markers

	Singular						Plural		
Class	1SG	2SG	3SG	LOG	1+2SG	Class	1PL	2PL	3PL
1	N-/me-	e-/we-	a-	mə̂-	de-	2	sê-	nyî-	bé-
3			Ń-/mé			4			Ń-/mé
5			á-/dé-			6			mé
7			é-			8			é'-/bé-
9			e-			10			é-
14			é'-/bé-						
19			é'-/bé-			13			á-/dé-

The capital *N-* represents a homorganic nasal. The prefixes divide into three tone classes; some carry a high tone (´), some a low tone (unmarked), and some a falling tone (ˆ). These tones change depending on the tense/aspect/mood forms of the verb, especially when the verbs are dependent or negative. Also the vowels of these prefixes change in some cases as they merge with the future tense and negative prefixes that follow the subject marker. These changes will not be described but can be observed in the verb tables in section 4.6.6.

The logophoric subject marker (LOG) *mə̂-* is used in reported speech to refer to the reported speaker.

---

[1]This could be analysed as a floating H tone prefix attached to the form with the L tone prefix.

4.4 Verb stems

The lexical meaning of the verb is carried by the stem which consists either of a root only or of a root plus an extension.

4.4.1 Verb roots

All verb roots consist of one syllable with one of the following shapes: CVC, CV, CVV or CVVC.

(248)   CVC   CV   CVV   CVVC
       wóg   bɛ́   síi   sɔɔm
      'to wash, rub on'   'to be'   'to iron'   'to hide'

CVC roots are the most common, CVVC roots the least common. CV roots are relatively few in number and most of them have tense/aspect formations which are different from the CVC roots. They include verbs such as *-dyɛ́* 'eat', *-mwɛ́* 'drink' and *-kɛ* 'go'. See the verb tables in section 4.6.6.

Some roots contain labialised (w) or palatalised (y) consonants as indicated in (249).

(249)   kwɛl   dyɛ́   hyɔ́ɔ   tyéem
       'cut'   'eat'   'sweep' 'stand'

4.4.2 Root tones

Each verb root has either a low or a high tone thus dividing the verbs into two tone classes. There are many verb pairs where tone is the only distinguishing mark between two lexical items (250).

(250) High tone verb roots Low tone verb roots
      bɛ́b 'spoil, be bad'   beb 'tie'
      hyɛ́ 'be warm, hot'   hyɛ 'come'
      lɔ́g 'leave'   lɔg 'stay behind'

4.4.3 Derivational affixes or verbal extensions

Akɔɔse has twelve derivational suffixes which immediately follow the root to make up the verb stem. These suffixes are also referred to as verbal extensions. They can be divided into two groups. The ones in the first group have the structure VC or V, are productive and in most cases

4.4 Verb stems

have their own identifiable meaning. The ones in the second group have the structure CVC, are not really productive and do not have an easily identifiable meaning. Verb extensions have no inherent tone but take the tone from the following morpheme by tone spreading.

4.4.4 Vowel initial extensions

Three extensions belong to this group which, as mentioned above, are productive. In other words, they can be added to many verb roots in order to add to the meaning of the stem. Each has one or two variant forms depending on the phonological context.

(251) -ed/-t   'causative'
      -ɛn/-n   'instrumental, reciprocal, comitative'
      -e/-'/-d   'applicative'

The -C variants are found before vowels, the -V(C) variants elsewhere. The -d variant of the applicative suffix is only found in CVV verbs (see verb 7 in tables 4.13–4.57).

These extensions may be added to a verb like -pém 'to carry' to get the stems in (252). On the right are indicated the number of verb stems found with these extensions in a set of 755 verbs with an extension.

(252) **pém**   'carry'
      pém-ed   'make carry, cause to carry'   166
      pém-ɛn   'carry with'   164
      pém-e   'carry for'   192

The distribution of the variants is illustrated in (253)–(255). On the left side the -C forms are given. On the right side are the -V(C) forms, which in this case are word final.

(253) **a-pém-t-é** → **apémté**   **a-N-pém-ed-H** → **ampéméd**
      3SG-carry-CAUS-PERF   3SG-PAST-carry-CAUS-H
      's/he made (somebody) carry (st.)'   's/he made (somebody) carry (st.)'

(254) **a-pém-n-e** → **apémné**   **a-N-pém-ɛn-H** → **ampémén**
      3SG-carry-INST-PERF   3SG-PAST-carry-INST-H
      's/he carried with (something)'   's/he carried with (something)'

(255) a-pém-'-e → apémmé or apé'mé   a-N-pém-e-H → ampémé
     3SG-carry-APP-PERF   3SG-PAST-carry-APP-H
     's/he carried for (somebody)'   's/he carried for (somebody)'

4.4.4.1 Rare extension -ɛl

There are two verbs with the extension -ɛl. No meaning/function can be assigned to it. Also, the roots do not exist independently from these stems.

(256) **kwag-ɛl**   'bite'   <   ??
     yag-ɛl   'throw'   <   ??

4.4.5 Consonant initial extensions

This group consists of nine extensions which, as mentioned earlier, can no longer be productively applied in the language and whose exact meanings are not discernable today. Each has two forms, a -CeC and a -CaaC form. As no unique meaning can be ascribed to any particular extension we simply give one verb each for illustrative purposes. The numbers indicate the number of stems with this extension found in a corpus of 755 extended verb stems.

(257) -ned/-naad **hyɔ́m-ned** 'go around'   83 < **hyɔ́m** 'stroll'
     -tɛn/-taan   **bom-tɛn**   'join together'   54 < **bom**   'meet'
     -ted/-taad   **chem-ted** 'make to understand'   40 < **chem** 'recognise'
     -led/-laad   **kíb-led**   'twist in pain'   22 < **kib**   'twist'
     -nɛn/-naan   **bwɔg-nɛn** 'hold firmly'   16 < **bwɔg** 'support'
     -lɛn/-laan   **sɔ́b-lɛn**   'mix with'   9 < **sɔb**   'be wet'
     -sɛn/-saan   **bom-sɛn**   'prepare'   8 < **boŋ**   'be good'
     -gɛn/-gaan   **tɔ́ŋ-gɛn**   'be correct'   4   ---
     -med/-maad   **hee-med**   'breathe'   3   ---

The -CaaC variant is a combination of the -CeC form and the imperfective marker[2] and occurs in all verbs marked for IMPF. See the example in (258).

(258) **a-wóg-laan**
     3SG-hear-EXT.IMPF
     'he is listening'   (see wóg-lɛn 'to listen')

---

[2] Historically, the CVC extensions may come from the sequence of two extensions interrupted by the IMPF suffix. There appears to be evidence for this in Londo, a Bantu language of the Oroko group (Bantu A11) (Friesen 2002:10).

4.4 Verb stems

4.4.6 -V(C) extensions illustrated

In this section I give some examples of each productive extension in order to illustrate the range of meanings expressed by the extensions. This material is basically repeated from Hedinger (1992).

4.4.6.1 -ed *'causative'*

The -*ed* suffix has in the large majority of cases the meaning 'to cause to X, to make somebody or something to X' where X stands for the unextended root.

(259)   chíb   'steal'   chíb-ed   'cause sb. to steal'
       kún   'sleep'   kún-ed   'cause sb. to sleep'
       yəg   'be red/ripe' yəg-ed   'cause st. to ripen, to make ripe/red'
       pɛn   'shine'   pɛn-ed   'cause to shine'

4.4.6.2 -ed *(formal suffix)*

In some verb stems the *-ed* extension is clearly present but has no meaning on its own. Such suffixes which are identical in form but not clearly identical in meaning to the causative extension described above have sometimes been referred to as formal suffixes. In some cases the root without the extension does not exist separately.

(260)   bág-ed   'verify'
       hɔ́b-ed   'stir'   hɔ́b   'to speak'
       sɛd-ed   'ask'   sɛd   'to ask'

4.4.6.3 -ɛn *'instrumental'*

The -*ɛn* suffix is relatively productive. Three functions can be distinguished on the basis of their meaning and their influence on verb valency.

Roots suffixed with instrumental -*ɛn* require a complement with the semantic function of instrument. This is the most frequently occurring of three formally identical extensions. As indicated in the right-most column, root final velar nasals drop out intervocalically.

(261) sum   'plant'   sum-ɛn   'plant with'
     see **ebúme** 'umbrella'   búm-ɛn   'cover with'
     chám   'cook'   chám-ɛn   'cook with'
     kaŋ   'tie'   kaa-n   'tie with'   < kaŋ+ɛn
     kób   'catch'   kób-ɛn   'catch with'
     lyóg   'fish (w.basket)'   lyóg-ɛn   'fish with'
     wúu   'kill'   wú-ɛn   'kill with'
     yáŋ   'fry'   yáa-n   'fry with'   < yáŋ+ɛn

4.4.6.4 -ɛn 'comitative'

The extension -ɛn 'comitative' expresses that the action being performed is accompanied by somebody or something.

(262) heb   'run away'   heb-ɛn   'elope with'
     húu   'return'   hwé-ɛn   'return with'
     hún   'fall'   hún-ɛn   'fall with'
     lóm   'send'   lóm-ɛn   'send sb. with'
     téd   'take'   téd-ɛn   'take with'
     bɛ́   'be'   bɛ́-ɛn   'be with'
     bíd   'go out'   bíd-ɛn   'go out with'
     bom   'meet'   bom-ɛn   'meet with'

4.4.6.5 -ɛn 'reciprocal'

The third -ɛn extension, with the meaning 'reciprocal' indicates that two or more agents act on each other in some way.

(263) báŋ   'fear'   báá-n   'fear each other'   < báŋ+ɛn
     dəŋ   'like, love'   dəə-n   'love each other'   < dəŋ+ɛn
     hɛn   'quarrel(?)'   hɛn-ɛn   'be at loggerheads'
     kɔɔ   'hate'   kɔɔ-n   'hate each other'   < kɔɔ+ɛn
     seb   'embrace'   seb-ɛn   'embrace'
     sɛl   'quarrel'   sɛl-ɛn   'quarrel'
     syə́ŋ   'abuse (verbal)'   syə́ə-n   'abuse each other'   < syəŋ+ɛn
     tɔ́m   'congratulate'   tɔ́m-ɛn   'hit palms together (in greeting)'
     -                              wág-ɛn   'resemble'
     wóŋ   'have, marry'   wóo-n   'be married'   < wóŋ+ɛn

4.4.6.6 -ɛn 'separative'

There are a number of verb stems with the extension -ɛn that can be interpreted as having the meaning 'separative' as in (264).³ However, this appears not to be very productive.

(264)   **chíb** 'steal'   **chíb-ɛn** 'steal from'
      choŋ 'survive'   **choo-n** 'get better from'   <   **choŋ + ɛn**
      dul 'draw, pull'   **dul-ɛn** 'take photograph, pull'
      hɛd 'want'   **hɛd-ɛn** 'ask from, want'
      kab 'divide, share'   **kab-ɛn** 'separate'
      kob 'take, receive'   **kob-ɛn** 'take from'
      kud 'have, get'   **kud-ɛn** 'get from'
      sog 'seize'   **sog-ɛn** 'take by force'

4.4.6.7 -ɛn *(formal suffix)*

There are also many stems which formally have the -ɛn extension but where no meaning can be attributed to the extension as such.

(265)   **bɛl** 'do'   **bɛl-ɛn** 'use'
      hɔ́b 'speak'   **hɔ́b-ɛn** 'rebuke'
      -    **lɔ́ə-n** 'be bent'   < ? **lɔ́ŋ + ɛn**
      sud 'descend'   **sud-ɛn** 'be sad, downcast'
      kib 'twist, bend'   **kib-ɛn** 'be twisted'

4.4.6.8 -e 'applicative'

This extension has two identifiable meanings: applicative and separative.

The -e 'applicative' is very productive and occurs in many lexical items. It indicates that the action or the state described is for the benefit or on behalf of somebody else.

---

³The term 'separative' is taken from Schadeberg (1982), but no claim is made that the form of this suffix is related to any suffix discussed in that article. However, the -e suffix in section 4.4.6.9 might be derived from one of those suffixes.

(266) chám   'cook'   chám-e 'cook for'
     húd   'remove'   húd-e   'remove for'
     lím   'dig'   lím-e   'dig for'
     boŋ   'be good'   boo   'care for'   < boŋ + e
     lóŋ   'build'   lóo   'build for'   < lóŋ + e
     wúu   'kill'   wúu⁴   'kill for'   < wúú + e

4.4.6.9 -e *'separative'*

There are the following stems with the extension -*e* which could be interpreted as having a 'separative' meaning. However, this is not very productive.

(267) (mwé 'drink')   míi⁵   'drink from, drink for'
      -                səl-e   'scrape off'
      -                síd-e   'go away from, come close to'
      -                syəə   'leave, get off or away'
      -                tyóg-e 'remove plant from ground'

4.4.6.10 -e *(formal suffix)*

Verb stems with the -*e* extension where no meaning can be attributed to either the root or the extension but only to the stem as a whole are the following.

(268) - bə́l-e   'burst into tears'
      - búb-e   'soften by fire'
      - bwóg-e   'begin, set out'
      - dúb-e   'believe'
      - láa⁶   'tell'
      - nyáa   'lick'

4.4.7   -CVC extensions illustrated

In this section I give examples of stems with -CVC extensions. These extensions are primarily used to differentiate separate lexical forms with no apparent inherent meaning, but there are some where a specific grammatical meaning may be abstracted.

---

⁴For the formal differences between "kill" and "kill for" compare verb stem type 6 and 7 in sections 4.6.5 and 4.6.6.

⁵*míi* is clearly derived from *mwé* 'drink', but not via a current derivational process.

⁶See verb stem type 7 in sections 4.6.5 and 4.6.6 for evidence of the presence of this extension.

4.4 Verb stems

4.4.7.1 -led

(269)
chum	'smell (itr.)'	chum-led	'sniff, smell (tr.)'
hóŋ	'make round'	hóŋ-led	'cause to roll'
kib	'twist, bend'	kib-led	'twist in pain'
-		hag-led	'struggle to do something'
-		swág-led	'beat all over the body'
-		wog-led	'struggle'

4.4.7.2 -lɛn

(270)
chóŋ	'dangle'	chóŋ-lɛn	'hang about'
həŋ	'change'	həŋ-lɛn	'change st.'
wóg	'hear, feel'	wóg-lɛn	'listen, taste st.'
-		kɔb-lɛn	'cross legs'

4.4.7.3 -med

Only three stems have been found with this extension.

(271)
(heed	'breathe')	hee-med	'breathe, sigh'
-		káa-med	'yawn'
-		paa-med	'escape from, get separated'

At first it is not clear whether these stems should be segmented after the *m* as CVV*m-ed*. However, these stems follow the inflectional paradigm of the stems with -CVC extensions.

4.4.7.4 -ned *'applicative'*

The -*ned* extension has three different meanings: applicative (272), comitative (273) and instrumental (274). Compare the same three meanings for the -*en* extension above.

(272)
ban-e	'put, keep'	ban-ned	'keep for'
boŋ	'be good'	boŋ-ned	'be good for'
láŋ	'read'	láŋ-ned	'tell st. to sb. for sb.'
pɛ	'arrive'	pii-ned[7]	'bring for'

---

[7] The relationship to the base form is due to an old derviational process affecting only a small number of verbs.

4.4.7.5 -ned *'comitative'*

(273)
chám	'cook'	chám-ned	'cook with (spice)'
chɔ́g-e	'climb'	chɔ́g-ned	'climb with sb.'
ləg	'remain with'	ləg-ned	'remain with'
lím	'dig'	lím-ned	'bury with'
naa ásē[8]	'lie down, sleep'	naŋ-ned	'sleep with'
síd-e	'come close'	síd-ned	'come/go with'
sob	'escape, leave'	sob-ned	'leave st. with'

4.4.7.6 -ned *'instrumental'*

Only two examples have been found of the *-ned* extension with this sense.

(274)
wɔ́m	'scratch, plane'	wɔ́m-ned	'plane st. with st.'
chɔ́g-e	'climb'	chɔ́g-ned	'climb with st.'

4.4.7.7 -nɛn

There are about a dozen stems with this extension. No common meaning could be detected except that in almost all of the stems there is an idea of intensity.

(275)
bwɔg-e	'hold down'	bwɔg-nɛn	'hold firmly, sit on eggs'
-		háŋ-nɛn	'insist on doing st.'
kun-e	'turn over'	kun-nɛn	'turn over as in wrestling'
ság	'dance, shake'	ság-nɛn	'thank sb.'
sóŋ	'knot up'	sóŋ-nɛn	'tighten, fasten'
-		swáŋ-nɛn	'strangle, hold tight'
təə <təŋ-e	'tie'	təŋ-nɛn	'insist, persist'
tóg	'be poor'	tóg-nɛn	'be in need'

4.4.7.8 -ted

Some items with this extension have an applicative (276) and some a causative meaning (277). However, there are as many others which do not have an identifiable meaning (278).

---

[8] *aseö* 'down' is a particle used to form many phrasal verbs.

4.4 Verb stems

(276) **béb**   'be bad, spoilt'   **béb-ted**   'destroy st. for sb.'
     chɔ́g-e   'climb, go up'   **chɔ́g-ted**   'lift for'
     hún   'fall'   **hún-ted**   'throw down for, fall on'
     kɔ́g   'germinate'   **kɔ́g-ted**   'hatch for'

(277) **bíd**   'go out'   **bíd-ted**   'cause to come out, produce'
     chem   'recognise'   **hem-ted**   'cause to understand'
     pém   'carry (on head)'   **pém-ted**   'cause to carry'
     tóm   'pass by'   **tóm-ted**   'cause to pass, serve'

(278) -   **boo-ted**   'begin'
     kwɛl   'cut'   **kwɛn-ted**   'cut into pieces'
     mwag-e   'sprinkle'   **mwag-ted**   'sprinkle, throw small stones'
     tim   'return'   **tim-ted**   'give back to'

4.4.7.9 -tɛn

Some stems with this extension appear to have an instrumental meaning (279), some a component of comitative (280) and a few a reciprocal meaning (281).

(279) **dog**   'deceive'   **dog-tɛn**   'deceive with'
     sóg   'stop'   **sóg-tɛn**   'support with'
     tín-ed   'push'   **tín-tɛn**   'push with'

(280) **hyɔ́m**   'stroll, wander'   **hyɔ́m-tɛn**   'turn round with'
     lad   'close, gather'   **lad-tɛn**   'put together with'
     nəg-ed   'run'   **nəg-tɛn**   'run with'

(281) -   **pen-tɛn**   'argue with'
     -                                     **pun-tɛn**   'meet with'

4.4.7.10 -sɛn

The following four lexical items have the extension *-sɛn* with no apparent grammatical meaning.

(282) kəg   'try'   kəg-sɛn   'try'
                               kɔg-sɛn   'punish'
      liŋ   'be angry'   liŋ-sɛn   'make someone angry with'
      boŋ   'be good'   boŋ-sɛn   'prepare'

4.4.7.11 -gɛn

Three lexical items in our corpus have the extension *-gɛn*.

(283) -   tóŋ-gɛn   'must, have to, meet
                                              accidentally, affront'
      -                        wóŋ-gɛn   'help'
      bóŋ   'try'   bóŋ-gɛn   'venture, try'

This extension only occurs after roots with final velar nasal *ŋ*. Since *g* does not exist stem initially except as part of prenasalised stops this extension may be better interpreted as underlyingly *-'ɛn* where the glottal stop becomes *g* after *ŋ*.

4.5 Extensions and valency changes

This section covers the correlation of verbal extensions with verb valency. By verb valency, I mean the subject and the number and kinds of verbal complements including object, indirect object, instrument, locative, etc. which are obligatorily present with a given lexical item. The addition of an extension to a verb root may require the addition of a complement such as a benefactive, instrumental or other noun phrase in the clause. In such a case, the valency is being increased as in (284)–(290). In other cases, the addition of an extension decreases the valency as in (291).

No attempt will be made to give an exhaustive treatment of verb valency in Akɔɔse. This would be too large a topic as each verb and each different sense of a verb has its own valency.

From a morpho-semantic point of view, three types of verb stems can be distinguished: simple stems which consist of a root only, complex stems which are derived from verb roots by the addition of an extension, and complex stems which are historically but not synchronically derived. In this section, I am interested only in the first two: what is the valency change caused by the addition of an extension to a simple stem. There are three possibilities: a valency increase, a valency decrease or no valency change. In the examples that follow, the subject is not always present in the form of an explicit NP.

4.5 Extensions and valency changes

4.5.1 Valency increasing -ed 'causative'

The addition of the -ed suffix has a valency increasing effect. Intransitive verbs describing a state or quality become transitive (284)–(285). When added to intransitive verbs the -ed suffix adds a causing agent as the new subject and the inherent subject becomes object. This can be diagramed as case frames where the variables α, β and γ represent the underlying semantic roles expressed by different grammatical relations [S, DO, etc.]. In the left column the verb without the extension is given, in the right column the verb with the extension.

	α		β	α
V	<NP[S]>	V-ed	<NP[S], NP[DO]>	

(284) Mwăn a-kún-ɛ'.   Nɛ́ɛ a-kún-t-ɛ'   băn.
      1.child 1-sleep-IMPF   1.mother 1-sleep-CAUS-IMPF 2.child
      'The child is sleeping.' 'Mother put the children to sleep.'

	α		β	α
V	<NP[S]>	V-ed	<NP[S], NP[DO]>	

(285) Nsule ń-yɔ́g-é.   Mod a-yəg-t-é   nsule.
      3.banana 3-ripe-PERF   1.person 1.ripe-CAUS-PERF 3.banana
      'The banana is ripe.'   'The man made the bananas ripen.'

When adding the -ed extension to transitive verbs, as in (286), the causee becomes indirect object, making the verb ditransitive. The causing agent takes up the normal subject position before the verb, and the causee occurs after the verb before the direct object.

	α	β		γ	α	β
V	<NP[S], NP[DO]>		V-ed	<NP[S], NP[IO], NP[DO]>		

(286) Mwăn a-chíb-é mɔné.   Mod a-chíb-t-é   mwăn mɔné.
      1.child 1-steal-PERF 3.money 1.person 1-steal-CAUS-PERF 1.child 3.money
      'The child stole money.' 'The man made the child steal money.'

4.5.2 The -ɛn extension

Each of the three -ɛn extensions has a different effect on the valency of the verb.

4.5.2.1 Valency increasing -ɛn 'instrumental'

Verbs with the instrumental -ɛn require an obligatory instrumental noun phrase. This noun phrase usually has an inanimate referent and always occurs after the direct object.

$$\begin{array}{ll} \quad\quad \alpha \quad\quad \beta & \quad\quad\quad \alpha \quad\quad \beta \quad\quad \gamma \\ V \quad <NP[S], NP[DO]> & V\text{-}\varepsilon n \quad <NP[S], NP[DO], NP[In]> \end{array}$$

(287) **N-sum-é   mbaangé.**   **N-súm-n-é   mbaangé   bwɛl.**
1SG-plant-PERF 10.cocoyams   1 SG-plant-INST-PERF 10.cocoyams 14.stick
'I planted cocoyams.'   'I planted cocoyams with a stick.'

(288) **A-yáá   súu.**   **A-yáŋ-n-é   súu   mǒl.**
1-fry.PERF 10.fish   1-fry-INST-PERF 10.fish 6.oil
'She fried fish.'   'She fried fish with/in oil.'

In (288) the oil might be interpreted as either instrument or comitative, i.e. whether oil is the instrument whereby the fish is cooked or whether it is what accompanies the fish in the process of cooking.

4.5.2.2 Valency increasing -ɛn 'comitative'

The addition of this extension requires an extra object. This object with comitative role follows the direct object. Note that in (290) there is no direct object.

$$\begin{array}{ll} \quad\quad \alpha \quad\quad \beta & \quad\quad\quad \alpha \quad\quad \gamma \quad\quad \beta \\ V \quad <NP[S], NP[DO]> & V\text{-}\varepsilon n \quad <NP[S], NP[DO], NP[Com]> \end{array}$$

(289) **Lóm   kálag.**   **Lóm-ɛ́n   mɔ́ kálag.**
2SG.send.IMP letter   2SG.send-COM.IMP he letter
'Send the letter!'   'Send him with the letter!'

$$\begin{array}{ll} \quad\quad \alpha & \quad\quad\quad \alpha \quad\quad \beta \\ V \quad <NP[S]> & V\text{-}\varepsilon n \quad <NP[S], NP[Com]> \end{array}$$

(290) **Mod   a-béd-é wén.**   **Mod   a-béé-n-é   mwǎn wén.**
1.person 1-be-PERF here   1.person 1-be-COM-PERF 1.child here
'The person was here.'   'The person was here with the child.'

4.5.2.3 Valency decreasing -ɛn 'reciprocal'

The addition of this extension has the effect of decreasing the valency. Inherently transitive verbs become intransitive as the undergoer of the action becomes incorporated in the subject. The subject has to be plural as two (or more) participants act on each other and therefore are agent and undergoer at the same time as in (291).

$$\begin{array}{lll} & \alpha \quad \beta & \alpha\beta \\ V & <NP[S], NP[DO]> & V\text{-}\varepsilon n \quad <NP[S]> \end{array}$$

(291) **A-kɔ́ɔ́   ane   mod.**   **Ábé   bad   bé-kɔ́ɔ́-n-é.**
1-hate.PERF 1.that 1.man   2.those 2.people 2.hate-REC-PERF
'He hates that man.'   'Those people hate each other.'

4.5.3   Valency increasing -e 'applicative'

The applicative extension has a valency increasing effect. The noun phrase which is the beneficiary of the action is added before the direct object of the verb as an indirect object.

$$\begin{array}{lll} & \alpha \quad \beta & \alpha \quad \gamma \quad \beta \\ V & <NP[S], NP[DO]> & V\text{-}e \quad <NP[S], NP[IO], NP[DO]> \end{array}$$

(292) **Bé-wúú   nzyɔg.**   **Bé-wúú-d-e ´   mɔ́   nzyɔg.**
2-kill.PERF 9.elephant   2-kill-APP-PERF him 9.elephant
'They killed an elephant.'   'They killed an elephant for him.'

(293) **Lóm   kálag.**   **Lóm-é   mɔ́   kálag.**
2SG.send.IMP 9.letter   2SG.send-APP.IMP him 9.letter
'Send the letter.'   'Send him the letter.'

The few examples above illustrate the kind of valency changes that take place when productive extensions are suffixed to verb roots. Each verb stem, whether simple, derived or with a formal extension, has its own valency. In fact, different senses of formally identical stems may have different valencies. In a complete account of the language this would have to be dealt with in a dictionary, giving for each verb the case frame indicating its valency.

4.6 Tense, aspect, negation and dependent forms

4.6.1 Tense and aspect

Akɔɔse has primarily a perfective/imperfective aspect distinction. In addition the verb may be marked for past and future tense. Tense and aspect combine to give the following six verb forms: perfect, present (imperfective), past, past imperfective, future and future imperfective. They can be analysed as forming the following system.

Table 4.3. The six primary verb tenses

	Perfective	Imperfective
Past	past perfective	past imperfective
	perfect	present imperfective
Future	future perfective	future imperfective

Table 4.4. The verb 'to wash' in the six primary verb tenses

	Perfective	Imperfective
Past	**anwóg** 'he washed'	**awógáá** 'he was washing'
	awógé 'he has washed'	**awógɛ'** 'he is washing'
Future	**ǎ⁺wóg** 'he will wash'	**ǎ⁺wógé'** 'he will be washing'

In tables 4.4 and 4.5 the subject marker *a-* '3SG' is written attached to the verb stem or tense marker, as is done in the current orthography.

The affixes that distinguish the verb forms above from each other are abstracted in table 4.5.

Table 4.5. Summary of tense/aspect markers

	Perfective		Imperfective
Past	**Ǹ-**	-´	-é'-áá
		-é	-ɛ'
Future	**â-**	-´	**dâ-** -é'

All *imperfective* forms have the suffix *-ɛ'* except for the minor verbs (which have -CV shape, see stem types 12–14 in section 4.6.5) which have *-ag*. Perfective is not marked, unless the final *H* tone is considered marking for this aspect.

4.6 Tense, aspect, negation and dependent forms

The past has a homorganic nasal *N-* prefix and a final *H* tone. The past imperfective has the past suffix *-áá* following the imperfective marker with which it merges completely.[9] The perfect has the suffix *-é* with a high tone. The present doesn't have a tense marker as such. It is marked by the imperfective marker and present meaning is understood in the relevant context. The future perfective is marked with the future marker *â-* plus a final *-H* tone. The future imperfective is also marked with the future marker *â-* plus the imperfective marker *-έ'*. The future marker merges with the subject marker *a-* that precedes it. The tone of the subject marker also combines with the tone of the tense marker to form various new tones.

In addition to these six primary verb tenses there are a number of minor tenses which will be presented later on.

4.6.2 Verb negation

All the primary verb forms have affirmative and negative forms. There is no word for "not" to negate verbs (but see section 6.1 for non-verbal negation). Negation is marked by a prefix which merges with adjacent person and tense markers.

The primary tenses in the negative are as follows:

Table 4.6. The verb 'to wash' in the primary negative verb tenses

	Perfective	Imperfective
Past	**enkênwɔ́gké**	**ewɔ́gaá**
	ewɔ́gɛé	**ewɔ́gέé**
Future	**êwɔ́gké**	**êwɔ́gέé**

The affixes which mark tense, aspect and negation in negative forms can be abstracted as in the following table.

Table 4.7. Summary of tense, aspect and negative markers

	Perfective		Imperfective	
Past	e-nkêN-	-'ɛ́	e-	-ɛ'-aá
	e-	-e -'ɛ́	e-	-ɛ́'-'ɛ́
Future	^-e-â-	-´-'ɛ́	^-e-â-	-ɛ́'-'ɛ́

---

[9]In some dialects and in CVV verbs the imperfective and the past marker do not merge.

The prefix that marks negation is *e-* which merges with the subject marker *a-* resulting in *e-* in table 4.6. (For subject markers for other persons see the tables for negative forms in section 4.6.6.) These negative forms also take the suffix -*'é*. It should be noted that this suffix does not occur in all negatives and also occurs in non-negative forms. Therefore no specific meaning can be assigned to it. The tone rules are complex and will not be described here (see Hedinger 1985 for details). Also note that the glottal stops in these forms disappear in most cases.

4.6.3 Dependent verb forms

In specific grammatical contexts, such as dependent clauses, relative clauses and questions, both affirmative and negative verb forms have distinct dependent forms. These will now be outlined.

The dependent affirmative and negative forms are as in the following two tables. Compare table 4.4 with table 4.8.

Table 4.8. Dependent forms of the verb 'to wash' (affirmative)

	Perfective	Imperfective
Past	ánwɔ́gké	áwɔ́gkáá
	áwɔ́gé	áwɔ́gɛé
Future	á↓wɔ́gké	á↓wɔ́géé

Negative verb forms with the exception of the future have two dependent forms labeled as S and O in table 4.9 (compare table 4.9 with table 4.6). The grammatical contexts (S and O) in which the dependent forms occur are described in section 4.6.4.

Table 4.9. Dependent forms of the verb 'to wash' (negative)

	Context	Perfective	Imperfective
Past	S	enkênwɔ́g	ewɔ́gaa
	O	énkênwɔ́gké	é↓wɔ́gaá
	S	ewɔ́ge	ewɔ́gé'/é
	O	é↓wɔ́gɛé	é↓wɔ́géé
Future	S	êwɔ́g	êwɔ́gé'

4.6 Tense, aspect, negation and dependent forms

The tones and affixes that mark these verbs as dependent are abstracted in the corresponding two tables below. Compare table 4.10 with table 4.8, and table 4.11 with table 4.9.

Table 4.10. Summary of dependent markers (affirmative)

	Perfective		Imperfective	
Past	´ -	-'ɛ́	´ -	
	´ -		´ -	-'ɛ́
Future	´ -	-'ɛ́	´ -	-'ɛ́

Table 4.11. Summary of dependent markers (negative)

	Context	Perfective		Imperfective	
Past	S		ø		-T*
	O	´ -	-'ɛ́	´ -	
	S		ø		ø
	O	´ -	-'ɛ́	´ -	-'ɛ́
Future	S		ø		ø

*The -*T* stands for a tonal suffix which may be high or low.

In table 4.12 I give the low tone verb -*pim* 'to throw away' in all the forms discussed above.

No attempt will be made in this description to give underlying forms and the rules necessary to generate all the possible verb forms. Instead, a representative sample of verb stems with all the forms resulting from the combination of tense, aspect, mood, negation and dependent forms are shown in section 4.6.6.

Table 4.12. Independent and dependent forms for -pim 'to throw away'

		I	S	O
Affirmative	Past perfective 'he threw'		ampǐm	ámpimmé
	Past imperfective 'he was throwing'		apimáá	ápímáá
	Present imperfective 'he is throwing'		apimɛ'/e	ápimɛɛ́
	Perfect 'he has thrown'		apimé	ápímé
	Future perfective 'he will throw'		ăpǐm	ápimmé
	Future imperfective 'he will be throwing'		ăpimé'/ɛ'	ápiméé
		I	O	S
Negative	Past perfective 'he did not throw'	enkêmpimmé	énkêmpimmé	enkêmpǐm
	Past imperfective 'he was not throwing'	ěpimaá	épimaá	ěpimaa
	Present imperfective 'he is not throwing'	ě⁺pímɛ́ɛ́	épimɛɛ́	ě⁺pímé'/é
	Perfect 'he has not thrown'	ěpimɛɛ́	épimɛɛ́	ěpime
	Future perfective 'he will not throw'	êpimmé		êpǐm
	Future imperfective 'he will not be throwing'	êpiméé		êpimé'

4.6.4 Distribution of dependent verb forms

As shown above, Akɔɔse has one independent and one or two dependent forms for affirmative and negative verbs, respectively. The clauses in which the dependent forms are used can be grouped into subject type and non-subject type dependent clauses.

4.6 Tense, aspect, negation and dependent forms

4.6.4.1 Subject type (S) dependent clauses

The subject type is broadly characterised by structures where no constituent has been moved from a position after the verb to a position before the verb. They are as follows:

-Wh-questions when the subject is questioned (see section 7.2.2.2–3)
-Topicalised clauses when the subject is topicalised (see section 7.3.1.1)
-Relative clauses when the subject is relativised (see. section 7.4.2.1)
-Conditional clauses beginning with *nzé* (see section 8.5.14)

These contexts require what I have chosen to call the **S** forms of the verb. In (294) I give examples in the affirmative form. In (295) are found examples in the negative form.

(294) **Mwǎn apimé mbaangé.**   I   'The child threw out the cocoyams.'

   Nzé apimé mbaangé?   I = S   Who threw out the cocoyams?'
   Mwǎn mɔ̂ apimé mbaangé.   I = S   'It is the child that threw out the cocoyams.'
   mwǎn awě apimé mbaangé   I = S   'the child which threw out the cocoyams'
   Nzé mwǎn apimé mbaangé, ...   I = S   'If the child threw out the cocoyams, ...'

(295) **Mwǎn ĕpimɛɛ́ mbaangé.**   I   'The child didn't throw out the cocoyams.'

   Nzé ĕpime mbaangé?   S   'Who didn't throw out the cocoyams?'
   Mwǎn mɔ̂ ĕpime mbaangé.   S   'It is the child that didn't throw out the cocoyams.'
   mwǎn awě ĕpime mbaangé   S   'the child which didn't throw out the cocoyams'
   Nzé mwǎn ĕpime mbaangé, ...   S   'If the child didn't throw out the cocoyams, ...'

4.6.4.2 Non-subject type (O) dependent clauses

In the non-subject type, either a non-subject complement or an adjunct has moved from a position after the verb to the beginning of the clause or the clause is introduced by a conjunction. They are as follows:

- Wh-questions where a non-subject complement is being questioned (see section 7.2.2.2–3)
- Topicalised clauses where a non-subject complement is topicalised (see section 7.3.1.1)
- Relative clauses where a non-subject complement is relativised (see section 7.4.2)
- Subordinate clauses introduced by *néɛ, ngáne, dɔ́ə, héɛ, háá, áde, wéɛ* (see chapter 8)

These contexts require the o form of the verb. The examples in (296) show the affirmative forms and in (297) show the negative forms.

(296) **Mwǎn apimé mbaangé.** I 'The child threw out the cocoyams.'

Chě mwǎn ápímé? O 'What did the child throw out?'
Mbaangé chə̂ mwǎn ápímé. O 'It is the cocoyams that the child threw out.'
mbaangé éche mwǎn ápímé O 'the cocoyams which the child threw out'
Áde mwǎn ápímé mbaangé, ... O 'When the child threw out the cocoyams, ...'

(297) **Mwǎn ěpimɛɛ́ mbaangé.** I 'The child didn't throw out the cocoyams.'

Chě mwǎn épimɛɛ́? O 'What did the child not throw out?'
Mbaangé chə̂ mwǎn épimɛɛ́. O 'It is the cocoyams that the child didn't throw out.'
mbaangé éche mwǎn épimɛɛ́ O 'the cocoyams which the child didn't throw out'
Áde mwǎn épimɛɛ́ mbaangé, ... O 'When the child didn't throw out the cocoyams, ...'

For other examples of these contexts and the corresponding use of verb forms see chapter 7.

4.6 Tense, aspect, negation and dependent forms   107

In tables 4.13–4.39 bold face, roman, and italic type styles are used to distinguish these formal differences in verbs.

4.6.5 The infinitive forms of the verbs illustrated

Table 4.13 contains the verbs used to illustrate the different verb forms. As described in section 4.2 there are two forms of the infinitive, one with an L and another with an H tone on the prefix. Both are listed below. The verbs with an H tone stem are shown in the left hand column, the verbs with an L tone stem in the right hand column. The CV structure of the root plus extension is given under stem type. A dash in the table indicates that no example for that pattern has been found.

Table 4.13. Infinitive form of verb types used

	Stem type	High tone verbs		Low tone verbs	
1	CVC	**awɔ́g*** / áꜜwɔ́g	'to wash'	**apim** / ápim	'throw away'
2	CVC-v	**awɔ́me** / áꜜwɔ́me	'to plane'	**akule** / ákule	'be sick'
3	CVC-vc	**awɔ́mɛd** / áꜜwɔ́mɛd	'to have planed'	**abomɛn** / ábomɛn	'meet with'
4	CVC-cvc	**awóglɛn** / áꜜwóglɛn	'to listen'	**abaŋned** / ábaŋned	'sew with'
5	CVV	**asíi** / áꜜsíi	'to iron'	**asuu** / ásuu	'pass air'
6	CVV	**abóo** / áꜜbóo	'to break'	—	
7	CVV-v	**aláa** / áꜜláa	'to chew'	**anyaa** / ányaa	'tear off'
8	CVV-vc	**akáad** / áꜜkáad	'to judge'	**akaad** / ákaad	'line (pot)'
9	CVŋ	**aláŋ** / áꜜláŋ	'to read'	**akəŋ** / ákəŋ	'shave'
10	CVŋ-v	**aláα** / áꜜláα	'to tell'	**anαα** / ánαα	'lie down'
11	CVŋ-vc	**ahyάαd** / áꜜhyάαd	'to burn st.'	**asoon** / ásoon	'purge'
12	CV	**adyɛ́** / áꜜdyɛ́	'to eat'	**akwɛ** / ákwɛ	'fall'
13	CV	**abɛ́** / áꜜbɛ́	'to be'	**abɛ** / ábɛ	'give'
14	CV	—		**akɛ** / ákɛ	'go'

*Usage of the type styles in tables 4.13 and 4.14:
bold: independent, dependent S-type
roman: dependent O-type

1–4 are CVC roots, 1 has no extension, 2 has a -V (-v) extension, 3 a -VC (-vc) extension, 4 a -CVC (-cvc) extension.

5–8 are CVV roots. 5 has high vowels which become semivowels when followed by -ɛ.

4.6 Tense, aspect, negation and dependent forms

6 contains a rounded back vowel which becomes *ɔə* when merging with following *-ɛ*.

7 has a -V (-v) extension, 8 a -VC (-vc) extension.

9–11 are CVŋ roots. 9 has no extension, 10 has a -V (-v) extension and 11 a -VC (-vc) extension.

12–14 are CV roots. These are a small number of verbs with irregular paradigms, i.e. they do not follow the regular pattern found in 1–11 and each displays its own peculiarities.

12 can be considered the most regular of the CV ones. 'To be' in 13 is regular but has an additional partial paradigm. 'To give' in 13 is best analysed as having a CV (*bɛ*) and a CVC (*bag*) stem. 14 has an irregular form in the perfect (see section 4.6.6.1) and in the immediate past (see section 4.6.7.7).

4.6.6 Major verb tenses

In the following subsections I give four tables for each of the six main tenses:

- the affirmative in all persons of the verbs *-wɔ́g* and *-pim*
- the affirmative of the fourteen pairs of high and low tone verbs in third-person singular/class 1
- the negative in all persons of the verbs *-wɔ́g* and *-pim*
- the negative of the fourteen pairs of high and low tone verbs in third-person singular/class 1

Especially note the behaviour of the tone on the person prefixes. The verbs with noun class concord prefixes behave like any prefixes with low or high tone.

The glosses are approximate as the meaning can vary according to context.

4.6.6.1 Perfect

The perfect is formed by the addition of the suffix *-é* to the stem. It indicates an action that was completed in the past with the result still in effect. For verbs expressing qualities or states, it affirms the state. In discourse, the perfect is used for the story-line.

Table 4.14. Perfect affirmative, singular and plural persons

1SG	**n-wɔ́gé** ń-wɔ́gé	'I washed'	**m-pimé** ḿ-pímé	'I threw away'
2SG	**e-wɔ́gé** é-wɔ́gé	'you washed'	**e-pimé** é-pímé	'you threw away'
3SG	**a-wɔ́gé** á-wɔ́gé	'he/she washed'	**a-pimé** á-pímé	'he/she threw away'
LOG	**mɔ̂-wɔ́gé** mɔ́-wɔ́gé	'LOG washed'	**mɔ̂-pimé** mɔ́-pímé	'LOG threw away'
1PL incl.	**de-wɔ́gé** dé-wɔ́gé	'we washed'	**de-pimé** dé-pímé	'we threw away'
1PL excl.	**sê-wɔ́gé** sé-wɔ́gé	'we washed'	**sê-pimé** sé-pímé	'we threw away'
2PL	**nyî-wɔ́gé** nyí-wɔ́gé	'you washed'	**nyî-pimé** nyí-pímé	'you threw away'
3PL	**bé-wɔ́gé** bé-wɔ́gé	'they washed'	**bé-pímé** bé-pímé	'they threw away'

It should be noted that the low root tone (right-hand column) is replaced by a high tone when preceded and followed by a high tone. In other words, there is an L/H root tone neutralisation in these forms.

4.6 Tense, aspect, negation and dependent forms

Table 4.15. Perfect affirmative, third-person singular

Stem	High tone verbs		Low tone verbs	
1 CVC	**a-wɔ́gé** á-wɔ́gé	'he washed'	**a-pimé** á-pímé	'she threw away'
2 CVC-v	**a-wɔ́mmé** á-wɔ́mmé	'he planed'	**a-kunlé** á-kúnlé	'he is sick'
3 CVC-vc	**a-wɔ́mté** á-wɔ́mté	'he had st. planed'	**a-bomné** á-bómné	'he met with'
4 CVC-cvc	**a-wóglέné** á-wóglέné	'he listened'	**a-baŋnédé** á-báŋnédé	'she sewed with'
5 CVV	**a-síí** á-síí	'she ironed'	**a-suú** á-súú	'he passed air'
6 CVV	**a-bóó** á-bóó	'it is broken'	—	
7 CVV-v	**a-láádé** á-láádé	'he chewed'	**a-nyaádé** á-nyáádé	'she tore off'
8 CVV-vc	**a-kááté** á-kááté	'he judged'	**a-kaaté** á-kááté	'she lined the pot'
9 CVŋ	**a-lɑ́ɑ́** á-lɑ́ɑ́	'she read'	**a-kəɔ́** á-kɔ́ɔ́	'he shaved'
10 CVŋ-v	**a-láŋgé** á-láŋgé	'he told'	**a-naŋgé** á-náŋgé	'she lay down'
11 CVŋ-vc	**a-hyáŋté** á-hyáŋté	'she burned st.'	**a-soŋné** á-sóŋné	'he purged'
12 CV	**a-dyédé** á-dyédé	'he has eaten'	**a-kwedé** á-kwédé	'he fell'
13 CV	**a-bédé*** á-bédé	'she was'	**a-bagé** á-bágé	'she gave'
14 CV	—		**a-kií** á-kíí	'he went'

*The verb 'to be' has these additional forms: unmarked: *a-dé*, emphatic?: *a-díī*, dependent: *á-díí* 'she is'.

4.6.6.2 Perfect negative

In the perfect negative tense the negative prefix *e-* merges with the CV variant of the person or class marker. Of interest here is that there are more forms for the negative than for the affirmative (see section 4.6.6.1).

Table 4.16. Perfect negative, singular and plural persons

1SG	**me-wɔ́gɛɛ́*** *me-wɔ́ge* mé-⁺wɔ́gɛɛ́	'I didn't wash'	**mě-pimɛɛ́** *mě-pime* mé-pimɛɛ́	'I didn't throw away'
2SG	**we-wɔ́gɛɛ́** *we-wɔ́ge* wé-⁺wɔ́gɛɛ́	'you didn't wash'	**wě-pimɛɛ́** *wě-pime* wé-pimɛɛ́	'you didn't throw away'
3SG	**e-wɔ́gɛɛ́** *e-wɔ́ge* é-⁺wɔ́gɛɛ́	'he/she didn't wash'	**ě-pimɛɛ́** *ě-pime* é-pimɛɛ́	'he/she didn't throw away'
LOG	**mɔ̂-wɔ́gɛɛ́** *mɔ̂-wɔ́ge* mɔ́-⁺wɔ́gɛɛ́	'LOG didn't wash'	**mɔ́ɔ̄-pimɛɛ́** *mɔ́ɔ̄-pime* mɔ́-pimɛɛ́	'LOG didn't throw away'
1PL incl.	**de-wɔ́gɛɛ́** *de-wɔ́ge* dé-⁺wɔ́gɛɛ́	'we didn't wash'	**dě-pimɛɛ́** *dě-pime* dé-pimɛɛ́	'we didn't throw away'
1PL excl.	**sê-wɔ́gɛɛ́** *sê-wɔ́ge* sé-⁺wɔ́gɛɛ́	'we didn't wash'	**séē-pimɛɛ́** *séē-pime* sé-pimɛɛ́	'we didn't throw away'
2PL	**nyî-wɔ́gɛɛ́** *nyî-wɔ́ge* nyí-⁺wɔ́gɛɛ́	'you didn't wash'	**nyî̄-pimɛɛ́** *nyî̄-pime* nyí-pimɛɛ́	'you didn't throw away'
3PL	**bé-wɔ́gɛɛ́** bé-⁺wɔ́ge bé-⁺wɔ́gɛɛ́	'they didn't wash'	**bé-pimɛɛ́** bé-pime bé-pimɛɛ́	'they didn't throw away'

*Usage of the type styles in tables 4.16 and 4.17:
bold: independent
italics: dependent S-type
roman: dependent O-type

4.6 Tense, aspect, negation and dependent forms

Table 4.17. Perfect negative, third-person singular

Stem	High tone verbs		Low tone verbs	
1 CVC	e-wɔ́gɛɛ́ e-wɔ́ge é-⁺wɔ́gɛɛ́	'he didn't wash'	ě-pimɛɛ́ ě-pime é-pimɛɛ́	'she didn't throw away'
2 CVC-v	e-wɔ́mmɛɛ́ e-wɔ́mme é-⁺wɔ́mmɛɛ́	'he didn't plane'	ě-kunlɛɛ́ ě-kunle é-kunlɛɛ́	'he isn't sick'
3 CVC-vc	e-wɔ́mtɛɛ́ e-wɔ́mte é-⁺wɔ́mtɛɛ́	'he didn't have st. planed'	ě-bomnɛɛ́ ě-bomne é-bomnɛɛ́	'he didn't meet with'
4 CVC-cvc	e-wɔ́glɛnɛɛ́ e-wɔ́glɛne é-⁺wɔ́glɛnɛɛ́	'he didn't listen'	ě-baŋnedɛɛ́ ě-baŋnede é-baŋnedɛɛ́	'she didn't sew with'
5 CVV	e-síi'έ e-síi é-⁺síi'έ	'she didn't iron'	ě-suu'έ ě-suu é-suu'έ	'he didn't pass air'
6 CVV	e-bóo'έ e-bóo é-⁺bóo'έ	'it didn't break'	—	
7 CVV-v	e-láadɛɛ́ e-láade é-⁺láadɛɛ́	'he didn't chew'	ě-nyaadɛɛ́ ě-nyaade é-nyaadɛɛ́	'she didn't tear off'
8 CVV-vc	e-káatɛɛ́ e-káate é-⁺káatɛɛ́	'he didn't judge'	ě-kaatɛɛ́ ě-kaate é-kaatɛɛ́	'she didn't line the pot'
9 CVŋ	e-láα'έ e-láα é-⁺láα'έ	'she didn't read'	ě-kəə'έ ě-kəə é-kəə'έ	'he didn't shave'
10 CVŋ-v	e-láŋgɛɛ́ e-láŋge é-⁺láŋgɛɛ́	'he didn't tell'	ě-naŋgɛɛ́ ě-naŋge é-naŋgɛɛ́	'she didn't lie down'
11 CVŋ-vc	e-hyáŋtɛɛ́ e-hyáŋte é-⁺hyáŋtɛɛ́	'she didn't burn st.'	ě-soŋnɛɛ́ ě-soŋte é-soŋtɛɛ́	'he didn't purge'
12 CV	e-dyédɛɛ́ e-dyéde é-⁺dyédɛɛ́	'he didn't eat'	ě-kwedɛɛ́ ě-kwede é-kwedɛɛ́	'he didn't fall'
13 CV	e-bédɛɛ́* e-béde é-⁺bédɛɛ́	'she wasn't'	ě-bagɛɛ́ ě-bage é-bagɛɛ́	'she didn't give'
14 CV	—		ě-kii'έ ě-kii é-kii'έ	'he didn't go'

*The verb 'to be' has a set of alternative forms: independent: ě-saá, dependent S-type: ě-sɛ and dependent O-type, é-saá 'she isn't'.

4.6.6.3 *Present imperfective*

The present imperfective tense is formed by adding the imperfective suffix -ɛ' to the verb stem. It is used for actions or processes going on in the present as well as for habitual actions. The imperfective suffix -ɛ' frequently elides to -e when not before a pause.

Table 4.18. Present imperfective, singular and plural persons

1SG	**n-wɔ́gɛ'/e*** ń-wɔ́gɛɛ́	'I am washing'	**m-pimɛ'/e** ḿ-pimɛɛ́	'I am throwing away'
2SG	**e-wɔ́gɛ'** é-wɔ́gɛɛ́	'you are washing'	**e-pimɛ'** é-pimɛɛ́	'you are throwing away'
3SG	**a-wɔ́gɛ'** á-wɔ́gɛɛ́	'he/she is washing'	**a-pimɛ'** á-pimɛɛ́	'he/she is throwing away'
LOG	**mə̂-wɔ́gɛ'** mə́-wɔ́gɛɛ́	'LOG is washing'	**mə̂-pimɛ'** mə́-pimɛɛ́	'LOG is throwing away'
1PL incl.	**de-wɔ́gɛ'** dé-wɔ́gɛɛ́	'we are washing'	**de-pimɛ'** dé-pimɛɛ́	'we are throwing away'
1PL excl.	**sê-wɔ́gɛ'** sé-wɔ́gɛɛ́	'we are washing'	**sê-pimɛ'** sé-pimɛɛ́	'we are throwing away'
2PL	**nyî-wɔ́gɛ'** nyɪ́-wɔ́gɛɛ́	'you are washing'	**nyî-pimɛ'** nyɪ́-pimɛɛ́	'you are throwing away'
3PL	**bé-wɔ́gɛ'** bé-wɔ́gɛɛ́	'they are washing'	**bé-pimɛ'** bé-pimɛɛ́	'they are throwing away'

*Usage of the type styles in tables 4.18 and 4.19:
bold: independent, dependent S-type
normal: dependent O-type

4.6 Tense, aspect, negation and dependent forms

Table 4.19. Present imperfective, third-person singular

Stem	High tone verbs		Low tone verbs	
1 CVC	a-wɔ́gɛ'/e á-wɔ́gɛɛ́	'he is washing'	a-pimɛ'/e á-pimɛɛ́	'she is throwing away'
2 CVC-v	a-wɔ́mmɛ' á-wɔ́mmɛɛ́	'he is planing'	a-kunlɛ' á-kunlɛɛ́	'he is sick'
3 CVC-vc	a-wɔ́mtɛ' á-wɔ́mtɛɛ́	'he is having st. planed'	a-bomnɛ' á-bomnɛɛ́	'he is meeting w.'
4 CVC-cvc	a-wɔ́glaan á-wɔ́glaanné	'he is listening'	a-baŋnaad á-baŋnaadté	'she is sewing w.'
5 CVV	a-síɛ' á-síɛ'ɛ́	'she is ironing'	a-suɛ' á-suɛ'ɛ́	'he is passing air'
6 CVV	a-bɔ́ə' á-bɔ́ə'ɛ́	'it is breaking'	—	
7 CVV-v	a-láadɛ' á-láadɛɛ́	'he is chewing'	a-nyaadɛ' á-nyaadɛɛ́	'she is tearing off'
8 CVV-vc	a-káatɛ' á-káatɛɛ́	'he is judging'	a-kaatɛ' á-kaatɛɛ́	'she is lining the pot'
9 CVŋ	a-lǽɑ' á-lǽɑ'ɛ́	'she is reading'	a-kəə' á-kəə'ɛ́	'he is shaving'
10 CVŋ-v	a-láŋgɛ' á-láŋgɛɛ́	'he is telling'	a-naŋgɛ' á-naŋgɛɛ́	'she is lying down'
11 CVŋ-vc	a-hyáŋtɛ' á-hyáŋtɛɛ́	'she is burning st.'	a-soŋnɛ' á-soŋnɛɛ́	'he is purging'
12 CV	a-dyâg* á-dyákē	'he is eating'	a-kwag á-kwaké	'he is falling'
13 CV	a-bâg á-bákē	'she is'	a-bagɛ' á-bagɛɛ́	'she gives'
14 CV	—		a-kag á-kaké	'he goes'

*Note that the -ag ending in 12, 13 and 14 reflects an earlier form of the imperfective suffix.

4.6.6.4 Present imperfective negative

The present imperfective negative is formed with the negative prefix *e-* which merges with the person or class marker and the imperfective suffix *-ɛ'* which merges with the *-'ɛ* suffix, when present. When the imperfective suffix *-έ'* is word final it is frequently reduced to *-é*.

Low tone verbs with low and falling tone prefixes for the independent (bolded) form have an optional variant with a raised high tone on the stem: *mě-piméé* or *mě-ˈpíméé*. This is not indicated in the following table.

Table 4.20. Present imperfective negative, singular and plural persons

1SG	**me-wɔ́géé*** *me-wɔ́gé'* mé-ˈwɔ́géé	'I am not washing'	**mě-piméé** *mě-ˈpímé'* mé-piméé	'I am not throwing away'
2SG	**we-wɔ́géé** *we-wɔ́gé'* wé-ˈwɔ́géé	'you aren't washing'	**wě-piméé** *wě-ˈpímé'* wé-piméé	'you aren't throwing away'
3SG	**e-wɔ́géé** *e-wɔ́gé'* é-ˈwɔ́géé	'he/she isn't washing'	**ě-piméé** *ě-ˈpímé'* é-piméé	'he/she isn't throwing away'
LOG	**mɔ̂-wɔ́géé** *mɔ̂-wɔ́gé'* mɔ́-ˈwɔ́géé	'LOG isn't washing'	**mɔ́ɔ̄-piméé** *mɔ́ɔ̄-ˈpímé'* mɔ́-piméé	'LOG isn't throwing away'
1PL incl.	**de-wɔ́géé** *de-wɔ́gé'* dé-ˈwɔ́géé	'we aren't washing'	**dě-piméé** *dě-ˈpímé'* dé-piméé	'we aren't throwing away'
1PL excl.	**sê-wɔ́géé** *sê-wɔ́gé'* sé-ˈwɔ́géé	'we aren't washing'	**sēē-piméé** *sēē-ˈpímé'* sé-piméé	'we aren't throwing away'
2PL	**nyê-wɔ́géé** *nyê-wɔ́gé'* nyí-ˈwɔ́géé	'you aren't washing'	**nyíī-piméé** *nyíī-ˈpímé'* nyí-piméé	'you aren't throwing away'
3PL	**bé-ˈwɔ́géé** *bé-ˈwɔ́gé'* bé-ˈwɔ́géé	'they aren't washing'	**bé-piméé** *bé-pimé'* bé-piméé	'they aren't throwing away'

*Usage of the type styles in tables 4.20 and 4.21:
bold: independent
italics: dependent S-type
roman: dependent O-type

4.6 Tense, aspect, negation and dependent forms

Table 4.21. Present imperfective negative, third-person singular

Stem	High tone verbs		Low tone verbs	
1 CVC	e-wɔ́géé e-wɔ́gé'/é é-ꜜwɔ́géé	'he isn't washing'	ě-piméé ě-ꜜpímé'/é é-piméé	'she isn't throwing away'
2 CVC-v	e-wɔ́mméé e-wɔ́mmé' é-ꜜwɔ́mméé	'he isn't planing'	ě-kunléé ě-ꜜkúnlé' é-kunléé	'he isn't sick'
3 CVC-vc	e-wɔ́mtéé e-wɔ́mté' é-ꜜwɔ́mtéé	'he isn't having st. planed'	ě-bomnéé ě-ꜜbómné' é-bomnéé	'he isn't meeting with'
4 CVC-cvc	e-wógláánné e-wóglaán é-ꜜwóglaánné	'he isn't listening'	ě-baŋnáádté ě-ꜜbáŋnáád é-baŋnáádté	'she isn't sewing with'
5 CVV	e-síé'ɛ́ e-síé' é-ꜜsíé'ɛ	'she isn't ironing'	ě-suɛ́'ɛ ě-ꜜsúɛ́' é-suɛ́'ɛ	'he isn't passing air'
6 CVV	e-bɔ́ɔ́'ɛ́ e-bɔ́ɔ́' é-ꜜbɔ́ɔ́'ɛ	'it isn't breaking'	—	
7 CVV-v	e-láádéé e-láádé' é-ꜜláádéé	'he isn't chewing'	ě-nyaadéé ě-ꜜnyáádé' é-nyaadéé	'she isn't tearing off'
8 CVV-vc	e-káátéé e-káaté' é-ꜜkáatéé	'he isn't judging'	ě-kaatéé ě-ꜜkáátéʼ é-kaatéé	'she isn't lining the pot'
9 CVŋ	e-láá'ɛ́ e-láá' é-ꜜláá'ɛ	'she isn't reading'	ě-kəɔ́'ɛ ě-ꜜkɔ́ɔ́' é-kəɔ́'ɛ	'he isn't shaving'
10 CVŋ-v	e-láŋgéé e-láŋgé' é-ꜜláŋgéé	'he isn't telling'	ě-naŋgéé ě-ꜜnáŋgé' é-naŋgéé	'she isn't lying down'
11 CVŋ-vc	e-hyáŋtéé e-hyáŋté' é-ꜜhyáŋtéé	'she isn't burning st.'	ě-soŋnéé ě-ꜜsóŋné' é-soŋnéé	'he isn't purging'
12 CV	e-dyáké e-dyág é-ꜜdyáké	'he isn't eating'	ě-kwaké ě-ꜜkwág é-kwaké	'he isn't falling'
13 CV	e-báké/ě-saá e-bág é-ꜜbáké	'she isn't'	ě-bagéé ě-ꜜbágé' ě-bagéé	'she isn't giving'
14 CV	—		ě-kaké ě-ꜜkág ě-kaké	'he isn't going'

4.6.6.5 Past

The past tense is formed with the homorganic nasal past tense prefix *Ǹ-* immediately before the verb stem. There is also a final high tone on the last tone-bearing unit, which may be deleted in some cases. The low tone on the past marker is realised as a downstep if immediately preceded and followed by high tones.

This verb form is used for past actions and background information in discourse.

Table 4.22. Past, singular and plural persons

1SG	**me-nwɔ́g*** mé-nˈwɔ́gké	'I washed'	**me-mpǐm** mé-mpimmέ	'I threw away'
2SG	**we-nwɔ́g** wé-nˈwɔ́gké	'you washed'	**we-mpǐm** wé-mpimmέ	'you threw away'
3SG	**a-nwɔ́g** á-nˈwɔ́gké	'he/she washed'	**a-mpǐm** á-mpimmέ	'he/she threw away'
LOG	**mɔ̂-nwɔ́g** mɔ́-nˈwɔ́gké	'LOG washed'	**mɔ̂-mpǐm** mɔ́-mpimmέ	'LOG threw away'
1PL incl.	**de-nwɔ́g** dé-nˈwɔ́gké	'we washed'	**de-mpǐm** dé-mpimmέ	'we threw away'
1PL excl.	**sê-nwɔ́g** sé-nˈwɔ́gké	'we washed'	**sê-mpǐm** sé-mpimmέ	'we threw away'
2PL	**nyî-nwɔ́g** nyí-nˈwɔ́gké	'you washed'	**nyî-mpǐm** nyí-mpimmέ	'you threw away'
3PL	**bé-nˈwɔ́g** bé-nˈwɔ́gké	'they washed'	**bé-mpǐm** bé-mpimmέ	'they threw away'

*Usage of the type styles in tables 4.22 and 4.23:
bold: independent, dependent S-type
roman: dependent O-type

4.6 Tense, aspect, negation and dependent forms

Table 4.23. Past, third-person singular

Stem	High tone verbs		Low tone verbs	
1 CVC	**a-nwɔ́g** á-nwɔ́gké*	'he washed'	**a-mpĭm** á-mpimmɛ́	'she threw away'
2 CVC-v	**a-nwɔ́mé** á-nwɔ́méɛ́	'he planed'	**a-nkulé** á-nkuléɛ́	'he was sick'
3 CVC-vc	**a-nwɔ́méd** á-nwɔ́médté	'he had st. planed'	**a-mbomén** á-mboménné	'he met with'
4 CVC-cvc	**a-nwóglén** á-nwóglénné	'he listened'	**a-mbaŋnéd** á-mbaŋnédté	'she sewed with'
5 CVV	**a-nsíí** á-nsíí'ɛ́	'she ironed'	**a-nsuú** á-nsuú'ɛ́	'he passed air'
6 CVV	**a-mbóó** á-mbóó'ɛ́	'it broke'	—	
7 CVV-v	**a-nláá** á-nláá'ɛ́	'he chewed'	**a-nnyaá** á-nnyaá'ɛ́	'she tore off'
8 CVV-vc	**a-nkáád** á-nkáádté	'he judged'	**a-nkaád** á-nkaádté	'she lined the pot'
9 CVŋ	**a-nláŋ** á-nláŋgé	'she read'	**a-nkɔ̆ŋ** á-nkɔ̆ŋgé	'he shaved'
10 CVŋ-v	**a-nlɑ́ɑ́** á-nlɑ́ɑ́'ɛ́	'he told'	**a-nnɑɑ́** á-nnɑɑ́'ɛ́	'she lay down'
11 CVŋ-vc	**a-nhyɑ́ɑ́d** á-nhyɑ́ɑ́dté	'she burned st.'	**a-nsoón** á-nsoónné	'he purged'
12 CV	**a-ndyé** á-ndyéɛ́	'he ate'	**a-nkwɛ̆** á-nkwɛɛ́	'he fell'
13 CV	**a-mbé** á-mbéɛ́	'she was'	**a-mbĕ** á-mbagké	'she gave'
14 CV	—		**a-nkĕ** á-nkɛɛ́	'he went'

*The *gk* spelling is phonologically /k/ but underlyingly it is /g/.

4.6.6.6 Past negative

The past negative is the most easily recognised of the negative verb foms. It is formed by the negative marker *e-* which merges with the subject/concord marker, followed by *nkêN-* immediately before the verb stem. It has the *-'έ* suffixed except in the dependent S-type form.

Table 4.24. Past negative, singular and plural persons

1SG	**me-nkê-nwɔ́gkɛ́***	'I didn't wash'	**me-nkê-mpimmɛ́**	'I didn't throw away'
	me-nkê-nwɔ́g		*me-nkê-mpĭm*	
	mé-nkê-nwɔ́gké		mé-nkê-mpimmé	
2SG	**we-nkê-nwɔ́gkɛ́**	'you didn't wash'	**we-nkê-mpimmɛ́**	'you didn't throw away'
	we-nkê-nwɔ́g		*we-nkê-mpĭm*	
	wé-nkê-nwɔ́gké		wé-nkê-mpimmé	
3SG	**e-nkê-nwɔ́gkɛ́**	'he/she didn't wash'	**e-nkê-mpimmɛ́**	'he/she didn't throw away'
	e-nkê-nwɔ́g		*e-nkê-mpĭm*	
	é-nkê-nwɔ́gké		é-nkê-mpimmé	
LOG	**mɔ̂-nkê-nwɔ́gkɛ́**	'LOG didn't wash'	**mɔ̂-nkê-mpimmɛ́**	'LOG didn't throw away'
	mɔ̂-nkê-nwɔ́g		*mɔ̂-nkê-mpĭm*	
	mɔ́-nkê-nwɔ́gké		mɔ́-nkê-mpimmé	
1PL incl.	**de-nkê-nwɔ́gkɛ́**	'we didn't wash'	**de-nkê-mpimmɛ́**	'we didn't throw away'
	de-nkê-nwɔ́g		*de-nkê-mpĭm*	
	dé-nkê-nwɔ́gké		dé-nkê-mpimmé	
1PL excl.	**sê-nkê-nwɔ́gkɛ́**	'we didn't wash'	**sê-nkê-mpimmɛ́**	'we didn't throw away'
	sê-nkê-nwɔ́g		*sê-nkê-mpĭm*	
	sé-nkê-nwɔ́gké		sé-nkê-mpimmé	
2PL	**nyî-nkê-nwɔ́gkɛ́**	'you didn't wash'	**nyî-nkê-mpimmɛ́**	'you didn't throw away'
	nyî-nkê-nwɔ́g		*nyî-nkê-mpĭm*	
	nyí-nkê-nwɔ́gké		nyí-nkê-mpimmé	
3PL	**bé-nkê-nwɔ́gkɛ́**	'they didn't wash'	**bé-nkê-mpimmɛ́**	'they didn't throw away'
	bé-nkê-nwɔ́g		*bé-nkê-mpĭm*	
	bé-nkê-nwɔ́gké		bé-nkê-mpimmé	

*Usage of the type styles in tables 4.24 and 4.25:
bold: independent
italics: dependent S-type
roman: dependent O-type

4.6 Tense, aspect, negation and dependent forms

Table 4.25. Past negative, third-person singular

Stem	High tone verbs		Low tone verbs	
1 CVC	**e-nkê-nwɔ́gkɛ́**	'he didn't wash'	**e-nkê-mpimmɛ́**	'she didn't throw away'
	e-nkê-nwɔ́g		*e-nkê-mpĭm*	
	é-nkê-nwɔ́gkɛ́		é-nkê-mpimmɛ́	
2 CVC-v	**e-nkê-nwɔ́mɛ́ɛ́**	'he didn't plane'	**e-nkê-nkulɛ́ɛ́**	'he wasn't sick'
	e-nkê-nwɔ́m		*e-nkê-nkulé*	
	é-nkê-nwɔ́mɛ́ɛ́		é-nkê-nkulɛ́ɛ́	
3 CVC-vc	**e-nkê-nwɔ́médtɛ́**	'he hadn't st. planed'	**e-nkê-mbomɛ́nnɛ́**	'he didn't meet with'
	e-nkê-nwɔ́méd		*e-nkê-mbomén*	
	é-nkê-nwɔ́médtɛ́		é-nkê-mbomɛ́nnɛ́	
4 CVC-cvc	**e-nkê-nwóglɛ́nnɛ́**	'he didn't listen'	**e-nkê-mbaŋnédtɛ́**	'she didn't sew with'
	e-nkê-nwóglén		*e-nkê-mbaŋnéd*	
	é-nkê-nwóglɛ́nnɛ́		é-nkê-mbaŋnédtɛ́	
5 CVV	**e-nkê-nsíí'ɛ́**	'she didn't iron'	**e-nkê-nsuú'ɛ́**	'he didn't pass air'
	e-nkê-nsíí		*e-nkê-nsuú*	
	é-nkê-nsíí'ɛ́		é-nkê-nsuú'ɛ́	
6 CVV	**e-nkê-mbóó'ɛ́**	'it didn't break'	—	
	e-nkê-mbóó			
	é-nkê-mbóó'ɛ́			
7 CVV-v	**e-nkê-nláá'ɛ́**	'he didn't chew'	**e-nkê-nnyaá'ɛ́**	'she didn't tear off'
	e-nkê-nláá		*e-nkê-nnyaá*	
	é-nkê-nláá'ɛ́		é-nkê-nnyaá'ɛ́	
8 CVV-vc	**e-nkê-nkáádtɛ́**	'he didn't judge'	**e-nkê-nkaádtɛ́**	'she didn't line the pot'
	e-nkê-nkáád		*e-nkê-nkaád*	
	é-nkê-nkáádtɛ́		é-nkê-nkaádtɛ́	
9 CVŋ	**e-nkê-nláŋgé**	'he didn't read'	**e-nkê-nkəŋgé**	'he didn't shave'
	e-nkê-nláŋ		*e-nkê-nkə̌ŋ*	
	é-nkê-nláŋgé		é-nkê-nkəŋgé	
10 CVŋ-v	**e-nkê-nláɑ́'ɛ́**	'he didn't tell'	**e-nkê-nnɑɑ́'ɛ́**	'she didn't lie down'
	e-nkê-nláɑ́		*e-nkê-nnaá*	
	é-nkê-nláɑ́'ɛ́		é-nkê-nnɑɑ́'ɛ́	
11 CVŋ-vc	**e-nkê-nhyɑ́ɑ́dtɛ́**	'she didn't burn st.'	**e-nkê-nsoónnɛ́**	'he didn't purge'
	e-nkê-nhyɑ́ɑ́d		*e-nkê-nsoón*	
	é-nkê-nhyɑ́ɑ́dtɛ́		é-nkê-nsoónnɛ́	
12 CV	**e-nkê-ndyáá**	'he didn't eat'	**e-nkê-nkwaá**	'he didn't fall'
	e-nkê-ndyé		*e-nkê-nkwě*	
	é-nkê-ndyáá		é-nkê-nkwaá	
13 CV	**e-nkê-mbáá**	'she wasn't'	**e-nkê-mbaké**	'she didn't give'
	e-nkê-mbé		*e-nkê-mbě*	
	é-nkê-mbáá		é-nkê-mbaké	
14 CV	—		**e-nkê-nkaá**	'he didn't go'
			e-nkê-nkě	
			é-nkê-nkaá	

4.6.6.7 Past imperfective

The past imperfective tense is formed by adding the suffixes -é' and -áá to the stem.[10] Note that the first of these merges with the second in most cases. Low root tones thus become high between two high tones neutralising the H/L contrast in stem minimal pairs.

This form is used to indicate an ongoing action in the past and background information in discourse, as well as the condition in conditional sentences.

Table 4.26. Past imperfective, singular and plural persons

1SG	**n-wɔ́gáá*** ń-wɔ́gáá	'I was washing'	**m-pimáá** ḿ-pímáá	'I was throwing away'
2SG	**e-wɔ́gáá** é-wɔ́gáá	'you were washing'	**e-pimáá** é-pímáá	'you were throwing away'
3SG	**a-wɔ́gáá** á-wɔ́gáá	'he/she was washing'	**a-pimáá** á-pímáá	'he/she was throwing away'
LOG	**mɔ̂-wɔ́gáá** mɔ́-wɔ́gáá	'LOG was washing'	**mɔ̂-pimáá** mɔ́-pímáá	'LOG was throwing away'
1PL incl.	**de-wɔ́gáá** dé-wɔ́gáá	'we were washing'	**de-pimáá** dé-pímáá	'we were throwing away'
1PL excl.	**sê-wɔ́gáá** sé-wɔ́gáá	'we were washing'	**sê-pimáá** sé-pímáá	'we were throwing away'
2PL	**nyî-wɔ́gáá** nyí-wɔ́gáá	'you were washing'	**nyî-pimáá** nyí-pímáá	'you were throwing away'
3PL	**bé-wɔ́gáá** bé-wɔ́gáá	'they were washing'	**bé-pímáá** bé-pímáá	'they were throwing away'

*Usage of the type styles in tables 4.26 and 4.27:
bold: independent, dependent S-type
roman: dependent O-type

---

[10] Some dialects pronounce n-wɔ́gáá as n-wɔ́gé'áá, m-pimáá as m-pimé'áá, etc. In other words, the underlying morphemes have not merged.

4.6 Tense, aspect, negation and dependent forms

Table 4.27. Past imperfective, third-person singular

Stem	High tone verbs		Low tone verbs	
1 CVC	**a-wɔ́gáá** á-wɔ́gáá	'he was washing'	**a-pimáá** á-pímáá	'she was throwing away'
2 CVC-v	**a-wɔ́mmáá** á-wɔ́mmáá	'he was planing'	**a-kunláá** á-kúnláá	'he was sick'
3 CVC-vc	**a-wɔ́mtáá** á-wɔ́mtáá	'he was having st. planed'	**a-bomnáá** á-bómnáá	'he was meeting with'
4 CVC-cvc	**a-wóglénáá** á-wóglénáá	'he was listening'	**a-baŋnédáá** á-báŋnédáá	'she was sewing with'
5 CVV	**a-síé'áá** á-síé'áá	'she was ironing'	**a-sué'áá** á-súé'áá	'he was passing air'
6 CVV	**a-bóó'áá** á-bóó'áá	'it was breaking'	—	
7 CVV-v	**a-láádáá** á-láádáá	'he was chewing'	**a-nyaádáá** á-nyáádáá	'she was tearing off'
8 CVV-vc	**a-káátáá** á-káátáá	'he was judging'	**a-kaátáá** á-káátáá	'she was lining the pot'
9 CVŋ	**a-lɑ́ɑ́'áá** á-lɑ́ɑ́'áá	'she was reading'	**a-kəɔ́'áá** á-kɔ́ɔ́'áá	'he was shaving'
10 CVŋ-v	**a-láŋgáá** á-láŋgáá	'he was telling'	**a-naŋgáá** á-náŋgáá	'she was lying down'
11 CVŋ-vc	**a-hyáŋtáá** á-hyáŋtáá	'she was burning st.'	**a-soŋnáá** á-sóŋnáá	'he was purging'
12 CV	**a-dyágáá** á-dyágáá	'he was eating'	**a-kwagáá** á-kwágáá	'he was falling'
13 CV	**a-bágáá** á-bágáá	'she was'	**a-bagáá** á-bágáá	'she was giving'
14 CV	—		**a-kagáá** á-kágáá	'he was going'

4.6.6.8 Past imperfective negative

The past imperfective negative is formed with the usual negative prefix *e-* which merges with the person or class marker, and the same suffixes found in the corresponding affirmative *-ɛ' -áá*. However, the tone on the imperfective marker is low giving a rising tone on the resulting combination *-aá*. Tonally these have the same pattern as the perfect negative, so it is the vowels of the suffixes which distinguish these two forms.

Table 4.28. Past imperfective negative, singular and plural persons

1SG	**me-wɔ́gaá***	'I wasn't washing'	**mě-pimaá**	'I wasn't throwing away'
	me-wɔ́gaa		*mě-pimaa*	
	mé-ꜜwɔ́gaá		mé-pimaá	
2SG	**we-wɔ́gaá**	'you weren't washing'	**wě-pimaá**	'you weren't throwing away'
	we-wɔ́gaa		*wě-pimaa*	
	wé-ꜜwɔ́gaá		wé-pimaá	
3SG	**e-wɔ́gaá**	'he wasn't washing'	**ě-pimaá**	'he/she wasn't throwing away'
	e-wɔ́gaa		*ě-pimaa*	
	é-ꜜwɔ́gaá		é-pimaá	
LOG	**mɔ̂-wɔ́gaá**	'LOG wasn't washing'	**mɔ́ɔ̄-pimaá**	'LOG wasn't throwing away'
	mɔ̂-wɔ́gaa		*mɔ́ɔ̄-pimaa*	
	mɔ́-ꜜwɔ́gaá		mɔ́-pimaá	
1PL incl.	**de-wɔ́gaá**	'we weren't washing'	**dě-pimaá**	'we weren't throwing away'
	de-wɔ́gaa		*dě-pimaa*	
	dé-ꜜwɔ́gaá		dé-pimaá	
1PL excl.	**sê-wɔ́gaá**	'we weren't washing'	**séē-pimaá**	'we weren't throwing away'
	sê-wɔ́gaa		*séē-pimaa*	
	sé-ꜜwɔ́gaá		sé-pimaá	
2PL	**nyî-wɔ́gaá**	'you weren't washing'	**nyíī-pimaá**	'you weren't throwing away'
	nyî-wɔ́gaa		*nyíī-pimaa*	
	nyí-ꜜwɔ́gaá		nyí-pimaá	
3PL	**bé-wɔ́gaá**	'they weren't washing'	**bé-pimaá**	'they weren't throwing away'
	bé-wɔ́gaa		*bé-pimaa*	
	bé-ꜜwɔ́gaá		bé-pimaá	

*Usage of the type styles in tables 4.28 and 4.29:
bold: independent
italics: dependent S-type
roman: dependent O-type

4.6 Tense, aspect, negation and dependent forms

Table 4.29. Past imperfective negative, third-person singular

Stem	High tone verbs		Low tone verbs	
1 CVC	e-wógaá e-wɔ́gaa é-ꜜwógaá	'he wasn't washing'	ě-pimaá ě-pimaa é-pimaá	'she wasn't throwing away'
2 CVC-v	e-wómmaá e-wɔ́mmaa é-ꜜwómmaá	'he wasn't planing'	ě-kunlaá ě-kunlaa é-kunlaá	'he wasn't sick'
3 CVC-vc	e-wómtaá e-wɔ́mtaa é-ꜜwómtaá	'he wasn't having st. planed'	ě-bomnaá ě-bomnaa é-bomnaá	'he wasn't meeting with'
4 CVC-cvc	e-wóglɛnaá e-wóglɛnaa é-ꜜwóglɛnaá	'he wasn't listening'	ě-baŋnedaá ě-baŋnedaa é-baŋnedaá	'she wasn't sewing with'
5 CVV	e-síɛ'aá e-síɛ'aa é-ꜜsíɛ'aá	'she wasn't ironing'	ě-suɛ'aá ě-suɛ'aa é-suɛ'aá	'he wasn't passing air'
6 CVV	e-bóo'aá e-bóo'aa é-ꜜbóo'aá	'it wasn't breaking'	—	
7 CVV-v	e-láadaá e-láadaa é-ꜜláadaá	'he wasn't chewing'	ě-nyaadaá ě-nyaadaa é-nyaadaá	'she wasn't tearing off'
8 CVV-vc	e-káataá e-káataa é-ꜜkáataá	'he wasn't judging'	ě-kaataá ě-kaataa é-kaataá	'she wasn't lining the pot'
9 CVŋ	e-láα'aá e-láα'aa é-ꜜláα'aá	'she wasn't reading'	ě-kəə'aá ě-kəə'aa é-kəə'aá	'he wasn't shaving'
10 CVŋ-v	e-lâŋgaá e-lâŋgaa é-ꜜlâŋgaá	'he wasn't telling'	ě-naŋgaá ě-naŋgaa é-naŋgaá	'she wasn't lying down'
11 CVŋ-vc	e-hyâŋtaá e-hyâŋtaa é-ꜜhyâŋtaá	'she wasn't burning st.'	ě-soŋnaá ě-soŋnaa é-soŋnaá	'he wasn't purging'
12 CV	e-dyágaá e-dyágaa é-ꜜdyágaá	'he wasn't eating'	ě-kwagaá ě-kwagaa é-kwagaá	'he wasn't falling'
13 CV	e-bágaá e-bágaa é-ꜜbágaá	'she wasn't'	ě-bagaá ě-bagaa é-bagaá	'she wasn't giving'
14 CV	—		ě-kagaá ě-kagaa é-kagaá	'he wasn't going'

4.6.6.9 Future

The future tense is formed with the prefix *â-* which merges with the subject/class prefix. There is also a stem final tone which is frequently elided in context. This form is used for future actions.

Table 4.30. Future, singular and plural persons

1SG	**mě-ˈwóg*** mé-ˈwógké	'I will wash'	**mě-pǐm** mé-pimmé	'I will throw away'
2SG	**wě-ˈwóg** wé-ˈwógké	'you will wash'	**wě-pǐm** wé-pimmé	'you will throw away'
3SG	**ǎ-ˈwóg** á-ˈwógké	'he/she will wash'	**ǎ-pǐm** á-pimmé	'he/she will throw away'
LOG	**mɔ́ɔ̄-ˈwóg** mɔ́-ˈwógké	'LOG will wash'	**mɔ́ɔ̄-pǐm** mɔ́-pimmé	'LOG will throw away'
1PL incl.	**dě-ˈwóg** dé-ˈwógké	'we will wash'	**dě-pǐm** dé-pimmé	'we will throw away'
1PL excl.	**séē-zˈwóg** sé-ˈwógké	'we will wash'	**séē-pǐm** sé-pimmé	'we will throw away'
2PL	**nyéē-ˈwóg** nyé-ˈwógké	'you will wash'	**nyéē-pǐm** nyé-pimmé	'you will throw away'
3PL	**bě-ˈwóg** bé-ˈwógké	'they will wash'	**bě-pǐm** bé-pimmé	'they will throw away'

*Usage of the type styles in tables 4.30 and 4.31:
bold: independent, dependent S-type
roman: dependent O-type

4.6 Tense, aspect, negation and dependent forms

Table 4.31. Future, third-person singular

	Stem	High tone verbs		Low tone verbs	
1	CVC	ǎ-ˈwóg á-ˈwógkɛ́	'he will wash'	ǎ-pǐm/ìm á-pìmmɛ́	'she will throw away'
2	CVC-v	ǎ-ˈwómé/e á-ˈwóméé	'he will plane'	ǎ-kulé/e á-kulɛ́ɛ́	'she will be sick'
3	CVC-vc	ǎ-ˈwóméd á-ˈwómédtɛ́	'he will have st. planed'	ǎ-bomén á-boménnɛ́	'he will meet with'
4	CVC-cvc	ǎ-ˈwóglén á-ˈwóglénnɛ́	'he will listen'	ǎ-baŋnéd á-baŋnédtɛ́	'she will sew with'
5	CVV	ǎ-ˈsíí á-ˈsíí'ɛ	'she will iron'	ǎ-suú á-suú'ɛ	'he will pass air'
6	CVV	ǎ-ˈbóó á-ˈbóó'ɛ	'it will break'	—	
7	CVV-v	ǎ-ˈláá á-ˈláá'ɛ	'he will chew'	ǎ-nyaá á-nyaá'ɛ	'she will tear off'
8	CVV-vc	ǎ-ˈkáád á-ˈkáádtɛ́	'he will judge'	ǎ-kaád á-kaádtɛ́	'she will line (pot)'
9	CVŋ	ǎ-ˈláŋ á-ˈláŋgɛ́	'she will read'	ǎ-kə̌ŋ á-kəŋgɛ́	'he will shave'
10	CVŋ-v	ǎ-ˈláá á-ˈláá'ɛ	'he will tell'	ǎ-naá á-naá'ɛ	'she will lie down'
11	CVŋ-vc	ǎ-ˈhyáád á-ˈhyáádtɛ́	'she will burn st.'	ǎ-soón á-soónnɛ́	'he will purge'
12	CV	ǎ-ˈdyé á-ˈdyéé	'he will eat'	ǎ-kwɛ̌ á-kwɛɛ́	'he will fall'
13	CV	ǎ-ˈbé á-ˈbéé	'she will be'	ǎ-bɛ̌/-bakɛ́ ? á-bɛɛ́	'she will give'
14	CV	—		ǎ-kɛ̌ á-kɛɛ́	'he will go'

4.6.6.10 Future negative

The future negative is characterised by the *e-* prefix which merges with the subject marker. All future negatives have a falling tone on the prefix for every person and class. The form given in bold also has the -*'é* suffixed stem finally.

Table 4.32. Future negative, singular and plural persons

1SG	**mê-wɔ́gkɛ́*** *mê-wɔ́g*	'I won't wash'	**mê-pimmɛ́** *mê-pĭm*	'I won't throw away'
2SG	**wê-wɔ́gkɛ́** *wê-wɔ́g*	'you won't wash'	**wê-pimmɛ́** *wê-pĭm*	'you won't throw away'
3SG	**ê-wɔ́gkɛ́** *ê-wɔ́g*	'he/she won't wash'	**ê-pimmɛ́** *ê-pĭm*	'he/she won't throw away'
LOG	**mɔ̂-wɔ́gkɛ́** *mɔ̂-wɔ́g*	'LOG won't wash'	**mɔ̂-pimmɛ́** *mɔ̂-pĭm*	'LOG won't throw away'
1PL incl.	**dê-wɔ́gkɛ́** *dê-wɔ́g*	'we won't wash'	**dê-pimmɛ́** *dê-pĭm*	'we won't throw away'
1PL excl.	**sê-wɔ́gkɛ́** *sê-wɔ́g*	'we won't wash'	**sê-pimmɛ́** *sê-pĭm*	'we won't throw away'
2PL	**nyî-wɔ́gkɛ́** *nyî-wɔ́g*	'you won't wash'	**nyî-pimmɛ́** *nyî-pĭm*	'you won't throw away'
3PL	**bê-wɔ́gkɛ́** *bê-wɔ́g*	'they won't wash'	**bê-pimmɛ́** *bê-pĭm*	'they won't throw away'

*Usage of the type styles in tables 4.32 and 4.33:
bold: independent, dependent O-type
italics: dependent S-type

4.6 Tense, aspect, negation and dependent forms 129

Table 4.33. Future negative, third-person singular

Stem	High tone verbs		Low tone verbs	
1 CVC	ê-wɔ́gkɛ́ ê-wɔ́g	'he won't wash'	ê-pimmɛ́ ê-pĭm	'she won't throw away'
2 CVC-v	ê-wɔ́mɛ́ɛ́ ê-wɔ́mɛ́	'he won't plane'	ê-kulɛ́ɛ́ ê-kulɛ́	'he won't be sick'
3 CVC-vc	ê-wɔ́mɛ́dtɛ́ ê-wɔ́mɛ́d	'he won't have st. planed'	ê-bomɛ́nnɛ́ ê-bomɛ́n	'he won't meet with'
4 CVC-cvc	ê-wɔ́glɛ́nnɛ́ ê-wɔ́glɛ́n	'he won't listen'	ê-baŋnɛ́dtɛ́ ê-baŋnɛ́d	'she won't sew with'
5 CVV	ê-síí'ɛ́ ê-síí	'she won't iron'	ê-suú'ɛ́ ê-suú	'he won't pass air'
6 CVV	ê-bóó'ɛ́ ê-bóó	'it won't break'	—	
7 CVV-v	ê-láá'ɛ́ɛ́ ê-láá	'he won't chew'	ê-nyaá'ɛ́ ê-nyaá	'she won't tear off'
8 CVV-vc	ê-káádtɛ́ ê-káád	'he won't judge'	ê-kaádtɛ́ ê-kaád	'she won't line the pot'
9 CVŋ	ê-láŋgɛ́ ê-láŋ	'she won't read'	ê-kəŋgɛ́ ê-kɔ̆ŋ	'he won't shave'
10 CVŋ-v	ê-láá'ɛ́ ê-láá	'he won't tell'	ê-naá'ɛ́ ê-naá	'she won't lie down'
11 CVŋ-vc	ê-hyáádtɛ́ ê-hyáád	'she won't burn st.'	ê-soónnɛ́ ê-soón	'he won't purge'
12 CV	ê-dyáá ê-dyɛ́	'he won't eat'	ê-kwaá ê-kwĕ	'he won't fall'
13 CV	ê-báá ê-bɛ́	'she won't be'	ê-bakɛ́ ê-bă̆g ??	'she won't give'
14 CV	—		ê-kaá ê-kĕ	'he won't go'

4.6.6.11 Future imperfective

The future imperfective is marked by the future prefix *â-* and the imperfective suffix *-έ'* which carries a high tone. The imperfective suffix is often simplified to *-e* with a low tone. This verb form is used for ongoing actions in the future.

Table 4.34. Future imperfective, singular and plural persons

1SG	**mě-ˈwɔ́gέ'/e*** mé-ˈwɔ́gέε	'I will be washing'	**mě-pimέ'/e** mé-pimέε	'I will be throwing away'
2SG	**wě-ˈwɔ́gέ'** wέ-ˈwɔ́gέε	'you will be washing'	**wě-pimέ'** wέ-pimέε	'you will be throwing away'
3SG	**ǎ-ˈwɔ́gέ'** á-ˈwɔ́gέε	'he/she will be washing'	**ǎ-pimέ'** á-pimέε	'he/she will be throwing away'
log	**mɔ̌ɔ̄-ˈwɔ́gέ'** mɔ́-ˈwɔ́gέε	'LOG will be washing'	**mɔ̌ɔ̄-pimέ'** mɔ́-pimέε	'LOG will be throwing away'
1PL incl.	**dě-ˈwɔ́gέ'** dέ-ˈwɔ́gέε	'we will be washing'	**dě-pimέ'** dέ-pimέε	'we will be throwing away'
1PL excl.	**sěē-ˈwɔ́gέ'** sέ-ˈwɔ́gέε	'we will be washing'	**sěē-pimέ'** sέ-pimέε	'we will be throwing away'
2PL	**nyěē-ˈwɔ́gέ'** nyέ-ˈwɔ́gέε	'you will be washing'	**nyěē-pimέ'** nyέ-pimέε	'you will be throwing away'
3PL	**bέ-ˈwɔ́gέ'** bέ-ˈwɔ́gέε	'they will be washing'	**bέ-pimέ'** bέ-pimέε	'they will be throwing away'

*Usage of the type styles in tables 4.34 and 4.35:
bold: independent, dependent S-type
roman: dependent O-type

4.6 Tense, aspect, negation and dependent forms

Table 4.35. Future imperfective, third-person singular

Stem	High tone verbs		Low tone verbs	
1 CVC	ǎ-ˈwógé'/e á-ˈwógéé	'he will be washing'	ǎ-pimé'/e á-piméé	'she will be throwing away'
2 CVC-v	ǎ-ˈwómmé' á-ˈwómméé	'he will be planing'	ǎ-kunlé' á-kunléé	'he will be being sick'
3 CVC-vc	ǎ-ˈwómté' á-ˈwómtéé	'he will be having st. planed'	ǎ-bomné' á-bomnéé	'he will be meeting with'
4 CVC-cvc	ǎ-ˈwógláán á-ˈwógláánné	'he will be listening'	ǎ-baŋnáád á-baŋnáádté	'she will be sewing with'
5 CVV	ǎ-ˈsíé' á-ˈsíé'é	'she will be ironing'	ǎ-sué' á-sué'é	'he will be passing air'
6 CVV	ǎ-ˈbóó' á-ˈbóó'é	'it will be breaking'	—	
7 CVV-v	ǎ-ˈláádé' á-ˈláádéé	'he will be chewing'	ǎ-nyaadé' á-nyaadéé	'she will be tearing off'
8 CVV-vc	ǎ-ˈkááté' á-ˈkáátéé	'he will be judging'	ǎ-kaaté' á-kaatéé	'she will be lining (pot)'
9 CVŋ	ǎ-ˈláá' á-ˈláá'é	'she will be reading'	ǎ-kəɔ́' á-kəɔ́'é	'he will be shaving'
10 CVŋ-v	ǎ-ˈláŋgé' á-ˈláŋgéé	'he will be telling'	ǎ-naŋgé' á-naŋgéé	'she will be lying down'
11 CVŋ-vc	ǎ-ˈhyáŋgté' á-ˈhyáŋgtéé	'she will be burning st.'	ǎ-soŋné' á-soŋnéé	'he will be purging'
12 CV	ǎ-ˈdyág á-ˈdyágké	'he will be eating'	ǎ-kwăg á-kwăgké	'he will be falling'
13 CV	ǎ-ˈbág á-ˈbágké	'she will be being'	ǎ-bagé' á-bagéé	'she will be giving'
14 CV	—		ǎ-kăg á-kăgké	'he will be going'

4.6.6.12 *Future imperfective negative*

The future imperfective negative is characterised by the negative prefix *e-* and the future prefix *â-* which merge with the subject marker, as well as by the imperfective maker *-é'* and the suffix *-é*. The latter is not present in the dependent subject form. All future negatives have a falling tone on the subject marker in all persons.

Table 4.36. Future imperfective negative, singular and plural persons

1SG	**mê-wɔ́géé*** mê-wɔ́gé'	'I won't be washing'	**mê-piméé** mê-pimé'	'I won't be throwing away'
2SG	**wê-wɔ́géé** wê-wɔ́gé'	'you won't be washing'	**wê-piméé** wê-pimé'	'you won't be throwing away'
3SG	**ê-wɔ́géé** ê-wɔ́gé'	'he/she won't be washing'	**ê-piméé** ê-pimé'	'he/she won't be throwing away'
LOG	**mâ-wɔ́géé** mâ-wɔ́gé'	'LOG won't be washing'	**mâ-piméé** mâ-pimé'	'log won't be throwing away'
1PL incl.	**dê-wɔ́géé** dê-wɔ́gé'	'we won't be washing'	**dê-piméé** dê-pimé'	'we won't be throwing away'
1PL excl.	**sê-wɔ́géé** sê-wɔ́gé'	'we won't be washing'	**sê-piméé** sê-pimé'	'we won't be throwing away'
2PL	**nyî-wɔ́géé** nyî-wɔ́gé'	'you won't be washing'	**nyî-piméé** nyî-pimé'	'you won't be throwing away'
3PL	**bê-wɔ́géé** bê-wɔ́gé'	'they won't be washing'	**bê-piméé** bê-pimé'	'they won't be throwing away'

*Usage of the type styles in tables 4.36 and 4.37:
bold: independent, dependent O-type
italics: dependent S-type

4.6 Tense, aspect, negation and dependent forms   133

Table 4.37. Future imperfective negative, third-person singular

Stem	High tone verbs		Low tone verbs	
1 CVC	ê-wɔ́gɛ́ɛ́ ê-wɔ́gɛ́'	'he won't be washing'	ê-pimɛ́ɛ́ ê-pimɛ́'	'she won't be throwing away'
2 CVC-v	ê-wɔ́mmɛ́ɛ́ ê-wɔ́mmɛ́'	'he won't be planing'	ê-kunlɛ́ɛ́ ê-kunlɛ́'	'he won't be sick'
3 CVC-vc	ê-wɔ́mtɛ́ɛ́ ê-wɔ́mtɛ́'	'he won't be having st. planed'	ê-bomnɛ́ɛ́ ê-bomnɛ́'	'he won't be meeting with'
4 CVC-cvc	ê-wɔ́gláánnɛ́ ê-wɔ́gláán	'he won't be listening'	ê-baŋnááté ê-baŋnáád	'she won't be sewing with'
5 CVV	ê-síɛ́'ɛ́ ê-síɛ́	'she won't be ironing'	ê-suɛ'ɛ́ ê-suɛ́'	'he won't be passing air'
6 CVV	ê-bɔ́ɔ́'ɛ́ ê-bɔ́ɔ́'	'it won't be breaking'	—	
7 CVV-v	ê-láádɛ́ɛ́ ê-láádɛ́'	'he won't be chewing'	ê-nyaadɛ́ɛ́ ê-nyaadɛ́'	'she won't be tearing off'
8 CVV-vc	ê-káátɛ́ɛ́ ê-káátɛ́'	'he won't be judging'	ê-kaatɛ́ɛ́ ê-kaatɛ́'	'she won't be lining the pot'
9 CVŋ	ê-lɑ́ɑ́'ɛ́ ê-lɑ́ɑ́'	'she won't be reading'	ê-kəə'ɛ́ ê-kəɔ́'	'he won't be shaving'
10 CVŋ-v	ê-láŋgɛ́ɛ́ ê-láŋgɛ́'	'he won't be telling'	ê-naŋgɛ́ɛ́ ê-naŋgɛ́'	'she won't be lying down'
11 CVŋ-vc	ê-hyáŋtɛ́ɛ́ ê-hyáŋtɛ́'	'she won't be burning st.'	ê-soŋnɛ́ɛ́ ê-soŋnɛ́'	'he won't be purging'
12 CV	ê-dyákɛ́ ê-dyág	'he won't be eating'	ê-kwakɛ́ ê-kwăg	'he won't be falling'
13 CV	ê-bákɛ́ ê-bág	'she won't be'	ê-bagɛ́ɛ́ ê-bagɛ́'	'she won't be giving'
14 CV	—		ê-kakɛ́ ê-kăg	'he won't be going'

4.6.7 Minor verb tenses

Under this heading I group a number of verb forms that do not easily fit into the system so far described.

4.6.7.1 Neutral

The neutral verb form consists of the verb stem plus the person marker with no tense or aspect marking. In high tone verbs the high root tone is optionally copied onto the verbal extension resulting in two variant forms, e.g. *a-wɔ́méd* or *a-wɔ́med*, *a-síí* or *a-síi*.

Low tone verbs have two forms distinguished by tone. In the first, the person marker for any person is simply prefixed to the stem and given an H tone. In the second, a further H tone is added to the stem leaving the inherent L tone as a floating L which causes the H stem tone to downstep.

The neutral verb form is frequently used in non-initial clauses of multi-clause sentences on the story-line in discourse.

Table 4.38. Neutral, singular and plural persons

1SG	**n-wɔ́g*** ń-wɔ́gké	'I wash'	**ḿ-pim**	**ḿ-ˈpím** ḿ-ˈpímmé	'I throw away'
2SG	**e-wɔ́g** é-wɔ́gké	'you wash'	**é-pim**	**é-ˈpím** é-ˈpímmé	'you throw away'
3SG	**a-wɔ́g** á-wɔ́gké	'he/she washes'	**á-pim**	**á-ˈpím** á-ˈpímmé	'he/she throws away'
LOG	**mɔ̂-wɔ́g** mɔ́-wɔ́gké	'LOG wash'	**mɔ́-pim**	**mɔ́-ˈpím** mɔ́-ˈpímmé	'LOG throw away'
1PL incl.	**de-wɔ́g** dé-wɔ́gké	'we wash'	**dé-pim**	**dé-ˈpím** dé-ˈpímmé	'we throw away'
1PL excl.	**sê-wɔ́g** sé-wɔ́gké	'we wash'	**sé-pim**	**sé-ˈpím** sé-ˈpímmé	'we throw away'
2PL	**nyî-wɔ́g** nyí-wɔ́gké	'you wash'	**nyí-pim**	**nyí-ˈpím** nyí-ˈpímmé	'you throw away'
3PL	**bé-wɔ́g** bé-wɔ́gké	'they wash'	**bé-pim**	**bé-ˈpím** bé-ˈpímmé	'they throw away'

*Usage of the type styles in tables 4.38 and 4.39:
bold: independent
roman: dependent O-type

4.6 Tense, aspect, negation and dependent forms

Table 4.39. Neutral, third-person singular

Stem	High tone verbs		Low tone verbs		
1 CVC	a-wɔ́g á-wɔ́gké	'he washes'	á-pim	á-ˈpím á-ˈpímmé	'she throws away'
2 CVC-v	a-wɔ́mé á-wɔ́méé	'he planes'	á-kule	á-ˈkúlé á-ˈkúléé	'he is sick'
3 CVC-vc	a-wɔ́méd á-wɔ́médté	'he has st. planed'	á-bomɛn	á-ˈbómɛ́n á-ˈbómɛ́nné	'he meets with'
4 CVC-cvc	a-wóglén á-wóglénné	'he listens'	á-baŋned	á-ˈbáŋnéd á-ˈbáŋnédté	'she sews with'
5 CVV	a-síí á-síí'ɛ	'she irons'	á-suu	á-ˈsúú á-ˈsúú'ɛ	'he passes air'
6 CVV	a-bóó á-bóó'ɛ	'it breaks'	—	—	
7 CVV-v	a-láá á-láádé	'he chews'	á-nyaa	á-ˈnyáá á-ˈnyáá'ɛ	'she tears off'
8 CVV-vc	a-káád á-káádté	'he judges'	á-kaad	á-ˈkáád á-ˈkáádté	'she lines the pot'
9 CVŋ	a-láŋ á-láŋgé	'she reads'	á-kəŋ	á-ˈkɔ́ŋ á-ˈkɔ́ŋgé	'he shaves'
10 CVŋ-v	a-láá́ á-láá́'ɛ	'he tells'	á-naα	á-ˈnáá́ á-ˈnáá́'ɛ	'she lies down'
11 CVŋ-vc	a-hyáád́ á-hyáád́té	'she burns st.'	á-soon	á-ˈsóón á-ˈsóónné	'he purges'
12 CV	a-dyɛ́ á-dyɛ́ɛ́	'he eats'	á-kwɛ	á-ˈkwɛ́ á-ˈkwɛ́ɛ́	'he falls'
13 CV	a-bɛ́ á-bɛ́ɛ́	'she is'	á-bɛ	á-ˈbɛ́ á-ˈbɛ́ɛ́	'she gives'
14 CV	—		á-kɛ	á-ˈkɛ́ á-ˈkɛ́ɛ́	'he goes'

4.6.7.2 Neutral negative

The neutral negative is easily recognisable by the *se-* prefix between the subject marker and the verb stem. It also has a final H tone which is realised on the last tone-bearing unit. As the person/concord prefixes keep their inherent tones, only the forms in third-person singular are given throughout this verb paradigm.

Table 4.40. Neutral negative, third-person singular

Stem	High tone verbs		Low tone verbs	
1 CVC	**a-se-wóg**	'he doesn't wash'	**a-se-pǐm**	'she doesn't throw away'
2 CVC-v	**a-se-wómé**	'he doesn't plane'	**a-se-kulé**	'he isn't sick'
3 CVC-vc	**a-se-wóméd**	'he doesn't have st. planed'	**a-se-bomén**	'he doesn't meet with'
4 CVC-cvc	**a-se-wóglén**	'he doesn't listen'	**a-se-baŋnéd**	'she doesn't sew with'
5 CVV	**a-se-síí**	'she doesn't iron'	**a-se-suú**	'he doesn't pass air'
6 CVV	**a-se-bóó**	'it doesn't break'	—	
7 CVV-v	**a-se-láá**	'he doesn't chew'	**a-se-nyaá**	'she doesn't tear off'
8 CVV-vc	**a-se-káád**	'he doesn't judge'	**a-se-kaád**	'she doesn't line (pot)'
9 CVŋ	**a-se-láŋ**	'she doesn't read'	**a-se-kɔ̌ŋ**	'he doesn't shave'
10 CVŋ-v	**a-se-láá**	'he doesn't tell'	**a-se-nɑɑ́**	'she doesn't lie down'
11 CVŋ-vc	**a-se-hyɑ́ɑ́d**	'she doesn't burn st.'	**a-se-soón**	'he doesn't purge'
12 CV	**a-se-dyé**	'he doesn't eat'	**a-se-kwě**	'he doesn't fall'
13 CV	**a-se-bé**	'she is not'	**a-se-bě**	'she doesn't give'
14 CV	—		**a-se-kě**	'he doesn't go'

4.6.7.3 Consecutive

The consecutive verb aspect is formed with the subject marker and the imperfective marker -é'. All subject markers carry a H tone.

There is some variation in that the -ɛ' suffix may be reduced to -e and the final H tone may be changed to low, e.g., á-ꜜwɔ́gé' or á-ꜜwɔ́gɛ' or á-ꜜwɔ́gé or á-ꜜwɔ́ge.

The consecutive aspect is used in discourse for actions following some other action as a consequence of that action. It is also used to indicate that an action is being repeated. In this case the verb itself is often repeated as in (298).

As the tone pattern is the same with all prefixes, only the third-person singular forms will be given in table 4.41.

Table 4.41. Consecutive, third-person singular

Stem	High tone verbs		Low tone verbs	
1 CVC	á-ꜜwɔ́gé'	'he washes'	á-pimé'	'she throws away'
2 CVC-v	á-ꜜwɔ́mmé'	'he planes'	á-kunlé'	'he is sick'
3 CVC-vc	á-ꜜwɔ́mté'	'he planes st.'	á-bomné'	'he meets with'
4 CVC-cvc	á-ꜜwógláán	'he listens'	á-baŋnáád	'she sews with'
5 CVV	á-ꜜsíé'	'she irons'	á-sué'	'he passes air'
6 CVV	á-ꜜbɔ́ɔ́'	'it breaks'	—	
7 CVV-v	á-ꜜláádé'	'he chews'	á-nyaadé'	'she tears off'
8 CVV-vc	á-ꜜkááté'	'he judges'	á-kaaté'	'she lines the pot'
9 CVŋ	á-ꜜlɑ́ɑ́'	'she reads'	á-kəə́'	'he shaves'
10 CVŋ-v	á-ꜜláŋgé'	'he tells'	á-naŋgé'	'she lies down'
11 CVŋ-vc	á-ꜜhyáŋgté'	'she burns st.'	á-soŋné'	'he purges'
12 CV	á-ꜜdyág	'he eats'	á-kwăg	'he falls'
13 CV	á-ꜜbág	'she is'	á-bagé'	'she gives'
14 CV	—		á-kăg	'he goes'

(298) Nέɛ   é-syɔ́gé   mendíb   áweéte   éminé'
      as   2SG-pour.PERF   6.water   there.inside   2SG.wring.CONS
      éminé'   éminé'.
      2SG.wring.CONS   2SG.wring.CONS
      'After you pour in water, you wring and wring and wring.'

4.6.7.4 Prior past I

The prior past tense I is marked by *kidé-* prefixed to the stem and by an H tone suffix. In H tone verbs the root tone is downstepped. This tense may historically come from a two-verb construction consisting of a finite verb with auxiliary function plus the main verb in the infinitive.

It occurs relatively infrequently in texts and is used to express events that occur prior to other events.

Table 4.42. Prior past I, third-person singular

Stem	High tone verbs		Low tone verbs	
1 CVC	a-kidé-ꜜwóg* á-kídé-ꜜwógké	'he already washed'	a-kidé-pĭm á-kídé-pimmɛ́	'she already threw away'
2 CVC-v	a-kidé-ꜜwómé á-kídé-ꜜwóméɛ́	'he already planed'	a-kidé-kulé á-kídé-kuléɛ́	'he is already sick'
3 CVC-vc	a-kidé-ꜜwóméd á-kídé-ꜜwómédté	'he had already st. planed'	a-kidé-bomén á-kídé-boménné	'he already met with'
4 CVC-cvc	a-kidé-ꜜwóglén á-kídé-ꜜwóglénné	'he already listened'	a-kidé-baŋnéd á-kídé-baŋnédté	'she already sewed with'
5 CVV	a-kidé-ꜜsíí á-kídé-ꜜsíí'ɛ	'she already ironed'	a-kidé-suú á-kídé-suu'ɛ	'he already passed air'
6 CVV	a-kidé-ꜜbóó á-kídé-ꜜbóó'ɛ	'it is already broken'	—	
7 CVV-v	a-kidé-ꜜláá á-kídé-ꜜláá'ɛ	'he already chewed'	a-kidé-nyaá á-kídé-nyaá'ɛ	'she already tore off'
8 CVV-vc	a-kidé-ꜜkáád á-kídé-ꜜkáádté	'he already judged'	a-kidé-kaád á-kídé-kaádté	'she already lined the pot'
9 CVŋ	a-kidé-ꜜláŋ á-kídé-ꜜláŋgé	'she already read'	a-kidé-kŏŋ á-kídé-kŏŋgé	'he already shaved'
10 CVŋ-v	a-kidé-ꜜláǻ á-kídé-ꜜláǻ'ɛ	'he already told'	a-kidé-nɑǻ á-kídé-nɑǻ'ɛ	'she already lay down'
11 CVŋ-vc	a-kidé-ꜜhyǻǻd á-kídé-ꜜhyǻǻdté	'she already burned st.'	a-kidé-soón á-kídé-soónné	'he already purged'
12 CV	a-kidé-ꜜdyé á-kídé-ꜜdyéɛ́	'he has already eaten'	a-kidé-kwĕ á-kídé-kwɛɛ́	'he already fell'
13 CV	a-kidé-ꜜbé á-kídé-ꜜbéɛ́	'she already was'	a-kidé-bĕ á-kídé-bɛɛ́	'she already gave'
14 CV	—		a-kidé-kĕ á-kídé-kɛɛ́	'he already went'

*Usage of the forms type styles in tables 4.42 and 4.43:
bold: independent
roman: dependent O-type

4.6.7.5 Prior past II

The prior past tense II is identical in all respects to the prior past I above except that *ké-* is used instead of *kidé-* and it appears to have the same use.

Table 4.43. Prior past II, third-person singular

Stem	High tone verbs		Low tone verbs	
1 CVC	**a-ké-ˈwɔ́g*** á-ké-ˈwɔ́gkɛ́	'he already washed'	**a-ké-pĭm** á-ké-pĭmmɛ́	'she already threw away'
2 CVC-v	**a-ké-ˈwɔ́mé** á-ké-ˈwɔ́méé	'he already planed'	**a-ké-kulé** á-ké-kuléɛ́	'he is already sick'
3 CVC-vc	**a-ké-ˈwɔ́méd** á-ké-ˈwɔ́médtɛ́	'he had already st. planed'	**a-ké-bomén** á-ké-bomɛ́nnɛ́	'he already met with'
4 CVC-cvc	**a-ké-ˈwóglén** á-ké-ˈwóglénnɛ́	'he already listened'	**a-ké-baŋnéd** á-ké-baŋnédtɛ́	'she already sewed with'
5 CVV	**a-ké-ˈsíí** á-ké-ˈsíí'ɛ	'she already ironed'	**a-ké-suú** á-ké-suu'ɛ	'he already passed air'
6 CVV	**a-ké-ˈbóó** á-ké-ˈbóó'ɛ	'it is already broken'	—	
7 CVV-v	**a-ké-ˈláá** á-ké-ˈláá'ɛ	'he already chewed'	**a-ké-nyaá** á-ké-nyaá'ɛ	'she already tore off'
8 CVV-vc	**a-ké-ˈkáád** á-ké-ˈkáádtɛ́	'he already judged'	**a-ké-kaád** á-ké-kaádtɛ́	'she already lined the pot'
9 CVŋ	**a-ké-ˈláŋ** á-ké-ˈláŋgɛ́	'she already read'	**a-ké-kɔ̆ŋ** á-ké-kɔ̆ŋgɛ́	'he already shaved'
10 CVŋ-v	**a-ké-ˈláá** á-ké-ˈláá'ɛ	'he already told'	**a-ké-ναά** á-ké-ναά'ɛ	'she already lay down'
11 CVŋ-vc	**a-ké-ˈhyáád** á-ké-ˈhyáádtɛ́	'she already burned st.'	**a-ké-soón** á-ké-soónnɛ́	'he already purged'
12 CV	**a-ké-ˈdyé** á-ké-ˈdyéɛ́	'he has already eaten'	**a-ké-kwĕ** á-ké-kwɛɛ́	'he already fell'
13 CV	**a-ké-ˈbé** á-ké-ˈbéɛ́	'she already was'	**a-ké-bĕ** á-ké-bɛɛ́	'she already gave'
14 CV	—		**a-ké-kĕ** á-ké-kɛɛ́	'he already went'

*Usage of the type styles:
bold: independent
roman: dependent O-type

4.6.7.6 Subsequent past

The subsequent past tense is marked by the *dê-* prefix and a final H tone. It is used to relate an event to a previous event. It is not found frequently. I only give examples for the third-person singular as the tonal pattern with all the other subject markers is readily predictable.

Table 4.44. Subsequent past, third-person singular

Stem	High tone verbs		Low tone verbs	
1 CVC	a-dê-wɔ́g	'before he washed'	a-dê-pĭm	'before she threw away'
2 CVC-v	a-dê-wɔ́mé	'before he planed'	a-dê-kulé	'before he is sick'
3 CVC-vc	a-dê-wɔ́méd	'before he had st. planed'	a-dê-bomén	'before he met with'
4 CVC-cvc	a-dê-wóglén	'before he listened'	a-dê-baŋnéd	'before she sewed with'
5 CVV	a-dê-síí	'before she ironed'	a-dê-suú	'before he passed air'
6 CVV	a-dê-bóó	'before it is broken'	—	
7 CVV-v	a-dê-láá	'before he chewed'	a-dê-nyaá	'before she tore off'
8 CVV-vc	a-dê-káád	'before he judged'	a-dê-kaád	'before she lined the pot'
9 CVŋ	a-dê-láŋ	'before she read'	a-dê-kɔ̆ŋ	'before he shaved'
10 CVŋ-v	a-dê-láá́	'before he told'	a-dê-naá́	'before she lay down'
11 CVŋ-vc	a-dê-hyáád	'before she burned st.'	a-dê-soón	'before he purged'
12 CV	a-dê-dyέ	'before he has eaten'	a-dê-kwĕ	'before he fell'
13 CV	a-dê-bέ	'before she was'	a-dê-bĕ	'before she gave'
14 CV	—		a-dê-kĕ	'before he went'

4.6 Tense, aspect, negation and dependent forms   141

4.6.7.7 Immediate past

There are two more forms which often are given the gloss 'as soon as V'. I call these forms immediate past and immediate future. They are used in adverbial clauses which link the main clause to a preceding event. The immediate past is negative in form as is clear from the form of the prefix. It also has unique tonal properties. The L stem tone of L tone verbs is raised to H. In forms with subject markers with inherent falling tones (LOG, 1PL, 2PL), there is an unusual upstep (ˈ) before the root which raises the following H tones.

Table 4.45. Immediate past, singular and plural persons

1SG	mě-wɔ́gé	'as soon as I washed'	mě-pímé	'as soon as I threw away'
2SG	wě-wɔ́gé	'as soon as you washed'	wě-pímé	'as soon as you threw away'
3SG	ě-wɔ́gé	'as soon as he washed'	ě-pímé	'as soon as she threw away'
LOG	mɔ̌ɔ̃-ˈwɔ́gé	'as soon as LOG washed'	mɔ̌ɔ̃-ˈpímé	'as soon as LOG threw away'
1PL incl.	dě-wɔ́gé	'as soon as we washed'	dě-pímé	'as soon as we threw away'
1PL excl.	sěē-ˈwɔ́gé	'as soon as we washed'	sěē-ˈpímé	'as soon as we threw away'
2PL	nyǐ̃-ˈwɔ́gé	'as soon as you washed'	nyǐ̃-ˈpímé	'as soon as you threw away'
3PL	bé-ˈwɔ́gé	'as soon as they washed'	bé-ˈpímé	'as soon as they threw away'

Table 4.46. Immediate past, third-person singular

Stem	High tone verbs		Low tone verbs	
1 CVC	ě-wɔ́gé	'as soon as he washed'	ě-pímé	'as soon as she threw away'
2 CVC-v	ě-wɔ́mmé	'as soon as he planed'	ě-kúnlé	'as soon as he is sick'
3 CVC-vc	ě-wɔ́mté	'as soon as he had st. planed'	ě-bómné	'as soon as he met with'
4 CVC-cvc	ě-wɔ́glèné	'as soon as he listened'	ě-báŋnédé	'as soon as she sewed with'
5 CVV	ě-síí	'as soon as she ironed'	ě-súú	'as soon as he passed air'
6 CVV	ě-bóó	'as soon as it broke'	—	
7 CVV-v	ě-láádé	'as soon as he chewed'	ě-nyáádé	'as soon as she tore off'
8 CVV-vc	ě-káátè	'as soon as he judged'	ě-káátè	'as soon as she lined the pot'
9 CVŋ	ě-láá́	'as soon as she read'	ě-kɔ́ɔ́	'as soon as he shaved'
10 CVŋ-v	ě-láŋgé	'as soon as he told'	ě-náŋgé	'as soon as she lay down'
11 CVŋ-vc	ě-hyáŋté	'as soon as she burned st.'	ě-sɔ́ŋné	'as soon as he purged'
12 CV	ě-dyédé	'as soon as he ate'	ě-kwédé	'as soon as he fell'
13 CV	ě-bédé	'as soon as she was'	ě-bágé	'as soon as she gave'
14 CV	—		ě-kíí	'as soon as he went'

4.6.7.8 Immediate future

The immediate future is the same as the perfective future but with the addition of the final suffix -'ɛ́ which replaces the final H of the future tense. Like the immediate past tense, this form is used in adverbial clauses which link the main clause to a preceeding event.

Table 4.47. Immediate future, singular and plural persons

1SG	mě-ˈwɔ́gkɛ́	'as soon as I will wash'	mě-pimmɛ́	'as soon as I will throw away'
2SG	wě-ˈwɔ́gkɛ́	'as soon as you will wash'	wě-pimmɛ́	'as soon as you will throw away'
3SG	ǎ-ˈwɔ́gkɛ́	'as soon as he/she will wash'	ǎ-pimmɛ́	'as soon as he/she will throw away'
LOG	mɔ̌ɔ̄-ˈwɔ́gkɛ́	'as soon as LOG will wash'	mɔ̌ɔ̄-pimmɛ́	'as soon as LOG will throw away'
1PL incl.	dě-ˈwɔ́gkɛ́	'as soon as we will wash'	dě-pimmɛ́	'as soon as we will throw away'
1PL excl.	sɛ́ɛ̄-ˈwɔ́gkɛ́	'as soon as we will wash'	sɛ́ɛ̄-pimmɛ́	'as soon as we will throw away'
2PL	nyɛ́ɛ̄-ˈwɔ́gkɛ́	'as soon as you will wash'	nyɛ́ɛ̄-pimmɛ́	'as soon as you will throw away'
3PL	bɛ́-ˈwɔ́gkɛ́	'as soon as they will wash'	bɛ́-pimmɛ́	'as soon as they will throw away'

4.6 Tense, aspect, negation and dependent forms

Table 4.48. Immediate future, third-person singular

Stem	High tone verbs		Low tone verbs	
1 CVC	ǎ-ꜜwɔ́gkɛ́	'as soon as he will wash'	ǎ-pimmɛ́	'as soon as she will throw away'
2 CVC-v	ǎ-ꜜwɔ́mɛ́ɛ́	'as soon as he will plane'	ǎ-kulɛ́ɛ́	'as soon as he will be sick'
3 CVC-vc	ǎ-ꜜwɔ́mɛ́dtɛ́	'as soon as he will have st. planed'	ǎ-bomɛ́nnɛ́	'as soon as he will meet with'
4 CVC-cvc	ǎ-ꜜwɔ́glɛ́nnɛ́	'as soon as he will listen'	ǎ-baŋnɛ́dtɛ́	'as soon as she will sew with'
5 CVV	ǎ-ꜜsíí'ɛ́	'as soon as she will iron'	ǎ-suú'ɛ́	'as soon as he will pass air'
6 CVV	ǎ-ꜜbóó'ɛ́	'as soon as it will break'	—	
7 CVV-v	ǎ-ꜜláá'ɛ́ɛ́	'as soon as he will chew'	ǎ-nyaá'ɛ́	'as soon as she will tear off'
8 CVV-vc	ǎ-ꜜkáádtɛ́	'as soon as he will judge'	ǎ-kaádtɛ́	'as soon as she will line the pot'
9 CVŋ	ǎ-ꜜláŋgɛ́	'as soon as she will read'	ǎ-kəŋgɛ́	'as soon as he will shave'
10 CVŋ-v	ǎ-ꜜláá'ɛ́	'as soon as he will tell'	ǎ-naá'ɛ́	'as soon as she will lie down'
11 CVŋ-vc	ǎ-ꜜhyáádtɛ́	'as soon as she will burn st.'	ǎ-soónnɛ́	'as soon as he will purge'
12 CV	ǎ-ꜜdyáá	'as soon as he will eat'	ǎ-kwaá	'as soon as he will fall'
13 CV	ǎ-ꜜbáá	'as soon as she will be'	ǎ-bakɛ́	'as soon as she will give'
14 CV	—		ǎ-kaá	'as soon as he will go'

4.6.7.9 Echo verb

There is one other verb form which is not a tense as such but is used as an echo verb in some verbal expressions. It consists of the verb stem and the suffix -*én* which carries a high tone. I call it an echo verb because its form is derived from the stem of the main verb in the same clause.

It occurs at the end of the clause after all the other clause complements or adjuncts. It should be noted that the VC part of the -CVC extensions (type 4 below) is replaced by the suffix -én.

Table 4.49. Echo verbs

Stem	High tone verbs		Low tone verbs	
1 CVC	wɔ́gén	'wash'	pimén	'throw away'
2 CVC-v	wɔ́mmén	'plane'	kunlén	'be sick'
3 CVC-vc	wɔ́mtén	'have planed'	bomnén	'meet with'
4 CVC-cvc	wɔ́glén	'listen'	baɲnén	'sew with'
5 CVV	síén	'iron'	suén	'pass air'
6 CVV	bɔ́ɔ́n	'break'	—	
7 CVV-v	láádén*	'chew'	nyaadén	'tear off'
8 CVV-vc	kááténˇ	'judge'	kaatén	'line (pot)'
9 CVŋ	lɑ́ɑ́n	'read'	kɔɔ́n	'shave'
10 CVŋ-v	láŋgén	'tell'	naŋgén	'lie down'
11 CVŋ-vc	hyáŋtén	'burn'	soŋnén	'purge'
12 CV	dyéén	'eat'	kwɛén	'fall'
13 CV	béén	'be'	bagén†	'give'
14 CV	—		kɛén	'go'

*or láán?
†or beén?

(299) ě-**bídé**   **bid-én**
    1.NEG-come.out   come.out-EN
    'as soon as he came out...'

(300) e-**kagáá**   wɛ   **kɛ-én**
    2SG-go.IMPF   2SG.PRO   go-EN
    'you were just going'

(301) **háa**   bé-**chénlé**   ane   kɔ́demod   **chénl-én**
    then   2-call.PERF   that   young.man   call-EN
    'then they called that young man...'

4.7 Verb moods

Akɔɔse distinguishes between imperative and hortative moods, as well as indicative which has been the focus up to this point. Both have a perfective and an imperfective form. In the negative these distinctions are neutralised giving only one negative form. These are described in the next sub-sections.

4.7.1 Imperative perfective

The imperative perfective is the shortest existing verb form. It consists of the verb stem plus a final H tone. It only exists for the second-person singular. For commands involving other persons, the hortative paradigm in section 4.7.3 is used.

The imperative perfective is used for making commands and requests.

Table 4.50. Imperative perfective, second-person singular

Stem	High tone verbs		Low tone verbs	
1 CVC	wóg	'wash!'	pĭm	'throw away!'
2 CVC-v	wómé	'plane!'	kulé	'be sick!'
3 CVC-vc	wóméd	'have planed!'	bomén	'meet with!'
4 CVC-cvc	wóglén	'listen!'	baŋnéd	'sew with!'
5 CVV	síí	'iron!'	suú	'pass air!'
6 CVV	bóó	'break!'	—	
7 CVV-v	láá	'chew!'	nyaá	'tear!'
8 CVV-vc	káád	'judge!'	kaád	'line (pot)!'
9 CVŋ	láŋ	'read!'	kŏŋ	'shave!'
10 CVŋ-v	láά	'tell!'	nαά	'lie down!'
11 CVŋ-vc	hyάάd	'burn!'	soón	'purge!'
12 CV	dyé	'eat!'	kwĕ	'fall!'
13 CV	bé	'be!'	bĕ	'give!'
14 CV	—		kĕ	'go!'

4.7.2 Imperative imperfective

The imperative imperfective consists of the verb stem plus the imperfective marker -é' with a high tone.

It is used as a more insistent imperative and only exists for the second-person singular. For other persons, the hortative imperfective paradigm in section 4.7.4 is used.

Table 4.51. Imperative imperfective, second-person singular

Stem	High tone verbs		Low tone verbs	
1 CVC	wógé'	'wash!!'	pimé'	'throw away!!'
2 CVC-v	wómmé'	'plane!!'	kunlé'	'be sick!!'
3 CVC-vc	wómté'	'have planed!!'	bomné'	'meet with!!'
4 CVC-cvc	wógláán	'listen!!'	baŋnáád	'sew with!!'
5 CVV	síé'	'iron!!'	sué'	'pass air!!'
6 CVV	bɔ́ɔ́'	'break!!'	—	
7 CVV-v	láádé'	'chew!!'	nyaadé'	'tear!!'
8 CVV-vc	kááté'	'judge!!'	kaaté'	'line (pot)!!'
9 CVŋ	láá'	'read!!'	kɔɔ́'	'shave!!'
10 CVŋ-v	láŋgé'	'tell!!'	naŋgé'	'lie down!!'
11 CVŋ-vc	hyáŋgté'	'burn!!'	soŋné'	'purge!!'
12 CV	dyág	'eat!!'	kwăg	'fall!!'
13 CV	bág	'be!!'	bagé'	'give!!'
14 CV	—		kăg	'go!!'

4.7.3 Hortative perfective

I am calling the verb forms in the following tables the HORTATIVE as a cover term for what is often called by a number of different terms. Here it covers imperative (2PL), jussive (1SG and 1PL), desiderative (3SG and 3PL) and intention.

The hortative is formed by a high tone person marker plus a final L tone on the stem. The L tone is especially noticeable in H tone verbs like 'wash' where the combination of the H stem tone and the L final tone results in a falling tone on the stem.

4.7 Verb moods   147

Table 4.52. Hortative perfective, singular and plural persons

1SG	ń-wɔ̂g	'I should wash!'	ḿ-pim	'I should throw away!'
2SG	é-wɔ̂g	'you should wash!'	é-pim	'you should throw away!'
3SG	á-wɔ̂g	'she should wash!'	á-pim	'she should throw away!'
LOG	mɔ́-wɔ̂g	'LOG should wash!'	mɔ́-pim	'LOG should throw away!'
1PL incl.	dé-wɔ̂g	'we should wash!'	dé-pim	'we should throw away!'
1PL excl.	sé-wɔ̂g	'we should wash!'	sé-pim	'we should throw away!'
2PL	nyí-wɔ̂g	'you should wash!'	nyí-pim	'you should throw away!'
3PL	bé-wɔ̂g	'they should wash!'	bé-pim	'they should throw away!'

Table 4.53. Hortative perfective, third-person singular

	Stem	High tone verbs		Low tone verbs	
1	CVC	á-wɔ̂g	'he should wash!'	á-pim	'she should throw away!'
2	CVC-v	á-wɔ́me	'he should plane!'	á-kule	'he should be sick!'
3	CVC-vc	á-wɔ́med	'he should have st. planed!'	á-bomen	'he should meet with!'
4	CVC-cvc	á-wóglɛn	'he should listen!'	á-baŋned	'she should sew with!'
5	CVV	á-síi	'she should iron!'	á-suu	'he should pass air!'
6	CVV	á-bóo	'he should break!'	—	
7	CVV-v	á-láa	'he should chew!'	á-nyaa	'he should tear off!'
8	CVV-vc	á-káad	'he should judge!'	á-kaad	'she should line (pot)!'
9	CVŋ	á-lâŋ	'she should read!'	á-kəŋ	'he should shave!'
10	CVŋ-v	á-lɑ́ɑ	'he should tell!'	á-nɑɑ	'she should lie down!'
11	CVŋ-vc	á-hyɑ́ɑd	'he should burn st.!'	á-soon	'he should purge!'
12	CV	á-dyê	'she should eat!'	á-kwɛ	'he should fall!'
13	CV	á-bê	'he should be!'	á-bɛ	'he should give!'
14	CV	—		á-kɛ	'he should go!'

4.7.4 Hortative imperfective

The hortative imperfective is similar to the hortative perfective except that, instead of just a final L tone, there is the full imperfective marker -ɛ' which bears an L tone. All persons have the same tone pattern.

Table 4.54. Hortative imperfective, third-person singular

Stem	High tone verbs		Low tone verbs	
1 CVC	á-wɔ́gɛ'	'he should wash!!'	á-pimɛ'	'he should throw away!!'
2 CVC-v	á-wɔ́mmɛ'	'he should plane!!'	á-kunlɛ'	'he should be sick!!'
3 CVC-vc	á-wɔ́mtɛ'	'he should have st. planed!!'	á-bomnɛ'	'he should meet with!!'
4 CVC-cvc	á-wóglaan	'he should listen!!'	á-baŋnaad	'he should sew with!!'
5 CVV	á-síɛ'	'he should iron!!'	á-suɛ'	'he should pass air!!'
6 CVV	á-bɔ́ə'	'he should break!!'	—	
7 CVV-v	á-láadɛ'	'he should chew!!'	á-nyaadɛ'	'he should tear off!!'
8 CVV-vc	á-káatɛ'	'he should judge!!'	á-kaatɛ'	'he should line (pot)!!'
9 CVŋ	á-láα'	'he should read!!'	á-kəə'	'he should shave!!'
10 CVŋ-v	á-láŋgɛ'	'he should tell!!'	á-naŋgɛ'	'he should lie down!!'
11 CVŋ-vc	á-hyáŋgtɛ'	'he should burn st.!!'	á-soŋnɛ'	'he should purge!!'
12 CV	á-dyâg	'he should eat!!'	á-kwag	'he should fall!!'
13 CV	á-bâg	'he should be!!'	á-bagɛ'	'he should give!!'
14 CV	—		á-kag	'he should go!!'

4.7.5 Imperative and hortative negative

In the negative imperative and the hortative negative, perfective and imperfective are not distinguished, i.e. there is only one form for each person. This form is characterised by the negative prefix *e-* which is merged with the subject marker, and the imperfective suffix *-ɛ́'* which carries an H tone. This verb form is used to make negative commands and give negative instructions.

4.7 Verb moods

Table 4.55. Imperative and hortative negative, singular and plural persons

1SG	me-wɔ́gé'	'I should not wash!'	mě-pimé'	'I should not throw away!'
2SG	we-wɔ́gé'	'don't wash!'	wě-pimé'	'don't throw away!'
3SG	e-wɔ́gé'	'he/she should not wash!'	ě-pimé'	'he/she should not throw away!'
LOG	mɔ̂-wɔ́gé'	'LOG should not wash!'	mɔ̌ɔ̄-pimé'	'LOG should not throw away!'
1PL incl.	de-wɔ́gé'	'let's not wash!'	dě-pimé'	'let's not throw away!'
1PL excl.	sê-wɔ́gé'	'let's not wash!'	séē-pimé'	'let's not throw away!'
2PL	nyî-wɔ́gé'	'don't wash!'	nyǐī-pimé'	'don't throw away!'
3PL	bé-↓wɔ́gé'	'they should not wash!'	bé-pimé'	'they should not throw away!'

Table 4.56. Imperative and hortative negative, third-person singular

Stem	High tone verbs		Low tone verbs	
1 CVC	e-wɔ́gé'	'he shouldn't wash!'	ě-pimé'*	'he shouldn't throw away!'
2 CVC-v	e-wɔ́mmé'	'he shouldn't plane!'	ě-kunlé'	'he shouldn't be sick!'
3 CVC-vc	e-wɔ́mté'	'he shouldn't have st. planed!'	ě-bomné'	'he shouldn't meet with!'
4 CVC-cvc	e-wɔ́gláán	'he shouldn't listen!'	ě-baŋnáád	'he shouldn't sew with!'
5 CVV	e-síé'	'he shouldn't iron!'	ě-sué'	'he shouldn't pass air!'
6 CVV	e-bɔ́ɔ́'	'he shouldn't break!'	—	
7 CVV-v	e-láádé'	'he shouldn't chew!'	ě-nyaadé'	'he shouldn't tear off!'
8 CVV-vc	e-kááté'	'he shouldn't judge!'	ě-kaaté'	'he shouldn't line (pot)!'
9 CVŋ	e-láá'	'he shouldn't read!'	ě-kɔɔ́'	'he shouldn't shave!'
10 CVŋ-v	e-láŋgé'	'he shouldn't tell!'	ě-naŋgé'	'he shouldn't lie down!'
11 CVŋ-vc	e-hyáŋgté'	'he shouldn't burn st.!'	ě-soŋné'	'he shouldn't purge!'
12 CV	e-dyág	'he shouldn't eat!'	ě-kwǎg	'he shouldn't fall!'
13 CV	e-bág	'he shouldn't be!'	ě-bagé'	'he shouldn't give!'
14 CV	—		ě-kǎg	'he shouldn't go!'

*The low tone following a rising tone subject marker is often raised to high as follows: ě↑pímé'.

4.7.6 Negative prohibitive

The negative prohibitive verb form is marked by a high tone subject marker followed by the prefix *de-* plus a final H tone on the verb stem. It has not been found frequently. It indicates a negative injunction.

Table 4.57. Negative prohibitive, third-person singular

Stem	High tone verbs		Low tone verbs	
1 CVC	á-dɛ-wóg	'he should not wash!'	á-dɛ-pĭm	'she should not throw away!'
2 CVC-v	á-dɛ-wómé	'he should not plane!'	á-dɛ-kulé	'he should not be sick!'
3 CVC-vc	á-dɛ-wómɛ́d	'he should not have st. planed!'	á-dɛ-bomɛ́n	'he should not meet with!'
4 CVC-cvc	á-dɛ-wóglɛ́n	'he should not listen!'	á-dɛ-baŋnɛ́d	'she should not sew with!'
5 CVV	á-dɛ-síí	'she should not iron!'	á-dɛ-suú	'he should not pass air!'
6 CVV	á-dɛ-bóó	'he should not break!'	—	
7 CVV-v	á-dɛ-láá	'he should not chew!'	á-dɛ-nyaá	'he should not tear off!'
8 CVV-vc	á-dɛ-káád	'he should not judge!'	á-dɛ-kaád	'she should not line (pot)!'
9 CVŋ	á-dɛ-láŋ	'he should not read!'	á-dɛ-kŏŋ	'he should not shave!'
10 CVŋ-v	á-dɛ-lɑ́ɑ́	'he should not tell!'	á-dɛ-nɑɑ́	'she should not lie down!'
11 CVŋ-vc	á-dɛ-hyɑ́ɑ́d	'he should not burn!'	á-dɛ-soón	'he should not purge!'
12 CV	á-dɛ-dyé	'he should not eat!'	á-dɛ-kwě	'he should not fall!'
13 CV	á-dɛ-bé	'he should not be!'	á-dɛ-bě	'he should not give!'
14 CV	—		á-dɛ-kě	'he should not go!'

5
The Verb Phrase

5.1 Introduction

Akɔɔse can have from one to three verbs in a clause. I will refer to these combinations of verbs as verb phrases (VP). The last verb in a verb phrase is always semantically the main verb. Any verb preceding the semantic main verb I call an *AUXILIARY VERB*, of which there are about seventy. The first verb has full inflection. Non-first verbs are either in the *infinitive*, *neutral* or *hortative* form, depending on the VP type.

There are three positions in the clause where verbs may appear. The first is between the subject and the complements. The second is between complements and obliques. The third position is clause finally where the echo verb occurs. This can be schematised as in (302).

(302) Subject   Complements   Obliques
      -----   Inflected -------------------- Infinitive ----------------------------- Echo
         S   Verb   IO DO Inst/Acc   Verb   InstP LocP TemP ManP Verb

The complements are the NPs required by the valency of the verb. The obliques are optional constituents which may be either PPs, NPs or AdvPs with the semantic function of instrument, locative, time, manner, etc.

There is always a verb in the first position which takes the tense/aspect/mood/negation marking. The serial VP, which can have up to three verbs (see section 5.3), appears in that position. The second position can only take a verb in the infinitive form (see the split VP in section 5.4). In the third position, only the echo verb with the suffix -*én* may occur (see section 5.7).

5.2 The simple verb phrase

The simple VP consists of one verb which is fully inflected for person/class, tense, aspect, mood, etc. It always occurs in the first position between subject and complement, either of which may or may not be present in a given clause, as shown in (303) where there is no subject NP and in (304) where there is no complement.

(303) **A-dyâg   ndyééd.**   'He is eating food.'
      1-eat.IMPF 9.food

(304) **Mod   a-wédé.**   'The man died.'
      1.person   1-die.PERF

(305) **Mod   a-n-sél-én   nyam   páá.**
      1.person 1-PAST-cut-INST 9.animal 9.knife
      'He cut up the animal with a knife.'

5.3 The serial verb phrase

The serial VP consists of two or three verbs. It occurs in the pre-complement position. The initial verb(s) belong(s) to the auxiliary class with aspectual, modal, adverbial, etc. marking. The final verb may be any verb and is semantically the main verb.

Each verb has a subject agreement prefix (subject marker) agreeing with the subject in person, number and noun class.

The first verb is fully inflected for tense/aspect, etc. However, non-first verbs are either in the neutral or hortative mood.

The examples in (306) have two verbs.

(306) a. **Bán   bé-kɛ   bé-wôŋ   bebaád.**
         2.RP 2-go.HORT   2-marry.HORT   2.women
         'They[1] said that they[1] should go and take a wife.'

b. **A-sébe   á-kɛ**   á   dyɔn.
   1-first   1-go   LOC   5.market
   'He first goes to the market.'

In (307) there is the particle *se* 'just' intervening between the two verbs. This is only possible in this type of VP.

(307) **Wě-ˈhéléé**   se   é-ˈsúm   akoŋ   áˈsé.
      2SG.NEG-can.IMPF   just 2SG-stick   5.spear   down
      'You cannot just stick the spear into the the ground.'

It should be noted that the subject marker referring to second person singular (2SG) has two different forms. This is due to the fact that underlyingly there is a negative marker following the first occurrence above requiring the corresponding variant of the subject marker (see table 4.2).

Example (308) shows a serial VP with three verbs (all occurring before the complement). The first (auxiliary) verb in the string is fully conjugated. The second (auxiliary) verb and the third (main) verb are in the neutral form. The third is semantically the main verb which has a direct object.

(308) **Bé-tə́ŋgéné**   **bé-sébé**   **bé-hɛd**   melâm.
      2-must.EXT.PERF   2-first   2-look.for   6.whiskey
      'They must first look for whiskey.'

The auxiliary verbs can be subdivided according to whether they can appear in first or second position in this VP type (see section 5.9).

5.4 The split verb phrase

There is one other VP which consists of two verbs. I call it the split VP because the two verbs are separated by the complement in transitive clauses.

The first verb in this kind of phrase is in the typical pre-complement position. Grammatically this is the main verb as it is fully inflected. Semantically, however, it is an auxiliary verb belonging to a small class of verbs with a variety of aspectual, modal or adverbial functions.

The second verb of this VP is in the position after the verb complements. Semantically this is the main verb as it determines which type of complements have to occur in the clause. Grammatically, on the other hand, it is downgraded as it always occurs in the L tone infinitive form.

(309) **Bad bé-bóótédé mɔ́ a-swágled á yŏl.**
2.people 2-begin.EXT.PERF 1.PRO INF-beat.EXT LOC body
'They began to beat him up.'

(310) **A-lómé me nkwě atéd.**
1-send.PERF 1SG.PRO 3.salt INF.take
'He sent me to get salt.'

In the negative, the particle *ké* 'even' is often found immediately after the first verb.

(311) a. **Séē-pedɛɛ́ ké kâd a-mad...**
1PL.NEG-arrive.PERF.SF even 9.cards INF-finish
'We had not even finished playing cards...'

b. **Séē-pedɛɛ́ ké a-bíd á metúbɛɛ...**
1PL.NEG-arrive.PERF.SF even INF-get.out LOC car
'We had hardly left the car...'

5.5 Phrasal verbs

Akɔɔse has phrasal verbs consisting of a verb stem plus the particle *áte*. The latter is clearly derived from the locational adverb with the same form meaning 'into' (see section 6.4.4.2).

(312) **lɛl** 'hard' > **lɛl áte** 'to be difficult'
    swag 'pass by ?' > **swagled áte** 'to rinse'
    — > **mwaŋ áte** 'to shine'

Semantically, the verb stem plus particle express a single concept which is not the sum of the meanings of its parts. In transitive clauses, phrasal verbs are separated like the verbs in the split VP, with the *áte* particle occurring in the post-complement position. In (313) and (314) the particle is separated from the verb and appears after the complement and before the oblique, if present, as in (314).

(313) **Yŏl e-kɔ́mé mod áte.**
9.body 9-tire.PERF 1.person áte
'The person was very surprised.'

(314) **Yǒl   e-bébé   mɔ́   áte   á   ndáb.**
9.body   9-bad.PERF   3SG.PRO   áte   LOC   house
'He had bad luck in the house.'

When the phrasal verb is used in a split VP, then both the verb and particle appear together in the post-complement position, as in (315).

(315) **Yǒl e-timé   mod   a-kɔ́m   áte.**
9.body 9-unexpectedly.PERF 1.person INF-tired áte
'The man had an unexpected surprise.'

There are several verbs which appear to be phrasal involving the locative adverb *ásē* 'down'. Most of them are more or less transparent having a directional meaning (316). However, there are some which are best treated as phrasal verbs because their meaning derivations are opaque, as in (317).

(316) **A-dyě   ásē.**   'She sat down.'
1-sit.PERF   down

(317) **Bé-tímé   ásē.**   'They settled their dispute.'
2-return.PERF   down

5.6 Infinitives and the verb phrase

In the split VP, we have seen one use of infinitives. There is another use of the infinitive in purpose clauses. Purpose clauses never have a subject NP because they are closely linked to the preceeding main clause with which they share the subject. These clauses begin with a verb in the infinitive but with a high tone prefix (see section 4.6.5). This is illustrated in (318).

Main clause   Purpose clause
(318) **Mod   asyəə́l a-n-sú   á   ndáb,   á-boŋsɛn   nsɔn   ḿmī.**
1.person 1.all   1-PAST-return LOC 9.house INF-prepare.EXT 3.work 3.his
'Everybody went home to prepare his work.'

5.6.1 Verb-verb infinitives

There are compound infinitives which contain two verbs. Both verbs are in the infinitive form and are linked by the associative marker for class 5. In purpose clauses, the first infinitive has an H prefix tone, the second an L prefix tone.

	Main clause		Purpose clause		
(319)	**Bé-bídé**	ébwɔ́g,	á-kɛ	dé	a-hɛd	bebaád.
	2-go.out.PERF	outside	INF-go	5.AM	INF-look.for	2.wife
	'They went out to go and look for wives.'

This verb-verb infinitive is structurally an associative phrase where two nouns are linked with the associative marker (AM), with the AM agreeing in noun class 5 with the first noun. There is a clear parallel, however, between this verb-verb construction and the serial VP in that the first verb has an auxiliary function and the second verb is semantically the main verb. Also, the noun following the second verb is the object of the verb-verb infinitive construction.

This compound infinitive not only occurs in purpose clauses but also as the second verb of a split VP as described above. Example (320) shows this infinitive in post-complement position:

(320) **Séē-hɛdɛɛ́** mehélé a-kɛ dé a-nəged.
2PL.NEG-want.PERF.SF 6.race INF-go 5.AM INF-run
'We didn't want to go and run the race.'

Note that both infinitives have a low tone prefix as is typical for the second verb in a split VP. Also note that *mehélé* 'race' is the object of *nəged* 'run' which is the second verb in the compound infinitive.

5.6.2 Verb-object infinitives

There is another compound infinitive similar to the one consisting of two verbs. It also involves an associative structure. The difference lies in the fact that the second element is not a verb but a noun. This noun is semantically the object of the infinitive verb. This type is only found in purpose clauses.

	Main clause				Purpose clause			
(321)	**Sê-n-kĕ**	á¹hín	mbwɛ	ń Sátedɛ́,	á-¹húd	dé	mélám	ásē.
	2PL-PAST-go	LOC.bush	3.day	3.AM Saturday	INF-remove	5.AM	6.trap	down
	'We went to the bush on Saturday to remove traps.'

5.7 Echo verbs

Akɔɔse has sentences like (322)–(324) which contain echo verbs.

(322) Ă-ˈsɔ́l-é   á   ndáb   sɔ́l-én...
      1.FUT-enter-IMPF   LOC   house   enter-EN
      'As soon as he entered the house...'

(323) A-soó-ˈaá   mɔ́   páá   soó-n.
      1-stab-DEV   1.PRO   9.cutlass   stab-EN
      'He immediately stabbed her with the cutlass.'

(324) A-kún-e   kún-én.
      1-sleep-IMFP   sleep-EN
      'He is only sleeping (i.e. is not dead).'

Formally, the echo verb repeats the verb stem of the main verb and has the suffix *-én* added to it (see section 4.6.7.9). In -CVC extensions, the *-én* replaces the VC part. Constructions with echo verbs have a range of adverbial and emphatic functions, the details of which need further study.

5.8 Intensification

Another structure which is used to indicate degree consists of *sede-* plus the verb stem of the main verb. The resulting verbal structure occurs in the post-complement position. It is parallel to the echo verb in that it copies the verb stem.

(325) a. É-ˈwúé   nyam   sede-wúu.
         2SG-kill.ITER 10.animal   INT-kill
         'You kill animals a lot.'

      b. nsyɔ́ŋ   ḿme   ń-kɔ́lé   sede-kəl
         3.gain   3.REL   3-big.PERF   INT-big
         'very big gain'

5.9 Auxiliary verbs

Verbs divide into different classes depending on their distribution in larger structures. There is a large open class of verbs referred to above as the semantic main verb which are found in the simple VP and in the infinitive verb position as well as the final verb in the serial VP.

There is also a group of around seventy verbs which I refer to as auxiliary verbs. These verbs occur as the first verb in the verb phrases described above. I call them verbs because they take verbal affixation just like the large open class in the simple VP. I call them auxiliary verbs because they have a qualifying function in the verb phrase which in other languages may be expressed by affixes, particles or adverbs.

The auxiliary verbs can also be classified according to their semantic content or function. More research needs to be done in this area. The classification below is, therefore, provisional and does not include all the auxiliaries.

5.9.1 Distributional subclasses

All auxiliaries may occur in the split VP with the exception of *belé* 'always' which only occurs in the serial VP.

The subclass which occurs as the initial verb in the serial VP consists of at least the following:

(326) bɛ   'still'   hyɛ   'to come'
       de   'still'   sébe   'first'
       bɛle   'always'   tim   'at last, instead, unexpectedly'
       hɛl   'be able to'   tóngɛn   'must'
       kɛ   'to go'

Occurring as second verb in the serial VP are at least the following:

(327) bé   'still'   hyɛ   'to come'
       kɛ   'to go'   sébe   'first'

It should also be noted that a large number of these auxiliary verbs also function as main verbs, often with a different meaning.

5.9.2 Semantic subclasses

Akɔɔse auxiliary verbs have a variety of semantic functions. They can therefore be subclassified according to these different functions. In what follows, I employ the terminology used by Longacre (1976:237–241). He uses terms like directionals, phasals, aspectuals, performatives, etc. to describe various features which are frequently expressed "as verbal affixes or as elements of the verb phrase (e.g. auxiliary verbs), but which may on occasion surface as full verbs or as whole clauses in some languages" (p. 237).

5.9 Auxiliary verbs

Below, the auxiliary verbs are categorised into different subgroups. It is clear that this classification needs further refinement. Some auxiliaries may have more than one semantic function and therefore belong to different classes. Some may contain components from more than one category and therefore fall simultaneously into two classes as, for example, *lóm* 'to send' which I am provisionally classifying as belonging to performatives and to directionals.

5.9.2.1 Aspectuals

These auxiliary verbs contribute an aspectual meaning.

(328) **bé/dé**   'still (incompletive)'
     bɛl   'always (repetitive, habitual)'
     mɛntɛn   'be used to, usually (repetitive, habitual)'
     yɔge   'always (repetitive, habitual)'
     tɔgɛn   'maintain, keep on (continuative)'
     ləg   'remain'

5.9.2.2 Phasals

Phasal auxiliary verbs focus on the beginning and end points of an action.

(329) **báde**   'begin (inceptive)'
     báne   'begin (inceptive)'
     booted   'begin (inceptive)'
     sél   'begin, start (inceptive)'
     léde   'start, in course of (inceptive)'
     maa   'finish (terminative)'
     mad   'finish (terminative)'
     madɛn   'finish with (terminative)'
     pɛ   '(negative form) hardly, not even (just before/after completing action)'

5.9.2.3 Modals

Modal auxiliary verbs indicate obligation, necessity, desire, intent, ability, etc.

(330) **tə́ŋgɛn**   'must (obligation/necessity)'
       wóŋ   'have to (obligation/necessity)'
       dəŋ   'like (desire)'
       hɛd   'want (desire/intent)'
       kəg   'try (intent)'
       koŋ   'intentionally (intent)'
       hɛl   'be able (ability)'
       kobe   '(negative form) be unable (ability)'
       chu   'dare'

The following modal auxiliary verbs also have to do with intention and its outcome.

(331) **bwéd**   'succeed in, manage to'
       wɛsɛn   'persevere'
       kog   'nearly'
       pon   'try, almost, nearly'
       kud   'fail'
       pan   'go wrong'
       boŋsɛn   'prepare'
       wóŋgɛn   'help'

5.9.2.4 Performatives

Performative auxiliary verbs have to do with verbal or mental activities.

(332) **cháŋ**   'beg'
       mwag   'allow'
       kwɛntɛn   'agree'
       báŋ   'refuse, be afraid'
       syəŋ   'abuse'

5.9.2.5 Cognitives

Cognitive auxiliary verbs indicate mental states.

(333) **bíí**   'know'
       chatɛn   'forget'

5.9.2.6 *Adverbials*

Adverbial auxiliary verbs have to do with the evaluation of an action.

(334) **boŋ**   'be good'
       chabned   'be far (distance)'
       kam   'be difficult'
       lɛl   'be hard, difficult'
       pádned   'abruptly'
       tóŋ   'carefully'
       tyə́g   '(negative form) easily'
       wámsɛn   'quickly'
       kóŋ   'really'
       lyə́ge   'instead'
       kɔ́m   'be tired'

5.9.2.7 *Temporals*

Temporal auxiliary verbs relate an action to another action in time.

(335) **kɔ́le**   'do first'
       sébe   'be first'
       dimtɛn   'be last'
       pɔ́l   'be early'
       lyɔg   'be early, long ago'
       syəg   'be long since'
       léb   'take/be a long time'
       lyɔge   'delay'
       mwɛ   'wait'
       tim   'at last (also: instead, surpass)'

5.9.2.8 *Directionals*

Directional auxiliary verbs involve verbs of movement.

(336) **kɛ/kag**   'go'
       hyɛ   'come'
       pɛ   'come, arrive'
       húu   'return'
       lóm   'send'
       hide   '(negative form) leave'

5.9.2.9 *Quantity*

These auxiliary verbs are used to indicate quantity or to make a comparison.

(337) **bud** 'be much, many'
 dɔ́g 'surpass'
 tóm 'exceed'
 tómtɛn 'more than'

5.9.3 Auxiliary verbs illustrated

Examples (338)–(347) illustrate selected auxiliaries in context. In (338) and (339), the auxiliaries are part of a serial verb phrase and, in the others, part of a split verb phrase.

(338) **Ane** mod **a-dé** **a-bónɛ'**.
 1.DEM 1.man 1-be 1-shout.IMPF
 'That man is still shouting.'

(339) **Boŋ** dé-sébe dé-sob chɔ́.
 then 1.2-first.HORT 1.2-leave.HORT 7.PRO
 'Then we first have to leave it.'

(340) **Bebaád** **bé-booted** medyɛ **a-kab**.
 2.women 2-begin 6.food INF-share
 'The women begin to share the food.'

(341) **Échê ekud é bebaád é-tɔ́ŋgéné** ḿmê nsimé **a-kud**.
 7.DEM 7.many 7.AM 2.women 7-must.PERF 3.DEM 3.blessing INF-receive
 'Those many women must receive those blessings.'

(342) **E-se-kwɛntén** me ádén akan **a-wógɛn**?
 2SG-NEG-agree 1SG 5.DEM 5.thing INF-hear
 'You don't agree to hear that thing from me?'

(343) **Asáŋ**, sôn, mmŏŋ **wě-chatáán** sé **a-sáŋ**.
 VOC.father please yourself 2SG.NEG-forget 2PL INF-bless
 'Father, please, don't forget to bless us.'

5.9 Auxiliary verbs

(344) **Sê-wamsén**   mwǎn   nhɔ́g   **a-kób.**
    2PL-quickly   1.child   1.one   INF-catch
    'We quickly caught one child.'

(345) Ǎ   mɔ́   mwěn   **mɔ́ɔ̄-hyě**   mɔ́   nzêd   **a-téde.**
    3SG.RP   1.PRO   1.himself   LOG.FUT-come   1.PRO   9.ring   INF-take.APP
    'He₁ said, he₁ himself will come to bring him₂ the ring.'

(346) **Bad**   **bé-budaá**   bebaád   **a-kɛɛn**   á   dɔ́gtɛɛ.
    2.people   2.NEG-many.IMPF.PAST   2.women   INF-go.ACC   LOC   maternity
    'Not many people were taking the women to the maternity.'

(347) **A-chuú**   **a-kɛ**   á   Kupéɛ.
    1-dare.PERF   INF-go   LOC   Kupe
    'He is not afraid to go up Kupe mountain.'

6
The Clause and Clause Constituents

Akɔɔse is an SVO (subject-verb-object) language. This is the constituent order in both main and subordinate clauses. The only exception to this is in clauses with the split VP described in chapter 5 where one of the two verbs present follows the object.[1]

Akɔɔse has verbal and non-verbal clauses. The non-verbal clause consists minimally of an NP and a demonstrative. The verbal clause consists minimally of a verb. Other constituents such as subject, direct object, indirect object, instrumental and locational complements may be present as required by the valency of the verb. Adjuncts of time, location, manner, etc. are also optionally present in the verbal clause.

6.1 Non-verbal clauses

Non-verbal clauses are presentative structures consisting of *noun phrase* plus *demonstrative*. Since they minimally consist of a noun followed by demonstrative, these clauses often are identical to a noun phrase consisting of noun plus demonstrative with attributive function. In non-verbal clauses, the demonstrative has predicative function. The grammatical structure of non-verbal clauses can be represented as in (348), in which the first part is a nominal complement NP followed by the demonstrative functioning as the subject.

---
[1] Whether the ancestor language from which Akóóse has developed had SOV or SVO order is left open.

(348) S → NP[NC]   DEM[Sub]

The demonstrative can be one of the three post-nominal forms: proximal, distal and far-distal, as illustrated in (349). The demonstrative has to agree in noun class with the nominal complement that preceeds it, exactly as in an NP.

(349) **Ndáb**   **ꜛnén.**   'This is a/the house.'
      9.house   9.this

      Ndáb   **ꜛnê.**   'That is a/the house.'
      9.house   9.that.DIST

      Ndáb   **ꜛníníí.**   'That is a/the house over there.'
      9.house   9.that.FAR.DIST

This structure can be negated by adding *saké* 'not' before the nominal complement (350), in which case the demonstrative becomes optional (351).

(350) <u>**Saké**</u>   **ndáb**   **ꜛnén.**   'This isn't a/the house.'
      not   9.house   9.this

      Saké   **echem**   **ndáb**   **ne.**   'That isn't my house.'
      not   9.my   9.house   9.that

(351) <u>**Saké**</u>   **ndáb.**   'This isn't a/the house.'
      not   9.house

Examples (350) and (351) have the structure in (352).

(352)
      S → (NEG) NP[NC] $\begin{Bmatrix} \text{DEM[Sub]} \\ \emptyset \end{Bmatrix}$

In the negative, temporal and locational adverbs can occur to deny an alternative assertion with focus on time or place not on existence.

(353) a. **Saké**   **bɔɔb.**   'It is not now.'
         not   now

b. **Saké   hén.**   'It is not here/at this point.'
   not   here

Non-verbal clauses are quite restricted in their use in that only deictic elements (demonstratives) are used as subject and no time reference is possible. When one wants a specific referent as subject, or wants to place the assertion in time, then a verbal clause with the copular verb 'to be' is needed.

6.2 Verbal clauses

The verbal clause has a minimum of one verb.

Akɔɔse is a pro-drop language, that is, the subject NP can be dropped without being replaced by a pronoun. It can be argued that the subject NP is underlyingly present as there is always subject-verb agreement on the verb. On the surface, however, the subject (Sub) is often absent, thus allowing for clauses consisting of a verb only.

Up to three complements may also be present depending on the valency of the verb. The verb valency may change due to the addition of verbal extensions as explained in section 4.5. Objects are not marked for their grammatical relation with the verb. These are strictly ordered with the indirect object (IO) immediately following the verb, followed by the direct object (DO) which in turn is followed by the instrument/accompaniment (Inst/Acc) complement. The indirect object typically has an animate or human referent. The direct object may be animate or inanimate.

The verbal clause with its nominal complements can therefore be represented as in (354).

(354) S → (NP[Sub]) VP (NP[IO]) (NP[DO])(NP[Inst/Acc]) (INF-V)

The INF-V stands for the position where the infinitive verb occurs.

The clause can also take adjuncts or obliques with the following semantic roles: instrument (Inst), location (Loc), time (Time), manner (Man), accompaniment (Acc) and benefactive (Ben). These follow the complements and the INF-V. It is quite common to find two locational phrases and two temporal phrases in the same clause. However, only one instrument or accompaniment element (either complement or adjunct) can occur in one clause. Locational and temporal phrases are frequently fronted for certain discourse functions. The order of these obliques is typically as in (355).

(355) …. (InstP/AccP) (LocP) (TimP) (ManP) (Echo-V)

An "echo verb" may follow the obliques, as discussed in section 5.7.[2]

In discourse contexts, the objects required by the transitivity of the verb may be absent due to pragmatic factors, for example when the referent has been mentioned recently. Full object NPs may be replaced by pronouns.

A particular tonal change takes place between verbs and objects in some environments. After some verb forms ending in an H tone, the L tone of the prefix of an object noun with an H tone root is replaced by a H tone.

```
              H        L H      H     H H
(356) téd-H  +  mendíb  →  téd  méndíb      'Take (the) water.'
      take-IMP    6.water
```

```
          H       L H              H H H
(357) ě-ꞌkóngéé + mendíb  →  ě-ꞌkóngéé méndíb  'It doesn't hold water.'
      9.NEG-hold.APP.PERF  6.water
```

I will first look at clauses with copular verbs and then at transitive and intransitive clauses.

6.2.1 Non-active clauses with copular verb *-bé/-dé* 'to be'

The verb 'to be' has two paradigms, a regular one based on the stem *-bé* with an H tone (see verb type 13 in section 4.6.6), and a more restricted irregular one described here. The irregular paradigm is as follows:

(358)
Context[3]	Affirmative	Negative
I	**a dé**	**ě saá**
S		**ě sɛ**
O	**á díí** [4]	**é saá**

The affirmative has underlyingly an H tone stem, the negative an L tone. Both tonally and segmentally, they must have developed from different sources.

---

[2]The position of the InstP needs to be further clarified. It often comes after ManP. This may be due to extraposition.

[3]I = independent clause, S = subject dependent clause, O = non-subject dependent clause. See section 4.6.4 for more details.

[4]There is another form a *díí* which appears to be emphatic or focussed. This needs further investigation.

6.2 Verbal clauses

There are no tense/aspect/mood distinctions in this paradigm. In order to express such categories, the regular paradigm is used.

The copular verb 'to be' is used to link complements to the subject with relations such as location, possession, class membership, existence, etc. (see examples (359)–(370)).

6.2.1.1 Location

Location can be expressed with prepositional (359) or adverbial (360) complements.

(359) a. **A-dé á ndáb.**
 1-be LOC 9.house
 'He is in the house.'

 b. **Nyóod é-dé épɔn tê.**
 10.bee 10-be LOC.7.hole in
 'The bees are inside the hole.'

(360) **A-dé hɛ́n.**
 1.be here
 'He is here.'

The verb 'to be' also allows for indirect objects as in (361).

                      IO   LocP
(361) a. **Nsɛsú ń-dé mɔ́ ékuu.**
 3.jigger 3-be 1.PRO LOC.7.foot
 'He has a jigger in his foot.'

              IO   LocP
 b. **Nzɛ́ a-dé mɛ hɛ́n?**
 who 1.be 1SG.PRO here
 'Who is here for me/in my place?'

6.2.1.2 Class membership

Class membership is expressed with nominal complements.

(362) **A-dé   meléede.**
     1-be   1.teacher
     'He is a teacher.'

(363) **Mɔ́   a-bédé   kɔ̂ŋ.**
     1.PRO   1-be.PERF   9.chief
     'He was chief.'

(364) **Ábem   besón   bĕn   bé-díĩ   beken   bé   békáálé.**
     2.my   2.friends   2.themselves   2-be   2.guest   2.AM   2.whiteman
     'My friends are white guests/visitors/foreigners.'

6.2.1.3 Abstract quality

Abstract qualities in this structure are expressed with nominal complements. This structure is used when the lexical item for a certain abstract quality has the form of a noun (365) and (366). If the lexical item is a verb, an intransitive clause is used (see (375) and (376)).

(365) **A-dé   ngíne.**
     1.be   9.strength
     'He is strong.'

(366) **E-báké   menyinge.**
     1.NEG-be.IMPF   6.joy
     'She isn't happy.'

6.2.1.4 Comparison

Clauses with 'to be' are used to express a quality by making a comparison with some other entity with that quality. The complement is a prepositional phrase with the preposition *nê*.

(367) **A-dé   nê   mwǎ   nsêd.**
     1-be   like   1.small   3.sunbird
     'He is like a small sunbird.'

6.2 Verbal clauses

6.2.1.5 Existence

Existence is also expressed with this clause type. Typically, there is no nominal complement. This structure with the verb 'to be' is used in discourse to introduce new participants or time settings.

(368) **Nsoosongɛ   nhɔ́g   a-bédé...**
      1.hunter   1.one   1-be.PERF
      'There was a hunter...'

(369) **Nhɔn   ḿ   mod   nhɔ́g   ḿ-bédé, a-wɔ́ŋ   bebaád   hǐin...**
      3.rich   3.AM   1.man   3.one   3-was   1-have   2.women   many
      'There was a rich man, he had many wives...'

(370) **Epun   ehɔ́g   é-bédé, ...**
      7.day   7.one   7-be.PERF
      'There was a day...'

6.2.2 Non-active clauses with copular verb -*wóŋ* 'to have'

The copular verb -*wóŋ* 'to have' is typically used for possession.

(371) **Ane   mod   a-wóó   mbód   hǐin.**
      1.DEM.DIST   1.man   1.have.PERF   10.goat   many
      'That man has many goats.'

(372) **Káb   e-wóó   ntende   á   mbíd   te.**
      9.antelope   9-have.PERF   3.stripes   LOC   9.back   in
      'The antelope has stripes on the back.'

(373) **mod   awé   a-wóó   ngíne**
      1.person 1.REL   1-have.PERF   9.power
      'the man who has power'

Compare (373) with (365) above for a very similar construction with *ngíne*.

6.3 Active clauses

6.3.1 Intransitive clauses

Intransitive clauses have a subject but no object (374). They are used for functions ranging from active verbs, to verbs expressing abstract qualities, to reciprocal verbs.

(374) S V
    Mwaád   a-kúnɛ'.
    1.woman   1-sleep.IMPF
    'The woman is sleeping.'

(375) **Anén   mmwaád   a-chuné.**
    1.DEM.PROX   1.woman   1-old.PERF
    'This woman is old.'

(376) **Mwǎ   dií   nén   a-yəgé = ꜛyéé.**
    1.small   5.palmtree   1.DEM.PROX   1-red.PERF = EXCL
    '(The palmnuts on) that small palm tree is ripe.'

The examples in (375) and (376) show verbs which express qualities. Weather phenomena are often expressed by these kinds of intransitive clauses.

(377) **Enyɛn   é-pɛnɛ'.**
    7.sun   7-shine.IMPF
    'The sun is shining.'

(378) **Mbúú   e-chɔ̂g.**
    9.rain   9-fall.IMPF
    'It is raining.'

6.3.1.1 Reciprocals

Reciprocal verbs are intransitive, involving plural subjects acting on each other in some way.

(379) **Ábé   bad   bé-kɔ́ɔ́né.**
    2.DEM.DIST   2.person   2-hate.REC.PERF
    'Those people hate each other.'

6.3 Active clauses

(380) **Etón ne esɛd bé-wágnɛ'.**
7.(fruit) and 7.(fruit) 2-resemble.REC.IMPF
'The eton and esed fruit resemble each other.'

6.3.2 Transitive clauses

Transitive verbs take an object noun phrase, as in (381) and (382).

(381) S V O
Bad bé-káá mbág.
2.people 2-tie.PERF 3.bundle
'The people tied the bundle.'

(382) V O
A-kóbé súu bwămbwam.
1-catch.PERF 10.fish much
'He caught a lot of fish.'

Some logically intransitive verbs take a cognate object. These are therefore grammatically transitive.

(383) V O
Bé-wóó lɔɔ.
2-laugh.PERF 13.laugh
'They laughed.'

Some transitive clauses have an object which is the result of a process.

(384) **A-kwedé ndóg.**
1-fall.PERF 9.deafness
'He became deaf.'

6.3.2.1 Reflexives

Reflexives are expressed by adding *yǎl* 'body' as object to the clause. This makes these clauses structurally transitive.

(385) S   V   O
       Kúlɛ   a-hɔ́bté   yɛ̆l.
       9.tortoise.PERS 1-shake.PERF 9.body
       'Tortoise shook himself.'

(386)   V   O   LOC
       A-bɔmé   yɛ̆l   á   ndɔɔb   tê
       1-knock.PERF 9.body LOC 9.ground in
       'He knocked himself on the ground.'

6.3.3 Ditransitive clauses

Clauses with ditransitive verbs have two objects, the indirect object always preceding the direct object.

(387) S   V   IO   O
       Ane   mod   a-bágé   mɔ́   mɔné.
       1.DEM 1.man   1-give.PERF 3SG.PRO   3.money
       'That man gave him money.'

(388)   V   IO   O
       Bé-bɛnláád   mwăn   mɔné.
       2-use.IMPF   1.child   3.money
       'They used the child's money.'

(389) S   V   IO   O
       Kúb   e-kɔ́gté   me   băn   saámbé.
       9.hen 9-hatch.CAUS.PERF 1SG.PRO 2.child   seven
       'The hen hatched seven chicks for me.'

6.3.3.1 Causatives

Some clauses with causative verbs are ditransitive.

(390) **A-pémté**   mɔ́   lɔ̆n.
       1-carry.CAUS.PERF   3SG.PRO   13.firewood
       'He₁ made him₂ carry firewood.'

6.3.4 Tritransitive clauses

There are clauses with verbs that can take three objects with the indirect object being optional. The instrument here is considered an object as it is required by the verb and is not introduced with a preposition. In other words, it is a complement of the verb, not an adjunct.

(391)
V	IO	O	Inst
Bé-dibnaad	(me)	saadîn	e'kii.
2-open.with.IMPF	1SG.PRO	9.tin	14.key

'They opened the sardine tin with a key (for me).'

(392)
V	IO	O	Inst
Bé-bɔ́mné	(me)	mwǎn	bwěl.
2-beat.with.PERF	1SG.PRO	1.child	14.stick

'They beat (my) child with a stick./They beat the child (for me) with a stick.'

6.3.5 Clauses with locational complements

Some verbs require, in addition to the objects, an element with goal (393) or source (394) as semantic roles. I labelled *bad* 'people' indirect object rather than object as it is into the foot that the jigger entered. The indirect object simply specifies the possessor of the foot.

(393)
S	V	IO	Loc	
Ḿmê	**nsɛsú**	**ń-sɔ́lé**	**bad**	**á**	**mekuu.**
4.DEM	4.jigger	4-enter.PERF	2.people	LOC	6.foot

'Those jiggers entered peoples' feet.'

(394)
V	IO	Loc	
E-nkêm-bídénné		**mɔ́**	**ábum.**
9.NEG-PAST.NEG-come.out.with.SF		4.PRO	LOC.5.stomach

'It wasn't born with them. (lit. It didn't come out with them from stomach.)'

6.3.6 Verbs with a clause as object (complement clauses, predicate complements)

Certain verbs can take either a NP (395) or a clause (396) as object complement. Such verbs have mainly to do with perception (397)–(398). There is no complementiser to introduce these sentential objects.

(395)   V   O
                   [N   Num]NP
         Bé-táné   bebaád   bébɛ.
         2-meet.PERF 2.woman 2.two
         'They met two women.'

(396)   V   O
                   [Sub   V   O]s
         A-táné   mmwaád   a-chyɛ   awɛ́.
         1-meet.PERF 1.woman 1-cry.IMPF 5.cry
         'I met the woman crying.'

(397) CONJ V   O
                             [Sub   V   echo-V   ]s
      Nzé e-nyéné   edíb   é-yɔ́gé   áte   yəg-én...
      if   2SG-see.PERF   7.stream 7-red.PERF inside red-EN
      'As soon as you see the river go red...'

(398) V   O
                   [Sub   V]s
      A-wógé   mod   a-bónɛ'.
      1-hear.PERF 1.person   1-shout.IMPF
      'He heard somebody shouting.'

6.4 Oblique phrases

Obliques or adjuncts are phrases in a clause that do not have a grammatical relation to the verb. They are optional and have the semantic roles of instrument, time, location, manner, etc. They are either NPs or PPs. The normal position is clause final, but they may be fronted for pragmatic and discourse purposes.

Shown below are obliques with the semantic roles of instrument, accompaniment, time and location.

6.4.1 Instrument phrases

Clauses may have one optional phrase indicating the instrument with which the action is being performed. They are always PPs with the preposition *ne*.

6.4 Oblique phrases 177

(399) a. **A-kudé   ekob   ne   aláá.**
1-close.PERF 7.door with 5.stone
'He locked the door with a stone.'

b. **A-habtédé   mɔ́   áte   ne   mekáá.**
1-tear.PERF 6.PRO into with 6.hands
'He tore it with his hands.'

c. **Ábé   bad   bé-límé   e'chog   ne   ngíne   echâb   ésyɔ̄ɔ̄l.**
2.those 2.people 2-dig.PERF 8.hole with 9.power 9.their 9.all
'Those people dug the holes with all their strength.'

6.4.2 Accompaniment phrases

Another optional adjunct is the accompaniment phrase which expresses either an animate or inanimate entity that accompanies the subject or the object. It is always in the form of a prepositional phrase with the preposition *ne*.

(400) a. **A-pɛɛné   mbyɛ́   ne   mecheeb.**
1-bring.PERF 10.dog with 6.bells
'I brought dogs with bells on.'

b. **Nsɛsú   ń-díi   ń-húɛ'   ne   nguu.**
3.jigger 3-still 3-come.IMPF with pigs
'Jiggers always come with pigs.'

c. **Nkáálé   a-pedé   ne   beken   ábe   á-kagk
alɔ́ged   á   ꜝTɔ́mbél.**
1.white.man 1-arrive.PERF with 2.guests 2.REL 1-go.IMPF.SF
INF.leave LOC Tombel
'The white man arrived with guests whom he had gone to pick up in Tombel.'

6.4.3 Time phrases

Time adjuncts can be NPs (401), adverbs (402)–(407) or PPs (408)–(409). Time adjuncts occur post-verbally but are often found fronted.

6.4.3.1 *Noun phrases*

NPs usually involve a term referring to some time element like day, daytime, night, week, year, etc.

(401) a. **Epun**   té   a-húene   nyam.
　　　　 7.day   every 1-return.with.IMPF   10.animal
　　　　 'Every day he brings back animals.'

　　　b. **Epun**   é   bín   ehɔ́g   bé-nwén   nkogé.
　　　　 7.day   7.AM   14.day   7.one   2-PAST.plant   3.sugarcane
　　　　 'One day they planted sugarcane.'

　　　c. **Mmê**   nkuu   ámpē   sê-nangé   ásē.
　　　　 3.that   3.night   also   2PL-sleep.PERF   down
　　　　 'That night too we slept.'

　　　d. **Sú**   ébɛ   mě-hyɛ   mwǎ   díí   nén   akwɛl.
　　　　 10.day   10.two   1SG.FUT-come   1.small   5.oil.palm   1.DEM   INF.cut
　　　　 In two days I'll come to cut down this small oil palm.'

6.4.3.2 *Time words*

Akɔɔse has the following time words.

(402)   **chii**   'today'
　　　 chǎn   'yesterday, tomorrow'
　　　 bɔɔb   'now'
　　　 bwéed   'later on, earlier on'
　　　 bɔ́ɔ́b/bɔ́ɔ́d   'long ago'

These time words can take nominal modifiers such as demonstratives (403) and relative clauses (404). For this reason they could be considered a subclass of nouns. There are, however, severe restrictions. In (403), the demonstrative is class 9, and in (404) and (405), the relative pronoun is class 8 which is not what one would expect from the initial consonant ("class prefix") of the head word. Nouns beginning with *ch* typically belong to class 7, nouns beginning with *b* typically belong to class 2 or 14.

6.4 Oblique phrases

(403) **chii**   **nέn**   'today (emphatic)'
today   9.DEM

      bɔɔb   **nέn**   'right now'
      now   9.DEM

(404) **chăn**   **ábe**   **é'-húɛ'**   'the next day'
next.day 8.REL 8-come.IMPF

      chăn   **ábe**   **é'-tómé**   'the previous day'
      next.day 8.REL 8-pass.PERF

(405) **A-hɛdɛ**   **me**   **anyén**   **chăn**   **ábe**   **é'-húɛ'**.
1-want.IMPF 1SG.PRO INF.see next.day 8.REL 8-come.IMPF
'He wants to see me tomorrow.'

Some of the time adverbs have clear noun forms. The examples in (406) show them with the addition of the class 14 prefix *e'-*.

(406) a. **menzii**   **mé**   **e'bɔ́ɔb**   'the roads of long ago'
       6.road   6.AM   14.past

      b. **bad**   **bé**   **e'chii**   'people of today'
        2.person 2.AM 14.today

Time reference to position on a clock is expressed with the use of the noun *ngɔ́ŋ* 'bell'. Interestingly, the modifier *děn* in (407b) is of class 5, which is the concord for the locative prefix *á-* which is not present here.

(407) a. **ngɔ́ŋ**   **waam**   'eight o'clock'
     9.bell   eight

     b. **ngɔ́ŋ**   **ntóób**   **děn**   'right at six o'clock'
     9.bell   six   5.itself

6.4.3.3 Prepositional phrases

Time may be indicated with PPs involving the locative marker *á-* as in (408).

(408) a. á⁺mbíd   e   póndé   'after some time'
       LOC.9.back   9.AM   9.time

   b. á⁺mbíd   e   nguse   é   e'pun   'after a few days'
      LOC.9.back 9.AM   10.some   10.AM   8.day

   c. á   kên   eche ...   'at the time when...'
      LOC   9.time   9.RE

There is another common time expression, apparently in the form of a PP containing the preposition *ne* (409a). This may, however, be a reduction of a longer form with the preposition *kə́ŋ* (409b).

(409) a. ne   chii   'until today'
        with   today

   b. kə́ŋ   ne   chii   nɛ́n   'until right to this day'
      until   with   today   9.DEM

6.4.4 Locational phrases

Locational phrases are either required by the verb in which case they are complements as in (410) or they are not part of the valency of the verb and are therefore optional elements as in (411).

(410) a. **A-húú**   **á**   **ahín.**
        1-return.PERF   LOC   5.bush
        'He returned from the bush.'

   b. **A-kií**   **á**   **ngaŋ**   **wê**   **ngaabobɛ.**
      1-go.PERF   LOC   9.divination   LOC   9.spider
      'He went for divination to the spider.'

(411) a. **A-hún-'ɛ**   **á**   **ndib**   **tê**   **sɔndɔmm.**
        1-fall-ADD   LOC   9.deep.water   in   IDEO
        'He then fell in the deep water, splash.'

   b. **A-táné**   **mwɛ̂**   **á**   **ndáb**   **te.**
      1-meet.PERF   friend   LOC   house   in
      'He met the friend in the house.'

6.4 Oblique phrases 181

 c. **A-nkób**   **kém**   **á**   **bwɛl**   **mîn.**
  1-PAST.catch   9.monkey   LOC   14.tree   on
  'He caught a monkey in the top of the tree.'

Note that in (412) the locational oblique is in the form of an NP without overt marking with a locative preposition. With the verb -sɔ́l 'enter', the goal apparently is in an object relation to the verb.

(412) **Sê-sɔ́lé**   **ḿmi**   **mŏto.**
  1PL-enter.PERF   6.his   6.car
  'We got into his car.'

Location can be expressed by PPs (413), by NPs (412), by locative adverbs (414)–(417) and by locative nouns (423)–(424).

6.4.4.1 Prepositonal phrases

Locational phrases with the locative preposition have been described in section 3.9.1. Some examples are repeated here.

(413) **á ndáb**   'at/to the house'
  á nzag tê   'in the farm'
  ámbīd e ndáb   'behind the house'
  wê ane mod   'to that person'
  áwem ndáb   'to/at my house'

6.4.4.2 Locative adverbs

Below, I am grouping several locative adverbs on the basis of certain similarities. The ones in (414) are particles, probably derived from nouns preceded by the locative marker *á-*. They express specific locations in relation to a given entity. See also section 3.9.1.

(414) **áte**   'in/inside'
  ásē   'down/under'
  ámīn   'on/on top'

The adverbs in (415) also have the locative marker *á-*, typically prefixed to nouns. However, there do not appear to be corresponding nouns without this prefix. They are used for location in relation to elevation (above or below) and for points of the compass. There appear to be only two terms for points on the compass and some disagreement as to whether they refer to the north-south or east-west axis.

(415) ákuu   'up, upstream, north, east'
     ámbəŋ   'down, downstream, south, west'
     áchāād   'over there'

The adverbs in (416) and (417) are used for deictic reference pointing to a certain location in relation to the speaker and the hearer. The forms with *h* have specific reference, the forms with *w* more general reference.

(416) áhed   'there, discourse deictic (specific)'
     áwed   'there, discourse deictic (general)'

(417) 'here'   'there'   'over there'
     hέn   hê   héníí   '(specific)'
     wén   wê   wíníí   '(general)'

It should be noted that the adverbs in (417) are related in form to the demonstratives (see section 3.3.1.2) and have the same deictic value. The first refers to a location close to the speaker, the second at a distance from the speaker and the third at a distance from both speaker and hearer.

The following adverb expresses proximity to some thing or location. When it is used, it is linked to the following noun with the conjunction *ne* 'and/with', as in (418b).

(418) a. bεmbεn   'nearby'

     b. bεmbεn   ne   kwέέd
        near   with   9.death
        'near death'

6.4.4.3 Adverbs with modifiers

Some locational adverbs can have nominal modifiers such as demonstratives (419), PPs (420) and relative clauses (421). This makes them heads of NPs. However, the selection of modifiers that can occur with a specific type of adverb is quite restricted.

6.4 Oblique phrases

(419) **hɛ́n**   **nɛ́n**
here   9.DEM
'right here'

(420) **bɛmbɛn**   **ne**   **nkog**
near   with   3.waist
'near the waist'

(421) **A-síté**   ane mwǎn **bɛmbɛn** wê ane mwǎn
1-come.close.PERF 1.that 1.child near   where 1.that 1.child
á-ndyɛ'ɛ́.
1-PAST.sit.SF
'He came close to the child near where he sat.'

6.4.4.4 Two locative phrases

It is very common that two locative obliques occur together in the same clause. Typical combinations are shown in (422).

(422) **áte**   **wén**   'inside here'
in   here

áwed   **ámīn**   'up there'
there   up

áwed   **áte**   'in there'
there   in

á   **búum**   **mîn**   **wê**   'there on the Buma tree'
LOC   buma.tree   up   there

6.4.4.5 The locative noun

There is one noun (*hŏm* 'place') with general reference to location that often comes in locational phrases. NPs with this noun as head accompanied by various modifiers are used as locational obliques in (423)–(424). These locatives take class 5 agreement. This is the only noun in class 5 with an *h-* prefix, probably a relic of a Bantu locative class. The relative pronoun in (424) is in its reduced form (see section 3.3.6.2).

(423) **hŏm   ahɔ́g**
    5.place 5.one
    'a certain place'

   hŏm démpée
   5.place 5.other
   'another place'

(424) **N-dibté   hom=ɛ́ɛ   e'chuu   é'-díí.**
      1SG-find.PERF   5.place=REL   14.honey   14-be
      'I found a place where there is honey.'

6.4.5   Manner phrases

Manner obliques may be PPs (6.4.5.1), adverbs (6.4.5.2) or ideophones (6.4.5.3). A clause may contain one or two manner obliques.

6.4.5.1 Prepositional phrases

Prepositional phrases with the preposition *nɛ́ɛ* 'as, like' are used to indicate the manner of an action by making a comparison.

(425) **A-kag   kwa kwa kwa   nɛ́ɛ   ngwaa.**
      1-go.IMPF   IDEO   like   9.partridge
      'He walks like a partridge.'

6.4.5.2 Manner adverbs

The adverbs in (426)–(430) are frequently used to indicate manner. This group of words is quite diverse. Some are nouns (426), some are adverbs (427), some are reduplicated, some appear to contain the locative marker *á-* (428) and some are compounds (429) consisting of *mwă* plus another word.

(426) **mehélé**   'quickness, race'
      mehélé mehélé   'quickly'

(427) **bwăam**   'well'
      bwămbwam   'well'
      bwambí   'well'
      hĭin   'much'
      ngên   'useless'

6.4 Oblique phrases

(428) **ámpē**   'again'
       ábwɔ́g   'immediately'
       ábwɔ́g-ábwɔ́g   'immediately'

(429) **mwǎmpīn**   'small, little'
       mwǎləəŋ   'slowly'

(430) **nyɔméɛ**   'slowly'

(431) **Nkóbémwăn mwěn a-nəgté mɔ́ mehélé.**
       1.baby.nurse   1.self   1-run.PERF   1.PRO   6.race
       'The baby nurse herself ran quickly.'

(432) **Héɛ ane mwăn á-tímé ámbīd ábwɔ́g-ábwɔ́g.**
       then   1.that   1.child   o.1-return.PERF   back   immediately
       'Then that child returned immediately.'

(433) **Bé-dɔ́ɔ́'áá ḿmê nkɔɔd bwambí.**
       2-rolled.up.IMPF.PAST   3.that   3.rope   well
       'They rolled up that rope well.'

6.4.5.3 Ideophones

Ideophones are another category of elements that are very commonly used to indicate manner (434), often to express the sound of an action (435). For a list of ideophones see appendix A.2. More research is needed in the area of ideophones.

(434) **byɔɔd**   'slowly'
       kwab   'dart suddenly'
       chóŋŋ   'thoughtfully'

(435) **paaa' paaa'**   'sound of wings'
       kwɔ́rɔ́rɔ́rɔ   'noise of whistle or insect'

(436) **Nê é-míne bwěm áte tɔ́rɔ́tɔ́tɔ́tɔ́tɔ́...**
       as   2SG-squeeze.IMPF   8.things   into   IDEO
       'As you squeeze the clothes *tɔ́rɔ́tɔ́tɔ́tɔ́*...(to get the water out)'

(437) **Káb-enyamɛ a-nyéné nyɛ̌ sánkala epɔn nén, a-sɔ́l.**
antelope-animal 1-see.PERF very big hole this, 1-enter
áweéte byób.
there.inside IDEO
'Antelope saw that huge hole, he entered into it *byób*.'

6.4.5.4 Manner particle

I list under manner phrases also the particle *nê* which we have seen elsewhere with the meaning 'that, like that'. It seems to function like other manner phrases in clause-final position and may be glossed as 'so, in this manner'.

(438) **Hé-'ɘɔ́ menyâ mé-sógé hê nê**
there-DEV 6.story 6-end.PERF there like.that
'So here the story ends.'

6.4.6 Other oblique phrases

Other oblique phrases are BENEFACTIVE and REASON. These appear to be expressed with PPs with the preposition *áyɔ̄le* 'because, for'. However, this usage appears to be a relatively recent way of expressing these functions and needs further study.

(439) Benefactive
áyɔ̄le ane mwǎn
for 1.DEM 1.child
'for that child'

(440) Reason
áyɔ̄le ane mwǎn
because.of 1.DEM 1.child
'because of that child'

6.5 Subject repetition for emphasis

There are sentences which appear to contain an object. However, this extra element is a pronoun co-referential with the subject and is used for emphasis.

(441) **n-kíí me**
1SG-go.PERF 1SG.PRO
'I am going. (lit. I have gone me)'

6.5 Subject repetition for emphasis

(442) aá   mə̂   mə́-kíí   mə́
     3SG.RP   3SG.PRO   LOG-go.PERF   3SG.PRO
     'he said, "I am going." '

In (442) there are two pronouns, one before the verb and one after it, both used to emphasise the subject (see also (431) and (564)).

7
Sentence Modifications

7.1 Introduction

In this section I discuss three formally related sentence modifications: questions, topicalisation, and relative clauses. What they all have in common is the movement of a constituent to the beginning of the sentence. Associated with this fronting are changes in the verb form for both affirmative and negative constructions.

After discussing these three modifications I will also look at FRONTING and VOCATIVES.

The examples in (444)–(446) are derived from the more basic form in (443). In each case, the direct object has moved from its position after the verb to the beginning of the sentence. In the question in (444), the object NP is a question word (*cheé*). In the topicalised sentence in (445), the fronted object NP contains the topic marker *bə̂*. In the NP in (446), a noun is modified with a relative clause. The object of the verb *-chán*, which is co-referential with the noun *bekasálée*, has moved to the front and is represented by the relative pronoun.

In every case where a constituent has moved to the front, the verb is in the dependent non-subject form (indicated with O in the gloss). Compare the tone on the verbs in (444)–(446) with (443). See also section 4.6.3.

(443) **Mmwaád a-chané bekasálɛɛ á dyɔn.**
1.woman 1-buy.PERF 2.casava LOC 5.market
'The woman bought casava in the market.'

(444) Question
Cheé á-cháné á dyɔn?
what o.1-buy.PERF LOC 5.market
'What did she buy in the market?'

(445) Topicalised
bekasálɛɛ bɔ̂ á-cháné á dyɔn...
2.casava 2.TOP o.1-buy.PERF LOC 5.market
'it was casava that she bought in the market...'

(446) Relative clause
Bekasálɛɛ [ábe á-cháné á dyɔn]...
2.casava 2.REL o.1-buy.PERF LOC 5.market
'The casava which she bought in the market...'

When the clause constituent concerned is the subject there is no movement to the front of the verb and consequently no change in verb form. The verbs are then the same as in the independent clause in (443). This is the case in affirmative sentences, as follows:

(447) Question
Nzé a-chané bekasálɛɛ?
who 1-buy.PERF 2.casava
'Who bought casava?'

(448) Topicalised sentence
mmwaád mɔ̂ a-chané bekasálɛɛ...
1.woman 1.TOP 1-buy.PERF 2.casava
'it was the woman who bought casava...'

(449) *Relative clause*
Mmwaád [awě a-chané bekasálɛɛ]...
1.woman 1.REL 1-buy.PERF 2.casava
'The woman who bought casava...'

When the verb in these subject type constructions is negative, the dependant-subject forms are used (see section 4.6.4). In (450), the negative form for independent clauses is used. By contrast, in (451)–(453), it is the dependant-subject forms (marked as s in the gloss) that are used. Note especially the verb endings.

(450) Statement (negative)
Nzɛlé ě-chanéɛ́ bekasálɛ́ɛ.
Nzelle 1.NEG-buy.IMPF.SF 2.casava
'Nzelle is not buying casava.'

(451) Question (negative)
Nzé ě-chané' bekasálɛ́ɛ?
who s.1.NEG-buy.IMPF 2.casava
'Who is not buying casava?'

(452) Topicalised sentence (negative)
Nzɛlé mɔ̂ ě-chané' bekasálɛ́ɛ.
1.Nzelle 1.TOP s.1.NEG-buy.IMPF 2.casava
'It is Nzelle who is not buying casava.'

(453) Relative clause
mod [awě ě-chané' bekasálé]...
1.person 1.REL s.1.NEG-buy.IMPF 2.casava
'the person who is not buying casava...'

I will now look at the three types of sentence modifications in more detail.

7.2 Questions

There are two general types of questions, POLAR or YES/NO QUESTIONS and CONTENT QUESTIONS. The main distinction between them is that the polar questions are marked by a sentence-final question clitic. Content questions, on the other hand, do not have a sentence-final question marker but instead contain a question word or phrase.

7.2.1 Yes/no questions

Yes/no questions (or polar questions) ask for the confirmation or negation of a proposition. They are marked by a sentence final clitic =ɛ.

(454) **Echem esóŋ é mod é-tómé wɛ hɛ́n=ɛ?**
7.my 7.short 7.AM 1.person 7-pass.PREF 2SG.PRO here=Q
'Has my short person gone past here? (riddle)'

(455) **Nzé e-nyéné etón e-sábnéd esɛd=ɛ?**
if 2SG-see.PERF 7.eton 2SG-pay.with esed=Q
'If you see eton fruit, do you pay with esɛd fruit? (proverb)'

(456) **E-nyéné anén mmwaád=ɛ?**
2SG-see.PERF 1.this 1.woman=Q
'Do you see this woman?'

The question marker frequently assimilates to the quality of vowel that it is attached to.

(457) **Aá ken nyí-maá a-bóg áte=e?**
3SG.RP Q 2PL-finish.PERF INF-break into=Q
'He asked, "Have you finished breaking them?" '

When the question marker follows a velar nasal, the nasal drops out and the question marker merges with the preceding vowel.

(458) **Nzé e-hyedé mŏl a-chɔm, e-téd mbeé e soo=o? < (soŋ=ɛ)**
if 2SG-come.PERF 6.oil INF-beg 2SG-take 9.pot 9.AM??= Q
'If you come to beg for some oil, do you bring a large(?) pot? (proverb)'

The question marker has some variant forms *-yeé*, *-eé*, *-ēē*. These have an additional function of emphasis. The use of the different forms depends on the phonological shape of the element to which they are attached: *-yeé* follows vowels, *-eé* follows consonants. The *-ēē* is a tonal variant not illustrated. One example follows:

(459) **Bé-kɛ bé-dyāg á ndɔɔb tê=yeé?**
2-go.HORT 2-eat LOC ground in=Q
'Should they go and eat on the ground?'

Responses to polar questions typically include one of the following particles to confirm or negate the question.

7.2 Questions 193

(460) ɛɛ 'yes'
   aay, kám 'no'

The two forms for a negative response are regional variants; the latter is characteristic of the northern dialects.

(461) **Aá ken nyí-maá a-bóg áte=e? Bán ɛɛ.**
   3SG.RP Q 2PL-finish.PERF NF-break into=Q PL.RP yes
   'He asked, "Have you broken them?"' 'They answered, "Yes."'

(462) **Aá a-mwéē, aá ken e-bíí? Aá kám!**
   3SG.RP VOC-friend 3SG.RP Q 2SG-know.PERF 3SG.RP no
   'He said, "Friend!" and asked, "You know what?"' 'He answered, no!'

7.2.2 Content questions

Content questions (also called information questions, question word questions or "wh-questions") are characterised by the presence of a question word or phrase. There is no sentence-final question particle as in yes/no (polar) questions. Content questions ask for information regarding one of the constituents of the clause.

7.2.2.1 Question words and phrases

The question words are given in (463) and (464).

(463) **nzé** 'who' human
   benzé 'who (pl.)' human
   chě 'what' non-human
   héé 'where' location
   chán 'how, what' manner, object

(464) **-héé** 'who, which' human/non-human
   -tóŋ 'how many' number

The question words in (463) stand for a whole NP or PP; the words in (464) replace a constituent of a noun phrase and agree in noun class with the head noun of the phrase (465). (For the agreement markers see tables 3.9 and 3.11.)

(465) **mod**   **a-héé**   'which man'
     1.person 1-which

     bad   **bé-tə́ŋ**   'how many people'
     2.peson 2-how.many

     sú   **é-tə́ŋ**   'how many days'
     10.day   10-how.many

Time and reason do not have a single question word but are expressed with a phrase (466) or clause (467) containing a question word.

(466) **póndé** **e-héé**   'when'
     9.time   9-which

(467) **chě**   **é-kə́ə́**   **bɔŋ** ... 'why (lit. what caused that)'
     what 7-cause.PERF then

(468) **chě** **é-dé** **nzɔm** **echě** ... 'why (lit. what is the reason which)'
     what 7-be 9.reason 9.REL

Example (467) is a clause linked to the main clause with the conjunction *bɔŋ/baŋ* 'then, but'. Example (468) is a copular clause that consists of a relative clause that modifies *nzɔm* 'reason'.

There are other question phrases asking for a specific NP constituent. Example (469) consists of the question word *nzé* 'who' preceding the noun and the suffix -*é* following it. See examples in (470). Also note that the tones of the noun are replaced by high tones in this construction.

(469) **nzé ... -é**   'which...'

(470) **nzé módé**   'which person'   < **mod**
     nzé chómé 'which thing'   < **chǒm**

Example (471) consists of *kân*[1] and -*héé* and a noun that is linked to the first noun with the associative marker. This is illustrated in (472).

(471) **kân** **e** ... **ehéé**   'what kind of...'
     9.kind 9.AM ... 9.which

---

[1] *kân* may be a loanword from English "kind."

7.2 Questions

(472) **kân e mwăn ehéé**   'what kind of child'
9.kind 9.AM 1.child 9.which

      kân e nló ehéé   'what kind of a head'
9.kind 9.AM 3.head 9.which

7.2.2.2 Position of question words

In subject questions, the question word is always in subject position (473) and no fronting past the verb can take place. The norm for other constituents is for the questioned element to be moved to the front of the clause (see (474) and (476)). It is also possible, but rare, for it to stay in its inherent position (see (475) and (477)).

(473) S-Q V O   Subject
      Nzé a-n-nyěn nzyɔg?
      who 1-PAST-see elephant
      'Who saw the elephant?'

(474) O-Q V   Object, fronted
      Nzé á-n↓-nyénné?
      who O.1-PAST-see.SF
      'Whom did he see?'

(475) V O-Q   Object, *in situ*
      A-n-nyěn nzé?
      1-PAST-see who
      'Whom did he see?'

(476) LOC-Q V   Location, fronted
      Héé á-kagké?
      where O.1-go.IMPF.SF
      'Where is he going?'

(477) V LOC-Q   Location, *in situ*
      A-kag héé?
      1-go.IMPF where
      'Where is he going?'

Also note that the movement of the questioned constituent to the beginning of the clause carries with it a change in verb form. The verbs in

(475) and (477) are the plain forms for those tenses, but the verbs in (474) and (476) are in the dependant form. Note especially the tone change on the subject prefix and the addition of a suffix.

7.2.2.3 More examples of questions

In this section, I give more examples of questions with fronted and *in situ* constituents. Examples (478) and (479) illustrate the question words *chě* 'what' and *chán* 'what/how'.

(478) S-Q   V   O   Subject
      Chě é-hyɔ́ɔde   ndáb?
      what 7-sweep.IMPF 9.house
      'What sweeps the house? (riddle)'

(479) O-Q   S   V   IO   Object, fronted
      Chán dǐn   á-díí   wɛ?
      what 5.name o.5-be.SF 2SG.PRO
      'What is your name?'

The examples in (480)–(484) contain question phrases. The question phrases in (480), (481) and (484) are NPs with question words as modifiers which agree in noun class with the head noun.

(480) S-Q   V   Subject
      Bad   bétɔ́ŋ   bé-bédé?
      2.people 2.how.many 2-be.PERF
      'How many people were there?'

(481) S-Q   V   Subject
      Mod   ahéé   á-bédé?
      1.person 1.which 1-be.PERF
      'What person was he?'

In (482), the question phrase consists of the question word *nzé* plus the generic noun for 'thing' and a final suffix *-é* as seen earlier in (469) and (470). The tone on the noun *chŏm* is raised to high.

7.2 Questions

(482) O-Q   V   LOC   Object, fronted
Nzé chómé á-m-bɛnlé áhed?
what 7.thing.SF O.1-PAST-do.SF there
'What kind of thing did he do there?'

In (483), the question phrase is an associative NP plus the question word *ehéé* that agrees with the first noun in the AssNP as seen earlier in (470) and (471).

(483) O-Q   V   Object, fronted
Kán e nnəké ehéé á-n-channé?
9.kind 9.AM 3.knife 9.which O.1-PAST-buy.SF
'What kind of knife did he buy?'

(484) V   O-Q   Object, *in situ*
A-n-chăn kúb étəŋ?
1-PAST-buy 10.fowl 10.how.many
'He bought how many fowls?'

(485) MAN-Q   V   O   Manner, fronted
Chán á-boŋsaanné n dyééd?
how O.1-prepare.IMPF.SF 9.food
'How does she prepare food?'

(486) TIME-Q   V   LOC   Time, fronted
Póndé ehéé á-pédé hén?
9.time 9.which O.1-arrive.PERF here
'When did she get here?'

(487) TIME-Q   V   Time, fronted
Sú étəŋ nyí-húú?
10.days 10.how.many O.2PL-return.PERF
'How many days ago did you (pl.) get back?'

(488) REASON-Q   V   LOC   Reason
Chě é-kɔ́ɔ́ baŋ á-kɛ á-dɔ́gtɛɛ?
what 7-cause.PERF then 1-go LOC-hospital
'What caused him to go to the hospital?'

(489) V REASON-Q Reason clause
We-wâmsɛnɛɛ́ apɛ, chĕ é-bédé nzɔm?
2SG.NEG-hurry.PERF.SF INF.come what 7-be.PERF 9.reason
'You didn't hurry, what was the reason?'

The last example should probably be interpreted as two clauses with the second more as an afterthought, not as closely integrated as in the preceding examples.

7.2.3 Leading questions

Questions that expect a positive response are introduced by one of the particles in (490). These particles are clearly related to the negative form of the reduced paradigm of the verb 'to be' (see section 6.2.1). They are interchangeable.

(490) **saá** 'is it not? (expecting positive answer)'
      haá 'is it not? (expecting positive answer)'

With either of these question particles one of the constituents is always fronted and the yes/no question suffix comes at the end.

(491)   O   V
    Saá awí mwaád bé-wúú=u?
    is.it.not 1.his 1.wife o.2-kill.PERF=Q
    'Didn't they kill his wife?'

(492)   LOC   V
    Saá áwí e'wóŋgé mé-m-bɛ́=ɛ?
    is.it.not LOC.his 14.marriage o.1SG-PAST-be=Q
    'Wasn't it to him I was married?'

7.2.4 Tag questions

Related to the above are the following tag questions which are used after a statement to elicit a confirming response. They contain the comparative preposition *nê* 'like' and the final question clitic.

(493) **Saá nê=ɛ?** 'Is it not so?'
     is.it.not so=Q

7.3 Topicalisation

	Haá	**nê = ɛ?**		'Is it not so?'		
	is.it.not	so = Q				

(494) **Mə́** a-n-kɛ̌ á mbwɔg, haá nê = ɛ?
 3SG.PRO 1-PAST-go LOC 3.prison is.it.not so = Q
 'He went to prison, didn't he?'

7.2.5 Indirect questions

For indirect questions see section 8.3.

7.2.6 Questions expressing doubt

Questions which express doubt are introduced by the particle *kéné*. It seems to be related to *ké* 'whether'. It could be glossed as 'is it the case that...?' or 'I wonder whether...?'.

(495) **Kéné** a-dé ndáb = ɛ?
 whether 1-be 9.house = Q
 'I wonder/doubt whether he is in the house?'
 'Is it the case that he is in the house?'

(496) **Kéné** e-kidé-bĕl = ɛ?
 whether 2SG-already-do = Q
 'Have you already done it?'

7.3 Topicalisation

Topicalisation in Akɔɔse is a formal process where a clause constituent is fronted and marked by the topic marker. There are also changes in the form of the verb as indicated in section 7.1.

(497) O V
 Mmwaád mə́ mé-ꜛwóŋgé.
 1.woman 1.TOP O.1SG.FUT-have.SF
 'It is the woman I'll marry.'

(498) O V
 Ndim ḿ mwán mə́ á-bóótédé a-swéɛn.
 3.corpse 3.AM 1.child 3.TOP O.1-begin.PERF INF-return.ACC
 'It is the corpse of the child he began to bring back.'

(499) S   V
    Awem   sáá   mə̂   **a-m-pɛɛ́.**
    1.my   1.father 1.TOP   1-PAST-come
    'It was my father who came.'

7.3.1 The topic marker

The topic marker (TOP) always comes at the end of the topicalised phrase. It agrees in noun class with the head of the NP which it topicalises.

(500) **ane**   **mod**   **mə̂**   'it is that man...'
      1.DEM   1.person   1.TOP

      ábé   **bad**   **bə̂**   'it is those people...'
      2.DEM   2.person   2.TOP

In **Akɔɔse** the topic markers resemble post-nominal distal demonstratives (see section 3.3.1.2) but differ in two ways. Within the topic marker, the vowel is *ə* with a falling tone in every class. Note that the demonstratives for classes 1 and 9 do not resemble their respective topic markers. The topic markers for all the different classes are shown in table 7.1.

Table 7.1. The topic markers

Class		Class	
1	mə̂	2	bə̂
3	mə̂	4	mə̂
5	də̂	6	mə̂
7	chə̂	8	bə̂
9	chə̂	10	chə̂
14	bə̂		
19	bə̂	13	də̂

The topic marker has a reduced variant form which is cliticised to the last element of the topicalised phrase =ɛɛ́. There is only one form of this clitic and there is no agreement with the head of the topicalised NP (see examples (505)–(511).

(501) **abum = ɛɛ́...**
      5.stomach = TOP
      'it is the stomach that...'

7.3 Topicalisation

áwed = ɛɛ́...
LOC.there = TOP
'it is there that...'

7.3.1.1 Topicalised clause constituents

Any constituent of a clause such as subject, object, indirect object, instrument, time, location, and manner phrase can be topicalised. Examples (502)–(504), (508) and (509) have the full form of the topic marker, the rest have the reduced form.

(502) **Akag   də̂**   á-dé   ngáb.   Subject
5.promise   5.TOP   5-be   money
'It is the promise that is money.'

(503) **Ntâŋ   awe   bé-chəgɛɛ́   bán Ngaasambɛɛ**   Subject
1.slave   1.who   O.2-call.IMPF.SF   2.RP (name)
mə̂   a-m-pɛén   mbaangé   ékɔ́ɔ́sē.
1.TOP   1-PAST-bring   9.cocoyam   LOC.Bakossi
'It was a slave called Ngaasambe who brought cocoyams to Bakossi.'

(504) **Mbwɛ́   ne   ngulɛɛ   bə̂   bé-bédé   aśon.**   Subject
9.dog   and   1.lizard   2.TOP   2-be.PERF   5.friendship
'It was the dog and lizard who were friends.'

(505) **Anén   mod = ɛɛ́**   a-wóó   échi   chŏm.   Subject
1.this   1.man = TOP   1-has.PERF   7.his   7.thing
'It is this man who has his own thing.'

(506) **Káb = ɛɛ́**   mɔ́   á-ꜜtédté.   Object
9.antelope = TOP   1.PRO   O.1.FUT-take.SF
'It is the antelope that he will take.'

(507) **Ábén   bad = ɛɛ́**   bé-nꜜ-cháá'ɛ́   mɔ́.   Object
2.these   2.people = TOP   O.2-PAST-bear.SF   3SG.PRO
'It is these people who were born to him.'

(508) **Bɔɔb   də̂**   nyábɔ́ɔ̄-ꜜdyɛ́ɛ́.   Time
now   5.TOP   O.2PL.3PL.FUT-eat.SF
'It is now that you (excl.) will eat.'

(509) **Mbwé echě e-chíbɛ,** <u>**á nsəl dɔ̂**</u> **bé-nyénɛé.** Location
9.dog 9.REL 9-steal.IMPF LOC mouth 5.TOP O.2-see.IMPF.SF
'The dog which steals, it is from its mouth that it can be seen. (proverb)'

(510) **Áwed=ɛé ń-kaké.** Location
there=TOP O.1SG-go.IMPF.SF
'It is there I am going.'

(511) **Kúb ne a-se-bíi aá,** <u>**waáb kúl=ɛé**</u> **mɔ́-tédé.** Object
9.fowl 9.that 1-NEG-know 1.RP 1.friend 9.tortoise=TOP O.LOG-take.PERF
'This fowl didn't know that it was his friend Tortoise he had taken.'

7.3.1.2 Topicalisation of predicate

In the following examples, it is the *predicate* that is topicalised. This is done by topicalising the cognate object, i.e. an object in nominal form which has basically the same meaning as the verb. In (512), the cognate object of the verb 'to sleep' is topicalised. Compare (512) with (513). In (514), the head of the topicalised phrase is the infinitive form of the verb. Infinitives only occur as topicalised cognate objects, never as unmarked objects of the same verb.

(512) **E'chɔ́ bɔ̂ á-kúnɛé.** Cognate object
14.sleep 14.TOP O.1-sleep.IMPF.SF
'Sleeping is what he is doing.'

(513) **A-kúnɛ e'chɔ́.** Unmarked
1-sleep.IMPF 14.sleep
'He is sleeping.'

(514) **A-kún dɔ̂ á-kúnɛé.** Infinitive
INF-sleep 5.TOP O.1-sleep.IMPF.SF
'Sleeping is what he is doing.'

7.4 Relative clauses

7.4.1 Structure

Relative clauses (RCs) are very common in Akɔɔse. They are used to modify the head noun of the noun phrase, and are used primarily with restrictive function.

7.4 Relative clauses

Typically, a relative clause in Akɔɔse has various characteristics, including the following:

- a HEAD NOUN which precedes the relative clause and which is part of its matrix clause;
- it always begins with a RELATIVE PRONOUN; the form of the relative pronoun is determined by the noun class of the head noun it qualifies; and
- a CONSTITUENT of the relative clause that is RELATIVISED (this may be the subject, direct object, indirect object, instrument, location phrase, time phrase or manner phrase).

Example (515) is an NP which may function as subject or object in a sentence. The NP *mwǎ mǐm* is the head noun which is qualified by a relative clause (in square brackets). The NP *mwǎ mǐm* is also the implied object of the relative clause which has been extracted from the position after the verb; *awě* is the relative pronoun (REL). The gap in the relative clause is marked by Ø.

(515) **mwǎ   mǐm   [awě   bé-m-bɛé   Ø   bá]**
      1.small 6.wine [1.REL O.2-PAST-give.SF Ø   3PL]
      'the little wine that they gave them'

The verb form changes depending on whether a subject or a non-subject constituent of the relative clause is relativised, as described in section 7.1.

7.4.2 Constituents relativised

The elements of a clause that can be relativised are indicated in table 7.2.

Table 7.2. Relativisation

Constituent	constituent relativised	relative pronoun	gapping	trace
Subject	yes	REL	yes	no
Direct object	yes	REL	yes	no
Indirect object	yes	REL	yes	no
Instrument	yes	REL	yes	no
Comitative	yes	REL	yes	no
Time	yes	REL/*áde*	yes	no
Location	yes	*wê/áde*	yes	+/−
Manner	no			
Possessor	no			
Verb	yes	áde	no	n/a

The following comments can be made:

- When subject, direct and indirect objects are relativised, a gap is left with no trace of the extracted constituent being left behind. The form of the relative pronoun is determined by the class of the head noun.
- Manner and possessors are never relativised.
- Instrument and accompaniment constituents are only relativised when they are complements, i.e. when no preposition is present but where there is the -*en* suffix on the verb. When they are adjuncts introduced by a preposition, they cannot be relativised.
- Time phrases are relativised with gapping and no trace. When the head noun is a temporal word or phrase, the relative pronoun *áde* is used. For other nouns, the usual relative pronoun is used.
- When a location is relativised, there are two possibilities: (1) gapping with no trace and (2) gapping where the trace is *ámīn*, *ásē* or *áte*. In other words, in the second case, the noun has been extracted from the locational phrase leaving a post-nominal element *in situ* (see section 7.4.2.6).
- Verbs, too, can be relativised. In such cases, the head noun is the verb in the infinitive form, i.e. with the class 5 prefix. The fully declined verb remains in its proper place in the relative clause.

Relativisation of different clause constituents is illustrated below.

7.4.2.1 Subject relativised

In (516), the subject can be said to be extracted and replaced by the relative pronoun. There is no trace left in the relative clause of the subject. Such gaps are indicated in the example sentences by Ø.

(516) **Bad   bésyɔ́ɔ́l   [ábe Ø bé-bédé áwed áte]...**
2.people 2.all   2.REL Ø 2-be.PERF there inside
'all the people who were inside there...'

7.4.2.2 Direct object relativised

When the direct object is relativised, a gap is left in its position in the relativised clause. A dependent verb form is used.

(517) **N-wóó   ḿmêm ntyɔ́g [ḿmē mod é-dipéé   Ø áte].**
1SG-have.PERF 3.my 3.box 3.REL 1.person o.1.NEG-open.IMPF.SF Ø into
'I have a box which nobody opens. (riddle)'

7.4.2.3 Indirect object relativised

As with the direct object, when the indirect object is relativised, a gap is left. The location phrase in (518) is an apposition to the head noun.

(518) **awêm nkáálé   ákuu wê [awě ḿ-bɛnlɛé   Ø nsɔ́n]**
1.my 1.white.man up   there [1.who o.1SG-do.IMPF.SF Ø work]
'the white man up there for whom I work'

7.4.2.4 Instrument relativised

Instruments can only be relativised when they are objects of the verb marked by the instrumental extension -ɛn. A gap is left as with other objects.

(519) **Mod   e'lûd   a-wóó   sém   [eche**
1.person 14.smith 1-have.PERF 9.hammer [9.REL
á-lúɛnɛé   páan echin   Ø].
o.1-hammer.INST.IMPF.SF 9.knife 7.colocasia Ø]
'The blacksmith has a hammer with which he hammers the kitchen knife.'

In (520), the relative clause is not adjacent to the relativised noun. Instead it has moved to the end of the matrix clause. This movement of material to the end is sometimes called HEAVY SHIFT.

(520) **Ngude** ě-saá me [eche ń-lôŋnɛé ndáb Ø].
9.strength 9.NEG-be 1SG.PRO [9.REL O.1SG-build.INST.IMPF.SG 9.house Ø]
'I do not have the strength to build a house.'

7.4.2.5 Accompaniment relativised

The constituent with the semantic role of accompaniment can be relativised provided it is marked by the extension -ɛn on the verb. Note that this extension is formally identical with the instrumental and the reciprocal. The interpretation as comitative comes from the semantics of the verb and the "object."

(521) **ene** **pél** **esyəɔ́l** [eche ń-dyéé<u>n</u>é Ø]
9.that 9.anger 9.all [9.REL O.1SG-sit.ACC.PERF Ø]
'all that anger which I had'

7.4.2.6 Location relativised

When a constituent indicating location is relativised, the head noun of the NP or PP is extracted. There may be gapping (522)–(524), or there may be a trace in the form of a locative adverb left in the position of the extracted location phrase. Compare (526) with (525) to see that the head noun *ndáb* has been extracted from the PP resulting in the locative adverb *áte* 'being left'.

(522) **Hŏm** [áde é-bánné mŏl Ø] mod e-bwémɛ́ɛ́
5.place [5.REL O.2SG-put.PERF 6.oil Ø] 1.person 1.NEG-throw.IMPF.SF
aláá áhedɛ.
5.stone there
'Where you put the oil, one doesn't throw stones.'

(523) **hŏm** [áde bé-nəgtɛé e'péndé Ø]
5.place [5.REL O.2-run.IMPF.SF 8.relay.race Ø]
'where they run the relay race'

7.4 Relative clauses

(524) **Dyad** [áde sóo dé-kaké Ø nén]
5.town [5.REL 1PL.2PL.PRO O.1PL.2PL.-go.IMPF.SF Ø so]
ngun chô é-dé áwed.
10.corn 10.TOP 10-be there
'In the town where we are going, there is corn.'

(525) **ndáb** [eché mɔ́ á-kɔ́gtɛɛ́ mekii mé kúb áte hê]
9.house [9.REL 1.PRO O.1-hatch.IMPF.SF 6.egg 6.AM 10.hen LOC.in there]
the house, where she hatches the eggs in there'

(526) **á ndáb te**
LOC 9.house in
'in the house'

(527) **Sê-bédé toŋ** [ádē sé-ké-dyě'ɛ́ Ø e'pun é'láán].
1PL-be.PERF 9.room [5.REL O.1PL-already-stay.SF Ø 8.days 8.three]
'We were in a room where we stayed for three days.'

In (522)–(525), the relative pronouns agree in class with the preceding head noun. However, in (527), the head noun is class 9 and the relative pronoun is class 5. It seems that agreement is once again on semantic grounds with class 5 being the typical concord for location (see section 2.3.4).

7.4.2.7 Time relativised

Relative clauses in which the time constituent is relativised can be divided into the following three subgroups: those whose head is an NP or a PP referring to time (528)–(530), those with a time "adverb" as a head (532)–(535) and headless relative clauses (536).

In (529), the relative pronoun agrees with the head noun (class 9) rather than with the time expression as a whole (which is class 5). Some speakers use this same noun without the locative marker *á* (530). This might explain the irregular agreement in (529).

(528) **póndé** [eche ḿ-bédé á Pəŋ á ndáb wê echem
9.time [9.REL O.1SG-be.PERF LOC Peng LOC house LOC.REL 9.my
sáŋ Ø]
9.father Ø]
'At the time I was in Peng in the house of my father.'

(529) á kên [echĕ mé-n-lómmé nyí Ø]
 LOC 9.time [9.REL O.1SG-PAST-send.SF 2PL.PRO Ø]
 'when I sent you'

(530) kên [echĕ bé-pédé áhîn tê Ø]
 9.time [9.REL O.2-arrive.PERF LOC.5.forest in Ø]
 'when they reached the forest'

In (531), the relative pronoun does not agree with the class of the head noun but is class 5 (which is the class for location and, by extension, for time).

(531) **mbwɛmbwɛ** [áde bé-ˈwúú'ɛ sáá Ø]
 9.morning [5.REL O.2.FUT-kill.SF 1.father Ø]
 'the morning when they will kill their father'

In (532)–(535), the relative clause begins with the class 5 relative pronoun to agree with the time adverb.

(532) saké **bɔɔb** [ádē bedógtɛɛ bé békáálé bé-pédé hén Ø]
 not now [5.REL 2.doctors 2.AM 2.whites O.2-come.PERF here Ø]
 'not now that western medicine has come here'

(533) **boŋchii nɛ́n** [áde mĭd mé-máá bad a-dibned Ø]
 but today 9.this [5.REL 6.eye O.6-finish.PERF 2.person INF-open Ø]
 'but today when peoples' eyes have been opened'

(534) **bwéed** [áde nyí-n-kangé ḿmê mɛl hŏm ahóg Ø]
 long.ago [5.REL O.2PL-past-tie.SF 6.those 6.tree 5.place 5.one Ø]
 'long time ago when you tied those sticks in one place'

(535) **bɔɔb-pəə́** [ádē mod-té á-wánlé mwă bwɛl
 now-DEV [5.REL 1.person-each O.1-hold.PERF 1.small 14.stick
 éˈ-káá nén Ø]
 C.7-hand this Ø]
 'so now that everybody holds a small stick in his hand'

The first part of (536) is an example of a headless relative clause functioning as a time adverbial clause. It is introduced by the class 5 relative pronoun but has no head noun. The second part is also a headless relative clause introduced with a locative relative pronoun.

7.4 Relative clauses

(536) [áde á-pédé Ø [wê ane mod á-díí]]
[5.REL O.1-reach.PERF Ø [LOC.REL 1.that 1.person O.1-be.SF]]
'when he arrived where that man was'

7.4.2.8 Verbs relativised

A very common type of relativisation is where the verb is relativised and appears as head in the nominalised/infinitive form. This kind of construction is frequently used in discourse as part of the linkage between sentences. The verb from the first sentence is the one which is relativised at the beginning of the following sentence (537)–(540). Other elements of the first sentence may also be repeated, as seen with 'the hollow tree' in (537).

(537) **Ebubwɔ́gɛ bɔ́ ngoó bé-dyɛ́ɛ́ éˈ-lóm é bwɛl tê.**
7.mongoose.PERS and 9.tiger.PERS 2-stay LOC-7.hollow 7.AM 14.tree in
A-dyɛɛ [áde bé-dyɛ́ɛ́ éˈ-lóm é bwɛl tê]...
INF-stay [5.RELO.2-stay.PERF LOC.7-hollow 7.AM 14.tree in]
'Mongoose and leopard lived in a hollow tree. Staying in the hollow tree...'

(538) **Bechóm bé-pédé. Áde apɛ [áde bé-pédé],**
2.husband 2-arrive.PERF 5.that INF.arrive [5.RELO.2-arrive.PERF]
né-'ɔ́ bé-pédé á ˈtébelɛ. Bé-dyɛ́ɛ́.
SO-DEV 2-arrive.PERF LOC table 2-sit
'The husbands arrived. Having arrived, they got to the table and sat down.'

(539) **Mbwɛ́ e-tóm mehélé éˈbwɔ́g á-kɛ dé a-téd ehidényam.**
9.dog 9-pass 6.running LOC.outside INF-go 5.AM INF-take 7.bone
A-téd [ádē á-tédé ehidényam], á-kɛ̄ēn áhîn tɛ́.
INF-take [5.REL O.1-take.PERF 7.bone] INF-go.with LOC.5.bush in
'The dog quickly ran outside to get the bone. Taking the bone, he ran with it into the forest.'

(540) **Bé-sɛ́nlé ásē nê. A-séle [áde bé-sɛ́nlé ásē],**
2-start.PERF down so. INF-start [5.RELO.2-start.PERF down]
bé-kag bé-kalɛ' á nzii...
2-go.IMPF 2-converse.IMPF LOC 9.road

'They set off. Setting off, they walked, they conversed on the way...' One way to explain the fact that these structures take the dependent non-subject (O-) type form of the verb rather than the unmarked one is to consider the infinitives as cognate objects that have been moved to the front even though sentences with such cognate objects *in situ* have not been observed.[2]

The example in (541) is from the peak of a story. Though the specific verb has not occurred in the previous clause, it is the logical consequence of what preceded.

(541) a-kɔ́m [ádē   mepab mé-máá   mɔ́   a-kɔ́m áte]...
     INF-tire [5.REL 6.wing O.6-finish.PERF 1.PRO INF-tire in]
     'complete tiredness of his wings...'

7.5 Fronting

Fronting of post-verbal constituents without topicalisation is also used in questions expecting a confirming answer, as in (542)–(545). This is a type of focus construction with the question particle *saá* (see also sections 7.2.3 and 7.2.4).

(542) **Saá áwī e'wóŋgé mé-m-béé Ø ?**   Location
     is.not LOC.his 14.marriage O.1SG-PAST-be.SF.Q Ø
     'Wasn't it to him I was married?'

(543) **Saá awí mwaád bé-wúû Ø ?**   Object
     is.not 1.his 1.wife O.2-kill.PERF.Q Ø
     'Was it not his wife they killed?'

(544) **Saá chɔ́ ń-lâŋgɛé wɛ=ɛ Ø ?**   Object
     is.not 7.PRO O.1SG-tell.IMPF.SF 2SG.PRO =Q Ø
     'Is this not what I am telling you?'

(545) **Saá Dyŏb nyí-chɔ́gáá Ø Lɔŋgɔnɛ?**   Indirect object
     is.not God O.2PL-call.IMPF.PAST Ø Longone.Q
     'Weren't you calling God Longone?'

In (546), the constituent in focus is moved still further to the left of *saá*.

(546) **Tɛɛ saá Ø bɔ́ bé-bédé nhɔn-ɛ?**   Subject
     1.father is.not Ø 2.PRO 2-be.PERF Ahon.member-Q
     'Our fathers, were they not members of the *Ahon* society?'

---

[2]For clauses with cognate objects see section 6.3.2.

7.6 Vocatives and politeness adverbs

Vocatives are terms of address. Names and other terms used as vocatives are preceded by the vocative marker *a*, with either H or L tone depending on the first stem tone of the following noun (see section 2.4.4; Enang 1994 and Hedinger and Hedinger 1994). Vocatives are always in sentence-initial position.

(547) **Ngəə aá, "A mwɛ́ɛ̄, hyăg, nyam e-kwedé á mbɛ́ɛ́."**
Leopard 1.RP VOC friend come.IMP 9.animal 9-fall.PERF VOC 1.trap
'Leopard said, "Friend, come, an animal has fallen into the trap." '

(548) **A-lâŋge ḿmê njun ḿ mod nén aá, "A sáŋ,**
1-tell.IMPF 3.that 3.old 3.AM 1.person that 1.RP VOC 9.father
koó mɛ."
keep.IMP 1SG.PRO
'He told that old man, "Father, keep me." '

(549) **Hɛ́ɛ ngəə á-chyɛɛnɛɛ́ mɔ́ áte aá, "A Kûl,**
There 1.leopard o.1-cry.IMPF.SF 1.PRO in 1.RP VOC 9.tortoise
chán, a mwɛ́ɛ̄, saá me n-tage hén nén-ɛ?"
how VOC friend is.not 1SG.PRO 1SG-suffer.IMPF here so-Q
'Then Leopard cried, "Tortoise, look, friend, am I not suffering here so much?" '

In the next two examples, the politeness adverb *sôn* 'please' is used. If present, it appears between the vocative and the main clause.

(550) **Sôn, cháá me ane mod, boŋ é-kɛɛne**
please beg.IMP 1SG.PRO 1.that 1.person then 1.NEG-take.HORT
me á ꜛkóte.
1SG.PRO VOC court.
'Please, beg that man for me that he should not take me to court.'

(551) **Aá, "A mwɛ́ɛ̄, sôn sôn aá, mɔ́-bɛlé ádê**
1.RP VOC friend please please 1.RP LOG.NEG-do.HORT 5.that
akan ámpē."
5.thing again
'He said, "Friend, please, please, I won't do this again." '

8
Complex Sentences

In this chapter, I describe sentences that consist of more than one clause. This includes various clause combinations, and I am also including here such structures as analytical causatives, adverbial clauses, reported speech and related structures. Relative clauses were treated in section 7.4.

8.1 Analytic causatives

In addition to the morphological causatives expressed by verbal extensions (see section 4.4.6.1), there are analytic causatives. They are expressed either by the causative verb *-kəŋ* 'to cause' or *-bɛl* 'to do/make' plus a clause linked with the conjunction *boŋ* 'then' (which has the following variant forms: *baŋ*, *boŋkên*, and *baŋkên*).

The subject of the causative verb is also often topicalised or relativised.

(552) **Aséle á yɔ́l dɜ̂ á-kɔ́ɔ́ baŋkên dyěsid**
 5.slowness 5.AM 9.body 5.TOP 5-cause.PERF then 5.crab
 dé-wóo nló.
 5.NEG-have.PERF 3.head
 'Slowness made the crab have no head.'

(553) **chom[-ɛ̄ɛ̄   é-kɔ́ɔ́   boŋ   ń-wɔɔ']   é-díi nɛ́n**
   7.thing-REL 7-cause.PERF then 1SG-laugh.IMPF.HORT 7-is that
   échén   kúb   édyé   hén
   10.those 10.hens 10.are here
   'The thing which makes me laugh is the fact that those hens are here.'

(554) **Chán   nzêd   é-bélé   boŋ   e-nyénnéd áwôŋ   ekwɛ?**
   how   9.ring O.9-make.PERF then 9-be.seen LOC.your 7.bag
   'How did the ring make it so that it could be seen in your bag?'

(555) **Ndɔ́g   echĕ   á-kwédé   e-bɛlé   mɔ́   e-wógéé   bwǎam.**
   9.deafness 9.REL O.1-fall.PERF 9-make.PERF 1.PRO 1.NEG-hear.IMPF.SF well
   'His becoming deaf (lit. the deafness which he fell) has made him not to hear well.'

8.2 Reported speech

In this section, I will describe reported speech and structures formally related to it such as intention (see section 8.2.6).

Akɔɔse has direct, indirect and semidirect speech. There is no contrast of markers that formally distinguishes between these three types. The way the different types of speech can be identified, however, is by the choice of person in pronouns and subject markers as well as by changes in tense and temporal and locational adverbs, etc. These will be described in section 8.2.3.

We can easily distinguish between the speech margin and the speech content in Akɔɔse.

8.2.1 Speech margin

Speech is typically introduced by a clause containing a verb of speech, thought, intention, etc. This is what I am calling a "speech margin." Such verbs have their own argument structure requiring a subject, an indirect object, an optional complementiser and a reporting particle (RP). This is then followed by the speech content functioning as direct object of the verb of speech, thought or intention.

(556) S   V   IO   O
   mwaád   a-lâŋgɛ   njóm   [nɛ́n aá...]
   1.wife   1-say.IMPF   1.male COMP 1.RP]
   'The wife said to her husband...'

8.2 Reported speech

The subject refers to the speaker, the indirect object to the addressee. The object is introduced by the optional complementiser (COMP) *nén* 'that' and the reporting particle (RP) *aá*, respectively. The subject, as in any Akɔɔse clause, may be absent. The subject marker is always from the person class (class 1/2).

The complementiser appears to be optional, but it is not clear whether its absence is significant.

The reporting particle has different forms for different persons, described in section 8.2.2.

8.2.2 Reporting particle

The RP has five different forms which agree with the subject in person and number.

Table 8.1. The reporting particle (RP)

	1st	2nd	3rd	Log
singular	mě	wě	aá	mɔ́ɔ̄
plural	bán			

In the singular there is a form for first, second and third person and a logophoric form. The latter is used when the verb in the speech margin has the logophoric subject marker (see (558)). The plural has one form for all plural speakers and for impersonal reporting.

(557) **a-hɔ́bé   aá   [...]**
      3SG-say.PERF 3SG.RP
      'he said...'

       n-lâŋge   nyí   nén   mě   [...]
       1SG-tell.IMPF 2PL.PRO COMP   1SG.RP
       'I told you...'

       chom=ɛ́ɛ   nyí-chəgeé   bán   [...]
       7.thing=REL   O.2PL-call.IMPF.SF   PL.RP
       'the thing which you call...'

       bé-lâŋge   mɔ́   nén   bán   [...]
       3PL-tell.IMPF 3SG.PRO COMP   PL.RP
       'they told him...'

In (558), there is speech within speech. When the speaker (A) in the second speech margin is the same as the speaker (A) in the first speech margin, then the logophoric subject marker (mɔ́-) and the logophoric reporting particle (mɔ́ɔ̄) are used in the embedded speech margin.

(558) *speech margin 1*
    A-láŋgé   **mɔ́**   **ámpē**
    3SG-tell.PERF   3SG-PRO   again
    A   B
                          speech margin 2
    "**E-wógé**   **chom=ɛ́ɛ**   **mɔ́-lâŋgeɛ́**   **wɛ**   **nɛ́n mɔ́ɔ̄** [...]?"
    2SG-hear.PERF 7.thing=REL LOG-tell.IMPF.SF 2SG.PRO COMP LOG.RP
    B   A   B   A
    'She told him again, "Do you hear what I am telling you... ?"'

When questions are reported *ken* is always added to the reporting particle. Compare table 8.2 with table 8.1.

Table 8.2. The reporting particle in questions (RP Q)

	1st	2nd	3th	Log
singular	**mě ken**	**wě ken**	**aá ken**	**mɔ́ɔ̄ ken**
plural	**bán ken**			

The following examples illustrate speech clauses containing questions. In (559), the verb of speech *láŋ* is not specific to questions. The reported question, however, is introduced with the question form of the reporting particle.

(559) **A-láŋgé ane mod**   **nɛ́n**   **aá**   **ken**   "**Cheé**
    1-tell.PERF 1.that 1.man COMP 3SG.RP Q   what
    é-hyédé   **a-bɛl**   **hɛ́n?**"
    O.2SG-come.PERF INF-do here
    'They asked the man, "What have you come to do here?"'

(560) **Bé-bootéd a-sɛded bán ken** "**Kân e**   **mwǎn ehéé**   **á-cháá?**
    2-begin   INF-ask   PL.RP Q   9.kind 9.AM 1.child 9.which 1-bear.PERF
    'They began to ask, "What kind of child has she borne?"'

8.2 Reported speech

Speech margins vary from full forms (556) and (559) to reduced forms (560) and (561), to the most minimal one consisting of the reporting particle only (562) and (563).

A common reduction is to have the subject and RP but no verb as in (561) where the speech margin only contains a subject and the RP.

(561) S RP [   ]
   Nyag **aá** **mɔ́-wōge** **pél.**
   9.cow 3SG.RP LOG-feel 9.anger
   'The cow says that she is angry.'

(562) RP
   aá   […]
   3SG.RP
   'he (said) that…'

(563) RP
   bán […]
   3SG.RP
   'they (said) that…'

The most reduced form of a speech margin (consisting of the reporting particle only) has been found in discourse at points of high tension where different speakers are introduced alternately by just the reporting particle.

The reporting particle is also frequently used in spoken discourse consisting of several sentences, with the RP being repeated before every clause or phrase whenever there is a pause (see (564)).

(564) **Ebwéŋgo** é-lâŋge   Ngo   nɛ́n 'Golden cat said to Leopard,'
      7.golden.cat o.7-tell.IMPF 9.leopard COMP
      aá   é-dyɛ   hɛ́n,   'Sit here.'
      3SG.RP 2SG-sit.HORT here
      aá   mwǎmpín ḿ   póndé,   'In a short while'
      3SG.RP 3.small   3.AM 9.time
      aá   ane mod   ǎ-pě,   'the man will come.'
      3SG.RP 1.that 1.man   1.FUT-come
      aá   mɔ̂   mɔ́-kií   mɔ́,[1]   'I̲ am going.'
      3SG.RP 3SG.PRO LOG-go.PERF 3SG.PRO
      aá   wě-ˈtáné   mɔ́   á   ndáb...[2] 'Wait for me in the
      3SG.RP 2SG.FUT-meet 3SG.PRO LOC 9.house   house...'

8.2.3   Direct, indirect and semidirect speech

Direct, indirect and semidirect speech are distinguished as follows:

In DIRECT SPEECH, the words are reported as spoken in the original speech situation, without adjustment to the current speech situation. That means that the participants are referred to as follows:

   Speaker   = first-person marking
   Addressee = second-person marking
   Others   = third-person marking

Temporal and spatial deixis (yesterday, today, tomorrow; here, there, etc.) are also unchanged from the original speech situation.

In INDIRECT SPEECH, the report is adjusted to the situation in which the speech is reported. This means that person assignment is according to the reporting situation.

SEMIDIRECT SPEECH is characterised by a combination of direct and indirect person reference. The speaker of a reported speech is referred to by indirect reference but the addressee of the reported speech by direct reference.

Person marking in the three types may be summarised as in table 8.3.

---

[1]This pronoun refers to the subject of the clause and is repeated for emphasis (see section 6.5).

[2]This last sentence is an example of semidirect speech.

8.2 Reported speech

Table 8.3. Person marking in the three types of speech

	Participant	Person marking
Direct speech	speaker	1st person
	addressee	2nd person
	other	3rd person
Indirect speech	speaker	3rd person or LOG
	addressee	3rd person
	other	3rd person
Semidirect speech	speaker	3rd person or LOG
	addressee	2nd person
	other	3rd person

In direct speech, the original speaker and addressees are referred to with first- and second-person references, respectively.

In indirect speech, speaker and addressee are referred to by third-person reference. There are special logophoric forms (subject marker and reporting particle) in the singular that are used for the person in the speech content who is also the speaker in the speech margin.

In semidirect speech, the speaker is referred to by third-person or logophoric forms as in indirect speech, but the addressee is referred to by second-person forms as in direct speech.

This can be illustrated with the following examples.

(565) Direct speech

               1st   2nd
Bé-láŋgé bɔ́ nɛ́n bán, "Amwéē bán, sê-dəɔ́ nyí a-wóŋ."
2-tell.PERF 2.PRO COMP PL.RP VOC.friend PL.RP 1PL-like.PERF 2PL.PRO INF-have
'They told them, "Friends, we would like to marry you." '

(566) Indirect speech

              3rd   3rd
Échê ngɔndéde é-kwéntěné bán, "Bé-ꜝwóŋ bɔ́."
10.DEM 10.girl 10-agree.PERF PL.RP 3PL.FUT-have 3PL.PRO
'Those girls agreed with them saying, "They will marry them." '

(567) Semidirect speech

		2ⁿᵈ		LOG	2ⁿᵈ	

Aá   ken,   "Nzé   e-kalé   metóm, mɔ́-bél   wɛ   chán?"
3SG.RP Q   if   2SG-tell.PERF 6.lie   LOG.FUT-do 2SG.PRO what
'He₁ asked, "If you told a lie, what shall he₁ (the speaker) do with you?"'

Each of these examples report what somebody said to somebody else. In (565) the speaker and addressees are referred to by first- and second-person forms; in (566), both are referred to in third-person forms. In (567), where the logophoric is a special kind of third-person form, the speaker is referred to with a third-person form and the addressee in a second-person form.

There are some interesting facts when compound pronouns (see section 3.11.3) are involved. Example (568) is in semidirect speech.

(568)

			2ⁿᵈ-3ʳᵈ	2ⁿᵈ	

Mwaád a-lângɛ   nchóm,   "Ngáne nyú⁺mɔ́³   nyî-dyě   nén...
1.wife 1-tell.IMPF 1.husband since   2PL.3SG.PRO 2PL-stay.PERF COMP

		LOG	2ⁿᵈ	

aá   mbwé=ɛ́ɛ̄   mɔ́-⁺wéé   aá,   é-kɛ
3SG.RP 3.day=REL   LOG.FUT-die 3SG.RP 2SG-go.HORT

	2ⁿᵈ		3ʳᵈ		

e-lɔ́géd   mɔ́⁴   á   soŋ   tê."
2SG-leave 3SG.PRO LOC 9.grave in
'The wife told her husband, "Since you and I have lived together... the day when I die, you go and put me in the grave."'

The compound pronoun *nyú⁺mɔ́* 'you and him' refers to the man and his wife. It is a combination of second and third persons, clearly reflecting semidirect speech. The subject concord prefix on the verb, however, can only express one person. It is, therefore, in the second-person plural to include both participants. The corresponding forms for direct and indirect speech would be as follows.

---

³The *mɔ́* here refers to the speaker, but could theoretically also refer to another person. In other words, in the pronouns there is no 3SG versus LOG distinction, as is found in the subject markers.

⁴Same as previous note.

8.2 Reported speech

(569)

1ˢᵗ 2ⁿᵈ	1ˢᵗ 2ⁿᵈ	
sóo	**de-**	'you and I (direct speech)'
1PL.2SG.PRO	1.2	
3ʳᵈ 3ʳᵈ	3ʳᵈ	
bú⁺mɔ́	**bé-**	'you and him (indirect speech)'
3PL.3SG.PRO	3PL	

8.2.4 Verbs of speech, perception and cognition

Verbs that appear in the speech margin can be considered a separate subclass of verbs, based on the fact that they may take the complementiser *nén* and/or the reporting particle. Semantically they range from verbs involving speech (570), hearing (571), vision (572), thought or knowledge (573) to the stating of facts (574). This list is not complete nor are the categories meant to be absolute. Also, further work needs to be done to identify the valency for each verb. Some verbs may or may not take an indirect object and the complementiser *nén*. This kind of information technically belongs in the dictionary as it is unique to each verb.

(570)
- **láŋ** 'read'
- **láa** 'tell'
- **hɔ́b** 'speak'
- **kal** 'tell'
- **kán** 'speak, shout'
- **bón** 'shout'
- **kémed** 'praise'
- **swéded** 'ask'
- **sɛded** 'ask'
- **cháŋ** 'beg, ask for'
- **timtɛn** 'reply'
- **kwɛntɛn** 'accept'
- **mwed** 'allow'
- **lébe** 'send message'

(571) **wóg** 'hear'

(572) **lúmed** 'show'
nyén 'see'
chem 'recognise'
nyénned 'to be seen'
tenled 'to be written'

(573) **bíi** 'know'
dúbe 'believe'
wóo mewêmtɛn 'have thoughts'
dúbned 'be believed'

(574) **bɛ́** 'be'
dé 'be'

8.2.5 Content clauses illustrated

The following sentences illustrate some of the verbs listed above. Except for the first three examples, they all use the plural RP.

Comparing (575) with (576), it can be seen that the former has an indirect object (the addressee, a human referent) whereas the latter has a direct object *ngan* 'proverb' referring to what is told in a noun form. The complementiser *nén* and the direct object never co-occur, which would suggest the COMP is really the head of the direct object with the content including the RP as apposition.

(575) **A-láŋgé mmwaád nɛ́n aá, "Téd   mpûb...**
1-tell.PERF 1.woman COMP 3SG.RP take.IMP 4.ground.dry.plantain
'He told the wife, "Take ground plantain..." '

(576) **Nkɔ́ɔ́sē   a-kalé   ngan   aá,   "Nzé mod**
1.bakossi.man 1-tell.PERF 9.proverb 3SG.RP if 1.person
a-wógé   ntyɔ́g, aá   ntyɔ́g ń-tɔgɛ.
1-hear.PERF 3.drum 3SG.RP 3.drum 3-make.noise.IMPF
'The Bakossi tell this proverb, "If somebody hears a drum, he says it talks." '

(577) **A-sɛde   mwaád á   kûl   nén   aá   héé   awoŋ**
1-ask.IMPF 1.wife 1.AM 9.tortoise COMP 3SG.RP where 1.your
njóm   á-díí.
1.husband o.1-be.PERF
'Then he asked the wife of Tortoise where her husband was.'

8.2 Reported speech

The following examples all have *bán* as the RP. What is interesting is that the subject of the speech margin is in the singular except for (581) where it is plural. There is therefore no agreement in person and number in content clauses as is the case in typical speech clauses. This may be for two reasons. One, *bán* may be used for other classes than class 1. Two, in (578) and (579), for example, what is heard or seen obviously comes from a source other than the one who experienced it. This needs further study.

(578) **me-n-wóg   nɛ́n   bán...**
      1SG-PAST-hear COMP PL.RP
      'I heard that...'

(579) **É-nyénnédé   nɛ́n   bán...**
      7-be.seen.PERF COMP PL.RP
      'It is seen that...'

(580) **É-n-dúbnéd   nɛ́n   bán** nzé a-m-bɛl   nê, echáa
      7-PAST-be.believed COMP PL.RP if 1-PAST-do so 7.birth
      é-¹bídaá   bwâm.
      7.NEG-come.out.IMPF.PAST well
      'It was believed that if she did so, the birth would not go well.'

(581) **Bé-wóó   mewêmtɛn nɛ́n   bán...**
      2-have.PERF 6.thought COMP PL.RP
      'They thought that...'

(582) **Enén pɔ́le   e-lúmte   sóo   nɛ́n   bán...**
      9.this 9.talk 9-show.IMPF 1PL.2SG.PRO COMP PL.RP
      'This story shows us that...'

(583) **Éked   émpēe é-dé   nɛ́n   bán   kɛ́n kɛ́n kɛn kɛ́lɛnkɛ́ŋ...**
      7.riddle 7.other 7-be COMP PL.RP IDEO
      'There is another riddle going like this...'

(584) **Anén mwǎ   nkalaŋ a-dé sóo   nɛ́n   bán...**
      1.this 1.small 3.story 1-be 1PL.2SG.PRO COMP PL.RP
      'We have this small story...'

(585) É-m-bé-'ɛ   mɔ́   mbéndé   nɛ́n   bán   nzé a-wóge   mehɔ́b
      7-PAST-be-ADD 1.PRO 9.law   COMP   PL.RP if 1-hear.IMPF   6.talk
      mé   nyam...
      6.AM 9.animal
      'He also had an injunction that when he hears an animal talk...'

8.2.6 Intention

The structure of reported speech is also used to express intention. These structures consist of the reporting particle plus a verb with the logophoric prefix (see (586)).

(586) Aá   mɔ́-kag.
      3SG.RP   LOG-go.IMPF.HORT
      'He intends to go. (lit. He said/thought that he should go.)'

8.3 Indirect questions

Indirect polar questions are introduced by the particle *ké* 'whether' or *nzé* 'if'. They are introduced by some of the speech margin verbs listed above. No complementiser or reporting particle is used.

(587) A-n-sɛdéd sé   nzé/ké   mod   a-sóme   kónénkááalé
      1-PAST-ask 1PL.PRO   if/whether   1.person 1-sell.IMPF   10.rice
      á   dyad tê.
      LOC town in
      'He asked us whether someone sells rice in town.'

(588) Me-bíi'ɛ́   ké   a-hɛle   á-pē   chii.
      1SG.NEG-know.SF   whether   1-can.IMPF   1-reach.NEUT   today
      'I don't know whether he can reach here today.'

(589) Me-bíi'ɛ́   ké   á   Nninɔɔ á-m-bēē   káa héé.
      1SG.NEG-know.SF   whether   LOC   Ninong o.1-PAST-be.SF or   where
      'I don't know whether he was in Ninong or somewhere else.'

8.4 Sentence pro-form

The object position in a speech clause may be filled with a pro-form instead of a sentence complement. The pro-form standing for a whole sentence is *nê* which is similar in form to the comparative preposition (see section 3.9.5.4) and the temporal conjunction used in discourse. As can be seen from example (590), the pro-sentence particle takes the place of the object of the speech verb, including the complementisers and content.

(590) Nzé   mod   a-hɔ́bé   nê   né   a-tə́ngéné.
      if   1.person 1-say.PERF   PRO.S   then 1-be.right.PERF
      'If the person says that then he is correct.'

8.5 Other clause combinations

Under this heading I will group a large number of clause combinations with a variety of temporal and logical relations.

8.5.1 And-coordination

Clauses indicating chronologically unordered actions may be simply juxtaposed without any link element. In (591) the activities carried out by a group of people are not ordered in any way.

(591) **Bé-dyâg,   bé-kale   pɔ́lɛ,   bé-kɔne   bwěm,   bé-ságe.**
      2-eat.impf 2-tell.impf 9.story   2-sing.impf 8.things   2-dance.impf
      Ábíníí   bé-side   nsóó...
      2.other   2-throw.impf 3.jubilation
      'They eat, tell stories, sing and dance. Others intone a jubilation...'

8.5.2 Or-coordination

The conjunction *káa* 'or' (also *ngéɛ*) is used in "or-coordination" to indicate an alternative. These conjunctions can be used for coordinating clauses (592)–(594), (596) as well as phrases (595).

(592) **Bé-m-bē̄   bé-sale   mɔ́   mekon,   bé-lōŋnē**
      2-PAST-be 2-cut.IMPF 1.PRO   6.pole   2-build.with.CONS
      ndáb   káa   bé-bɛnlé   mɔ́   áyɔ̄le hyǒn.
      10.houses   or   2-use.CONS 6.PRO as 19.firewood
      'They were cutting poles for him, and built houses with them or used them for firewood.'

The alternative expressed may be in relation to polarity (593)–(594), subject, verb (595), object, location (596), etc.

(593) **Láá sé ké mod á-sábe káa e-sápé'.**
tell.IMP 2PL.PRO whether 1.person 1-pay.HORT or 1.NEG-pay.IMPF.IMP
'Tell us whether the person should pay or not.'

(594) **Me-bíí'ɛ́ ké mě-chěm mɔ́ káa**
1SG.NEG-know.SF whether 1SG.FUT-recognise 1.PRO or
mê-chemmɛ́.
1SG.NEG.FUT-recognise.SF
'I don't know if I will recognise him or not.'

(595) **M-bíí-'ɛ nén mě bé-ˈchámé sóo**
1SG-know.PERF-ADD COMP 1SG.RP 2.FUT-cook.APP 1PL.2SG.PRO
ngun káa bé-nyáŋ.
10.corn or 2-fry
'I also know that they will either cook corn for us or fry it.'

In "or-coordination," the part that is the same in both alternatives is often elided in the second alternative (as *ngun* 'corn' in (595)).

(596) **Me-bíí'ɛ́ ké á Nninɔɔ á-m-bēē káa héé.**
1SG.NEG-know.SF whether LOC Ninong 1-PAST-be or where
'I don't know whether he was in Ninong or somewhere else.'

8.5.3 But-coordination

Denied alternatives are also expressed by juxtaposition (597), the relationship between the two clauses being derived from the meaning of the individual clauses. However, the conjunction *baŋ/boŋ* 'then, but' can also be used to link the two clauses, though the meaning 'but' is not inherent to this conjunction but is derived from the context (598).

(597) **Ě-kaké ásō, a-timne mbíd.**
1.NEG-go.SF ahead 1-return.with back
'He does not go forward, but backwards.'

(598) **Bé-hɔ̂ŋlaad aláá, boŋ bé-tīntēē dɔ́.**
2-roll.IMPF 5.stone but 2.NEG-push.CAUS.IMPF.SF 5.PRO
'They roll the stone, but don't push it.'

8.5.4 Temporal sequence

There are a number of ways temporal sequences are indicated. Simple juxtaposition (599) is very common. The conjunction that indicates temporal sequence is *boŋ* 'then' (600) with its variants *baŋ* (601), *boŋkên* and *baŋkên*. In (601) and (602), the tense of the second verb is future, but the clause introduced by *baŋ* has the sense 'before' with the same time reference as in the first clause.

(599) **A-húd,   á-tīmēd áwī,   á-pɛ   á   ndáb   te   ámpē...**
1-remove 1-transfer LOC.his 1-arrive LOC house in again
'He takes it out, transfers it to his own (trap), he arrives at the house...'

(600) **Ngáne   nguu é-pédé   hén,   boŋ   á-sɛté   mɔ́   aá...**
as 9.pig O.9-come.PERF here then 1-ask.CONS 1.PRO 3SG.RP
'As pig arrived here, she asked him...'

(601) **...kɔ́ɔ́ŋ   ḿ-mád mbum   a-hɔ́ŋ,   baŋ   ă-hɔ̄b   aá**
till 3-finish 9.seed INF-be.round then 1.FUT-say 3SG.RP
nsɛsú   ń-dé   mɔ́   ékuu.
3.jigger 3-be 1.PRO LOC.7.foot
'...when it has become a lump, he will say that he has a jigger in his foot.'

(602) **Sê-pedé   áwed,   baŋ   mbúu   ĕ-bootéd   a-chɔ́.**
1PL-arrive.PERF there then 9.rain 9.FUT-start INF-fall
'We will reach there before it will start to rain.'

8.5.5 Prior action

Whether an event took place *before* another can be indicated in two different ways. One is by marking the clause expressing the subsequent action with the conjunction *boŋ/boŋkên* and the verb in the future tense (603).

(603) **A-húd,   á-tīmēd   áwī,   á-pɛ   á   ndáb   te   ámpē,**
1-remove 1-transfer LOC.his 1-arrive LOC house in again
boŋkên ă-nyĕm   ngəə   ásē.
then 1.FUT-wake.up 1.leopard.PERS down
'He removed it, transferred it to his own trap, arrived home before he woke up Loepard.'

Another way of explicitly indicating prior action is where the subsequent action is marked on the verb with the *dê-* prefix (604)–(606) (see also section 4.6.7.6). The order of the two clauses may be reversed (606).

(604) **Mě-kě** é⁺hálé, <u>ngandembúú e-dê-pě.</u>
 1SG.FUT-go LOC.7.Douala 9.Christmas 9-SUBS-arrive
 'I will go to Douala before Christmas.'

(605) **Sé-kaá** é⁺hálé, <u>ngandembúú e-dê-pě.</u>
 1PL.NEG.FUT-go.SG LOC.7.Douala 9.Christmas 9-SUBS-arrive
 'We will not go to Douala before Christmas.'

(606) <u>**Ngandembúú e-dê-pě,**</u> mě-kě é⁺hálé.
 9.Christmas 9-SUBS-arrive 1SG.FUT-go LOC.7.Douala
 'Before Christmas, I will go to Douala.'

8.5.6 Beginning and end points

There are two conjunctions used to introduce clauses that constitute the beginning or the end points of an action: *kɔ́ɔ́ŋ* 'until' (607)–(609) and *taa/ etaa* 'since' (610)–(613).

(607) **Bé-kálé póle hê,** <u>kɔ́ɔ́ŋ sê-kɔ́m.</u>
 2-tell.PERF 10.story there until 1PL-be.tired
 'They told stories until we were tired.'

(608) **A-bédé á díí sé wê ámpē,** <u>kɔ́ɔ́ŋ á-pē á ndáb.</u>
 1-be.PERF LOC 5.palm under there again until 1-go LOC 9.house
 'He was again under the palm tree until he went home.'

(609) **Nɛɛ bé-ké-bóó'é,** <u>kɔ́ɔ́ŋ áde bé-nyéné bán é-máá</u>
 as 2-PRIOR-break.SF until when O.2-see.PERF PL.RP 7-finish
 a-pɛ átintê bɔb.
 INF-reach LOC.middle now
 'They split (cocoa) until (when) they saw that they had done half of it.'

(610) **Bé-⁺nyénéé enyɛn** <u>taa</u> **bé-sɔ́lé.**
 2.NEG-see.PERF.SF 7.sun since 2-enter.PERF
 'They hadn't seen the sun since they entered.'

8.5 Other clause combinations 229

(611) **Aá ken taa mə̂-n-húú, a-bón kə́ŋ se bwéed?**
3SG.RP Q since LOG-PAST-return 1-shout until right long.before
'He asked whether since he returned he has been shouting for a long time.'

(612) **Me-nyénéé wɛ, taa de-húɛ ámbīd á**
1SG.NEG-see.IMPF.SF 2SG.PRO since 1+2-return.IMPF LOC.back LOC
Yawonde.
Yaoundé
'I haven't seen you since we returned from Yaoundé.'

(613) **Etaa de-húɛ ámbīd á Yawonde, me-nyénéé**
since 1+2-return.IMPF LOC.back LOC Yaoundé 1SG.NEG-see.IMPF.SF
wɛ.
2SG.PRO
'Since we returned from Yaoundé, I haven't seen you.'

8.5.7 Purpose

Purpose is expressed by means of infinitive clauses (614)–(617) which always follow the main clause (for infinitives see sections 4.6.5 and 5.6). There is a small pause between the two clauses, and the subject in both main and purpose clauses is the same.

(614) **Mod asyəə́l a-n-sú á ndáb, á-boŋsɛn nsɔn ḿmī.**
1.person 1.all 1-PAST-return LOC house INF-prepare 3.work 3.his
'Everybody went home to prepare his work.'

(615) **M-pém-'ɛ mpage ḿ mbaaŋgé á nló, á-kɛɛn**
1SG-carry-ADD 4.sucker 4.AM 10.cocoayam LOC 3.head INF-take
á Bekúme.
LOC Bekume
'I also carried cocoyam suckers on my head, to take them to Bekume.'

(616) **Ngo a-tóm mehélé áhîn tê á-kɛ dé á-tán**
9.tiger 1-pass quickly LOC.5.bush in INF-go 5.AM INF-meet
mwǎnyaŋ.
1.brother
'The tiger quickly ran into the forest to meet his brother.'

(617) **Sé-n-kĕ áhīn mbwɛ ń sátedé, á-hūd dé**
1PL-PAST-go LOC.5.bush 3.day 3.AM Saturday INF-remove 5.AM
mélám ásē á Kupéɛ.
6.trap down LOC Kupe
'We went to the forest on Saturday to remove the traps at Mt. Kupe.'

Purpose clauses can also be more integrated into the main clause as in (618)–(620) (see also section 5.6).

(618) **A-kií mendíb a-bwəŋ.**
1-go.PERF 6.water INF-draw
'He went to draw water.'

(619) **bad ábe bé-hyɛ sé éché kaké a-hɔdɛn**
2.people 2.REL 2-come 2PL.PRO 10.DEM 10.cocoa INF-remove.from.shell
'people who came to remove for us the cocoa from the shells'

(620) **Edímékəl é-lómé me nkwĕ a-téd élōm.**
7.spirit 7-send.PERF 1SG.PRO 3.salt INF-take LOC.7.hole
'The spirit sent me to take salt from the hole.'

There is third way of expressing purpose. When subjects of the two clauses are different, the clause or sentence that expresses purpose is introduced by a minor purpose clause *ábɛl nén* 'so that' (621)–(622).

(621) **Nzé a-wóó mɔné, a-hɛle á-bɛ mɔ́, á-bɛl nén**
if 1-have.PERF 3.money 1-can 1-give 1.PRO INF-do that
ádê hŏm á-suuned mɔ́.
5.that 5.place 5-return.HORT 1.PRO
'If he has money, he can give it to him, so that the place returns to his ownership.'

(622) **Ndyéd eché e-boó chê bé-bagɛɛ́ mɔ́, á-bɛl nén**
9.food 9.REL 9-be.good 9.TOP 2-give.IMPF.SF 1.PRO INF-do that
á-wôŋ yŏl e bwâm.
1-have.HORT 9.body 9.AM good
'It is the good food they give her with the purpose of making her strong.'

In (623), the purpose clause, which typically follows the main clause, is fronted.

(623) **Á-nyīme**   nkog   ámīn, etɔ́l   é-nyênnedɛɛ́   ké
      INF-cross.over 3.log up   7.space 7.NEG-be.seen.PERF.SF   even
      mwătiíd.
      little
      'For crossing over the log, not even a small space can be seen.'

8.5.8 Reason and cause

A clause that expresses reason is typically introduced by *áyɔ̄le* 'because'[5] and follows the main clause.

(624) **Mod-té**   **a-mwédé**   tɔ́mbɛlɛ   nhɔ́gé   nhɔ́gé, **áyɔ̄le**
      1.person-each   1-drink.PERF 9.glass   9.one   9.one   because
      bad   **bé-m-buú.**
      2.people   2-PAST-be.many
      'Each person drank only one glass, because there were many people.'

(625) **Hê**   **e'sélɛ**   **nyamɛ**   **á-tímé**   **a-bíd**   **á**
      there   14.duiker   9.animal.PERS   O.1-at.last.PERF INF-come.out   LOC
      kwééd te,   **áyɔ̄le**   **nyɛ̆**   **sáŋkala debyéé**   **awɛ̆**   **a-wóó.**
      9.death in   because   1.very   1.big   5.wisdom   1.REL   1-have.PERF
      'Then the duiker at last escaped death because of his very great wisdom.'

When a reason clause precedes the main clause, it is introduced by *ngáne*, *née* or *néngāne* 'as' (626)–(629). The verbs in clauses beginning with *ngáne*, *née* or *néngāne* take the dependent form (see section 4.6.3).

(626) **Ngáne**   **bé-n-lāā'ɛ̄**   sé   bán   séɛ̄-naá   á   Lobɛɛ,
      as   O.2-PAST-tell.SF   2PL.PRO   PL.RP   1PL.FUT-sleep LOC   Lobe
      nê   **á-bélé**   **sê-wâmsɛnɛɛ́**   **a-syəə**   á   **Kómbé.**
      that   O.1-make.PERF   1PL.NEG-hurry.PERF.SF   INF-leave   LOC   Kumba
      'Since they told us that we will sleep at Lobe, we didn't hurry to leave Kumba.'

(627) **Ngáne**   **bad**   **bé-nkê-m-bommé**   á   **móto,**
      as   2.people   2-NEG-PAST-meet.SF   LOC   6.car
      nê   **á-bel**   **ndulémóto á-kēēn**   sé   á   **Mbongɛ.**
      this   INF-make   1.driver   1-take   1PL.PRO   LOC   Mbonge
      'Since the people didn't meet at the car, the driver took us to Mbonge.'

---

[5]Another conjunction with the same function is *ebánjá* 'because' (a loan word from Douala).

(628) **Nɛɛ** nyag é-wúú nló áte, nzé bé-bágé
as 9.cowo.9-strong.PERF 3.head inside if 2-give.PERF
bɔ́ mebíi mé nyag, né bɔ̂ bê-wúú'ɛ
2.PRO 6.milk 6.AM 9.cow then 2.PRO 2.FUT.NEG-be.strong.SF
nló áte=e?
3.head in=Q
'Since cows are stubborn, if one gives cows milk to them (the children), won't they become stubborn?'

(629) Aá **néngāne** mwéē á-kwágté me, aá me
3SG.RP as friend O.1-shame.PERF 1.PRO 3SG.RP 1SG.PRO
ámpē mě-kwāgēd mɔ́.
also 1SG.FUT-shame 1.PRO
'Since my friend embarrassed me, so I will embarrass him too.'

8.5.9 Result

Result clauses are introduced by the minor clause *nê á-bélé*, *nê á-bɛl* 'that made' (630)–(631). Subject agreement in the minor clause is *á-* of class 5 suggesting that the first clause is seen as the subject. Class 5 is often used for adverbial expressions.

(630) **Ngáne bé-n-lāā'ē** sé bán, séē-naá á Lobɛɛ, **nê**
as O.2-PAST-tell.SF 2PL PL.RP 2PL.FUT-sleep LOC Lobe that
á-bélé sê-wâmsɛnɛé a-syəə á Kómbé
5-make.PERF 2PL.NEG-hurry.PERF.SF INF-leave LOC Kumba
'Since they told us that we will sleep at Lobe, we didn't hurry to leave Kumba.'

(631) **Ngáne bad bé-nkêm-bommé á mŏto, nê**
as 2.people 2-PAST.NEG-meet.SF LOC 9.car this
á-bɛl ndulémóto á-kēēn sé á Mbongɛ
5-made 1.driver he-took us to Mbonge
'Since the people didn't meet at the car, the driver took us to Mbonge.'

The result clause may be unmarked when it precedes the reason clause as in (632)–(633).

8.5 Other clause combinations

(632) **Mod-té   a-mwédé   tómbɛlɛ   nhógé nhógé, áyɔ̄le**
      1.person-each 1-drink.PERF 1.glass 1.one 1.one because
      bad   bé-m-buú.
      2.people 2-PAST-be.many
      'Each person drank one glass, because there were many people.'

(633) **Hê   e'sélɛ   nyamɛ   á-tímé   a-bíd   á**
      there 14.duiker 9.animal.PERS o.1-at.last.PERF INF-come.out LOC
      kwééd te, áyɔ̄le   nyɛ́ sánkala debyéé awɛ̌ a-wóó.
      9.death in because 1.very 1.big 5.wisdom 1.REL 1-have.PERF
      'The duiker in the end escaped death because of his great wisdom.'

(634) **Ngo   ě-chué'ɛ́   á-bíd   á   dyad tê   ámpē, á-bāŋ**
      9.tiger 9.NEG-dare.SF INF-come.out LOC 5.town in again INF-fear
      á   bad.
      5.AM 2.people
      'The tiger dreaded to come back to town for fear of the people.'

The result may also be introduced by *áyɔ̄le nɛ́n* 'because of this' (635)–(636).

(635) **Áyɔ̄le   nɛ́n... ene   káne   e   mmwaád a-bɛlé**
      because this 9.that 9.kind 9.AM 1.woman 1-always.PERF
      á-kudé   metake   ámbīd   e   póndé.
      1-get.CONS 6.suffering LOC.9.back 9.AM 9.time
      'Because if this...this kind of woman always suffers afterwards.'

(636) **...áyɔ̄le   nɛ́n bé-bɛlé   bé-hēdē   mɔ́ mwǎ melâm.**
      because this 2-always.CONS 2-put.CONS 1.PRO 1.small 6.whiskey
      '...because of this they always give him a small whiskey.'

8.5.10 Means

Means is expressed by the causative expression *-kɔ̌ŋ boŋkên* (637) and (638).

(637) **Lǎl   chɔ̂   é-kɔ̌ŋ   boŋkên   a-bíd   échōg   te wê.**
      9.ladder 9.FOC o.9-cause that 1-come.out LOC.7.hole in there
      'The ladder helped him come out of the hole.'

Means may also be expressed in relative clauses:

(638) **Chom=ɛɛ é-kɔ̌ŋ boŋkên a-bíd echōg te wê, é-saá.**
7.thing=REL 7-cause that 1-come.out LOC.7.hole in there 7-not.be
'There was nothing with which to climb out of the hole.'

8.5.11 Concessive

Concessive clauses are introduced by *kénéɛ* 'even though, although'. This marker appears to be composed of *ké* 'even, if' plus *néɛ* 'as, like'. The concessive clause may precede or follow the main clause (639)–(641).

(639) **Bé-bɔme mɔ́ áyɔ̄le echîb, kénéɛ a-dé a-chíbɛ.**
2-beat.IMPF 1.PRO because 7.theft still 1-be 1-steal.IMPF
'They beat him because of theft, but still he keeps stealing.'

(640) **Kénéɛ é-nyénɛé ḿmê mepɔke nê, ké mə mɔ̂-dyáké.**
even.though 2SG-see.IMPF.SF 6.that 6.fine.food that even 1.PRO
LOG.NEG-eat.IMPF.SF
'Even though you see this nice food, I don't eat any.'

(641) **Séē-tagɛé, kénéɛ sé-kágáá hom=ɛɛ sê-kíí'é.**
1.PL.NEG-suffer.IMPF.SF even.though 1.PL-go.IMPF.past 5.place=REL
1PL.NEG-go.PERF.SF
'We don't suffer, even though we were going to a place we have not gone before.'

Another type of concessive is formed by *ké...né* 'even though' where the concessive clause is marked by *ké* and the second clause is marked by *né* (642)–(643).

(642) **Ké ndyéd=ɛɛ́ é-dyēdɛé hén, né ǎ-dyē hǒm démpēe.**
even.if 9.food=TOP 1.NEG-eat.PERF.SF here then 1.FUT-eat
5.place 5.other
'Even if he doesn't eat food here, he will eat in another place.'

8.5 Other clause combinations

(643) **Ké** akwɛ dɜ̂ **â-n-kwě,** **né** ǎ-kɜ̌g mwě ḿme
even.if 5.fall 5.TOP O.1-past-fall then 1.FUT-try 3.year 3.REL
ń-húɛ'ɛ.
3-come.IMPF.SF
'Even if he fails his exams, he will try next year.'

8.5.12 Contra-expectation

Contra-expectation may be unmarked except for the fact that the verb is negative. However, when it is in focus, it can be marked by the conjunction *baŋ* 'but' as in (644)–(645).

(644) **Aá á-chəg** mɔ́ mbəŋ, **kénɛɛ** ngəə
1.RP1-call.HORT 1.PRO 3.nickname although 9.leopard.PERS
ě-hɛlɛé ḿmê mbəŋ a-chəg
1.NEG-can.PERF.SF 3.that 3.nickname INF-call
'He said that he should call him names, even though Leopard wasn't able to do it.'

(645) **N-dímté** akâŋled á múú, baŋ dé-kwɛntɛnɛɛ
1SG-put.out.PERF 5.ember 5.AM 3.fire but 5.NEG-agree.PERF.SF
a-dím.
INF-go.out
'I tried to put out the embers of the fire, but they wouldn't go out.'

8.5.13 Circumstantial

The following three ways to express a circumstantial clause have been noted: the circumstantial clause is introduced with *áde/ê* (646)–(648); it is introduced with *kuné* 'not-knowing, perhaps' (649)–(651); and with *ésebán* 'without' (652).

(646) **Cheé á-nyéné** me á yɔ̌l, **áde** á-pake
what O.1-see.PERF 1SG.PRO LOC 9.body 6.REL O.1-arrive.IMPF.SF
me a-hɔ́bɛn nén?
1SG.PRO INF-talk.with thus
'What do you see in me, that you begin to abuse me like that?'

(647) **A-chénlédáá** mɔ́ mwǎnyaŋ, **ê** bé-bɔ́mé mɔ́ bwɛl.
1-call.for.IMPF.SF 1.PRO 1.brother as 2-beat.PERF 1.PRO 14.stick
'He called his brother, when they beat him with a stick.'

(648) Sé   bán   séē̄-pě   áwed,   né   m-maá
     1PL.PRO PL.RP 1PL.FUT-reach there   then   1SG-finish.PERF
     a-chiited   wê ekwan,   ê̂   n-kɔ́mé.
     INF-be.soft like pudding   as   1SG-be.tired.PERF
     'Before we arrived there, I was soft like pudding since I was tired.'

(649) A-wógé   esaád   nkuu   nén,   kuné   mwǎn   a-wédé.
     1-hear.PERF 7.shout 3.night this   not.knowing   1.child 1-die.PERF
     'He heard shouting in the night, not knowing that the child had died.'

(650) Kɔ́ŋné ásōg   mbwé   é-timé   a-bíd   hŏm
     until LOC.5.end 9.dog   9-at.last.CONS INF-come.out   5.place
     ahɔ́g,   kuné   mbɔm   chô   bé-naneé.
     5.one not.knowing   9.python 9.TOP O.2-chase.IMPF.SF
     'Until at the end the dog came out one place, not knowing it was the python he was chasing.'

(651) Bán,   "A-mwéē̄,   mbwé   e   benyamé kě   á-nɔn
     2.RP   VOC-friend 9.dog 9.AM   ancestor go.IMP   1-see.HORT
     syáā̄   ekide   áte   kuné   mod   nhɔ́g a-dé hê   bɔɔb."
     1+2.PL.PRO 7.place   into   maybe   1.person 1.one 1-be here now
     'They (said), "Friend, dog, go look at the place for us perhaps there is one person there now."'

(652) A-wɛ́, ésebán   a-cháá   mwǎn.
     1-die without 1-bear.PERF   1.child
     'She died, without having borne a child.'

8.5.14 Conditional

Conditional clauses are typically introduced by *nzé* 'if, when' (653)–(657).

(653) Nzé   a-n-tán   nyam   á   mbéé wê   ngəə,   a-húd,
     if   1-PAST-meet   9.animal LOC trap of   1.leopard.PERS 1-remove
     á-tīmēd   áwī.
     1-return.CONS LOC.his
     'If he came across an animal in the trap of the leopard, he would remove it and put it into his own.'

8.5 Other clause combinations

(654) Aá **nzé** nyam e-hɔ́be dyam nê, aa
1.RP if 9.animal 9-say.IMPF 5.something like.this 1.RP
e-tyɔ́géé a-kɛ.
9.NEG-difficult.IMPF.SF INF-go
'If an animal says something like this, it will easily escape.'

(655) **Nzé** mbeé e-léné mendíb, e-hé mémpée.
if 9.pot 9-dry.up.PERF 6.water 2SG-put 6.other
'If the water dries up, you put more.'

(656) **Nzé** bé-hīde échê mbéndé á mbīd,
if S.2.NEG-follow.PERF 10.those 10.law LOC back
é-yɔ́ké a-bé nén mwǎn á-kud mbéb.
10-always.PERF INF-be COMP 1.child 1-get 9.bad
'If they don't follow these laws, bad will always happen to the child.'

(657) **Pɔpé** e-kútɛ', **nzé** ĕ-yəge bwâm.
9.papaya 9-crack.APP.IMPF if S.9.NEG-ripe.PERF well
'The papaya is cracking, if it is not fully ripe.'

The clause that follows the condition is often unmarked, but it may be marked by *né* 'then' (658)–(660) giving the structure *nzé...né* 'if...then'.

(658) **Nzé** akwɛ=ɛ́ɛ́ á-kwédé, **né** ê-kəké mwĕ ḿme
if 5.fall=TOP O.1-fall.PERF then 1.NEG.FUT-try.SF 3.year 3.REL
ń-húɛ'-ɛ?
3-come.IMPF-Q
'If he fails his exam, will he not try next year?'

(659) **Nzé** kúb e-kɔ́gté bǎn saámbé, **né** e-kəgé.
if 9.hen 9-hatch.PERF 2.child seven then 9-succeed.PERF
'If a hen hatches seven chicks, it has been successful.'

(660) **Nzé** nsóó ń-sídté, **né** akan á-bóó.
if 3.ululation 3-throw.CAUS.PERF then 5.thing 5-be.good.PERF
'If nsoo has been sung, then things are good.'

Negative conditions are introduced by *ésebán*, *ésebé* 'unless, only if, without'. Compare (661) with (662).

(661) **Maa   mê-sábéé   wɛ   mɔné   ámpē, ésebán**
      1SG.PRO.DEV 1SG.NEG.FUT-pay.IMPF.SF 2SG.PRO 3.money again unless
      e-peenédé   awêm   mwaád ádī   aláá   á   ndóŋ.
      2SG-bring.PERF 1.my   1.wife 5.her 5.stone 5.AM 9.pepper
      'I will not pay you until you return my wife's grinding stone.'

(662) **Mĕ-sāb   wɛ   mɔné,   ésebán e-peenédé   awêm**
      1SG.FUT-pay 2SG.PRO 3.money only.if 2SG-bring.PERF 1.my
      mwaád ádī   aláá   á   ndóŋ.
      1.wife 5.her 5.stone 5.AM 9.pepper
      'I will pay you only if you return my wife's grinding stone.'

The above listing is not exhaustive. There are other connectives which I have not illustrated, as for example, *nzé se* 'if not'.

8.6 Comparative clauses

Comparatives may consist of two complete clauses as in (663). However, most of the time the part introduced by the conjunction *tóma* 'more than' is less then a clause, e.g. an NP.

(663) **A-yəgɛ   ngáne etón   é-yəgɛé.**
      1-be.red.IMPF like 7.eton.fruit o.7-red.IMPF.SF
      'It is as red as the eton fruit.'

8.7 Summary list of conjunctions

áde, â, ê	'as, when'
áyɔ̄le	'because'
baŋ	'and, then, but'
baŋkên	'then'
bə́	'and, with'
boŋ	'then, but, before'
boŋkên	'then, before'
bɔɔpəá, bɔɔpɔɔ́ (< bɔɔb + -'ə́/-'ɔ́)	'now then'
də́ə̄	'then'
ebánjá	'because'
ésebán	'without, unless'
ésebé	'unless'
hâ, háā (< hê + -'aa´ ?)	'then, so'

8.7 Summary list of conjunctions

hɛ́ dɔ́ə	'from thence'
hɛ́ɛ, hɛ́ɛ̄ (< hɛ̂ + -'ɔ́ ?)	'then, so then'
káa	'or'
ké	'whether, if, even if'
kénɛ́ɛ	'although, even so'
kɔ́ɔ́ŋ	'until'
kɔ́ŋse	'right into'
kuné	'not knowing, perhaps'
ndíí	'since'
ne	'and'
né	'then'
nédē (< nê + adé)	'so, that is'
nɛ́ɛ	'as, when'
né-'ɔ́ɔ́	'therefore, so'
ngé	'or'
nzáa (< nzé + -'aa?)	'or'
nzé	'if, when'
taa, etaa	'since'

9

Negation

Akɔɔse has mainly clausal negation. There is no constituent negation. There are a few lexical items that are negated by reduplication.

9.1 Clause negation

Both verbal and non-verbal clauses can be negated.

9.1.1 Verbal clauses

Negation in verbal clauses is expressed morphologically in the verb. It involves a combination of a verb prefix, tonal changes and an extra suffix in certain cases. There are four prefixes indicating negative: *e-*, *nkê-*, *se-* and *de-*. The first is the most common in that it appears in most verb forms. It is also the most elusive as it merges with other prefixes (person/concord and tense markers) and can only be isolated by internal reconstruction (Hedinger 1985a).

To illustrate the *e-* prefix, the following examples of the perfect and present imperfective are given, contrasting the affirmative form with the corresponding negative. As can be seen, the *a-* changes to *e-* in the negative, the negative also has an extra suffix, and the tone on the aspect suffix changes to the opposite from the inherent tone. (For more examples see sections 4.6.6.1–4.6.6.4.)

(664) a-wɔ́g-é   <   a- wɔ́g-é   'he/she washed'
       e-wɔ́g-ɛέ   <   a-e-wɔ́g-e-'ɛ́   'he/she didn't wash'

(665) a-wɔ́g-ɛ'   <   a- wɔ́g-ɛ'   'he/she is washing'
       e-wɔ́g-έέ   <   a-e-wɔ́g-έ'-'ɛ́   'he/she isn't washing'

The marker *nkê-* only occurs in the past perfective negative verb form together with the negative marker *e-* (compare (666) with (667)). See also section 4.6.6.5–4.6.6.6.

(666) **a-n-wɔ́g**   'he/she washed'

(667) **e-nkê-n-wɔ́gké**   'he/she didn't wash'

The suffix found in each of the negative forms above, although present in each of the forms here, cannot be considered a negative suffix as it is not present in the dependent S-forms of these verbs (see section 4.6.2), and it also appears in positive dependent forms (see section 4.6.3).

The prefix *se-* appears only in the neutral negative (668); compare with the affirmative forms in (669). See also sections 4.6.7.1–4.6.7.2.

(668) **a-se-pĭm**   'he/she doesn't throw it away'
      1-NEG-throw

(669) **á-pim**   'he/she throws it away'
      á-ˈpím

The prefix *dɛ-* appears only in the negative prohibitive (see section 4.7.6).

(670) **á-dɛ-pĭm**   'let him not throw away'
      1-NEG-throw

9.1.2   The verb 'to be'

The verb 'to be', in addition to the fully regular forms based on *-bé* (see stem type 13 in table 4.13), has an irregular form *-dé* for which the negative is *-saá* and related forms (see section 6.2.1).

(671) **ĕ-saa**   'he/she is not'
      a-dé   'he/she is'

9.2 Non-verbal clauses

Non-verbal clauses are negated with the particle *saké* 'it is not', which has a dialectal variant *haké*. The demonstrative pronoun can be omitted as in (672b), or present as in (673).

(672) a. **Ndáb   nén.**   'This is a house.'
         9.house   9.DEM

    b. **Saké   ndáb.**   'This isn't a house.'
         NEG   9.house

(673)   **Saké   ndáb   nén.**   'This isn't a house.'
         NEG   9.house   9.DEM

9.3 Lexical negation

At the lexical level, there are no morphemes to change the inherent lexical meaning into the opposite. However, there are a few generic nouns which, when reduplicated, have negative meaning.

(674) **modmod**   'nobody'   see   **mod**   'person'
      chŏmchŏm   'nothing'   see   **chŏm**   'thing'
      dyamdyam   'nothing'   see   **dyam**   'thing/matter'

Whenever they are used, the accompanying verb is always negative, too. It could therefore be said that reduplication is not the sole indicator of negation.

(675) **Nyaá   mɔ́-'ɛ   e-lângɛɛ́   mɔ́   dyamdyam.**
      1.mother   1.PRO-ADD   1.NEG-tell.PERF.SF 1.PRO nothing
      'Mother she too didn't tell him anything.'

9.4 Miscellaneous negative items

There are several lexical items that have a negative component, most of them introduced elsewhere. They are listed here for completeness' sake.

Example (676) is equivalent to an echo question in English, seeking confirmation from the interlocutor after making a statement (see sections 7.2.3 and 7.2.4).

(676) ...saá nέε?   '...is it not?'

The following three examples show negative conjunctions. Example (677) is a conjunction, with a meaning that could be paraphrased with the negative form of the verb 'to know'. It comes at the beginning of a clause.

(677) **Kuné...**   'Not knowing...'

Example (678) is a conjunction and preposition which appears to be derived from the neutral negative form of the verbs 'to be' and 'to put'.

(678) **ésebé, ésebán**   'unless, without'

Example (679) is a negative conjunction, consisting of the conjunction *nzé* and the negative particle *se*.

(679) **nzé se**   'if not'

Example (680) looks like it might be an ideophone or adverb. We have only two examples.

(680) **ndindɔ́ndɔg**   'unconcerned, unresponsive, no reply'

Appendix A
Lexical Notes and Special Word Forms

A.1. Numerals

Below is a sample of numerals. The first section lists the numerals as they are used for counting; the second section lists them as they appear in a noun phrase with the noun *mod/bad* 'person/people'.

Because of the influence of English, people rarely use this numeral system. This means that the larger numerals are seldom used, and children often have difficulty using them correctly.

Numerals used for counting

1	e'hóg
2	é'bɛ
3	é'láán
4	é'niin
5	é'táan
6	ntóób
7	saámbé
8	waam
9	abog

10	dyôm
20	móóbɛ
30	mô méláán
40	mô méniin
50	mô métáan
60	mô mé ntóób
70	mô mé saámbé
80	mô mé waam
90	mô mé abóg
100	mbwókɛl (póg)
200	mbwókɛl ébɛ
400	mbwókɛl éniin
1000	ekálé (éhóg)
2000	e'kálé é'bɛ
1 million	edun

Numerals used in a noun phrase

1 person	mod nhóg		
10 people	mod/bad dyôm		
11 people	mod/bad dyôm ne nhóg	or	dyôm á mod/bad ne nhóg
12 people	mod/bad dyôm ne bébɛ		
13 people	mod/bad dyôm ne béláán		
14 people	mod/bad dyôm ne béniin		
15 people	mod/bad dyôm ne bétáan		
16 people	mod/bad dyôm ne ntóób		
17 people	mod/bad dyôm ne saámbé		
18 people	mod/bad dyôm ne waam		
19 people	mod/bad dyôm ne abog		
20 people	mod/bad móobɛ	or	mô mé bad mébɛ
21 people	mod/bad móobɛ ne nhóg	or	mô mé bad mébɛ ne mod nhóg
27 people	mod/bad móobɛ ne saámbé		
30 people	mod/bad mô méláán	or	mô mé bad méláán
70 people	mod/bad mô mé saámbé	or	mô mé bad saámbé
99 people	mod/bad mô mé abog ne abog	or	mô mé bad mébɛ abog ne abog
100 people	mod/bad mbwókɛl		
101 people	mod/bad mbwókɛl póg ne nhóg		
102 people	mod/bad mbwókɛl póg ne bébɛ		
106 people	mod/bad mbwókɛl póg ne ntóób		

Lexical Notes and Special Word Forms

110 people	mod/bad mbwɔ́kɛl pɔ́g ne dyôm
111 people	mod/bad mbwɔ́kɛl pɔ́g ne (mod/bad) dyôm ne nhɔ́g
112 people	bad mbwɔ́kɛl pɔ́g ne dyôm ne bébɛ
118 people	mbwɔ́kɛl e mod pɔ́g ne (bad/mod) dyôm ne waam
120 people	mbwɔ́kɛl e mod pɔ́g ne (bad/mod) mô mébɛ
121 people	mbwɔ́kɛl e mod pɔ́g ne (bad/mod) mô mébɛ ne nhɔ́g
122 people	mbwɔ́kɛl e mod pɔ́g ne (bad/mod) mô mébɛ ne bébɛ
129 people	mbwɔ́kɛl e mod pɔ́g ne (bad/mod) mô mébɛ ne abog
200 people	mbwɔ́kɛl é bad ébɛ *or* bad mbwɔ́kɛl ébɛ
201 people	mbwɔ́kɛl é bad ébɛ ne mod nhɔ́g
202 people	mbwɔ́kɛl é bad ébɛ ne bad bébɛ
203 people	mbwɔ́kɛl é bad ébɛ ne bad béláán
206 people	mbwɔ́kɛl é bad ébɛ ne bad ntóób
210 people	mbwɔ́kɛl é bad ébɛ ne bad dyôm
220 people	mbwɔ́kɛl é bad ébɛ ne bad mô mébɛ
221 people	mbwɔ́kɛl é bad ébɛ ne mô mé bad mébɛ ne nhɔ́g
222 people	mbwɔ́kɛl é bad ébɛ ne mô mé bad mébɛ ne bébɛ
223 people	mbwɔ́kɛl é bad ébɛ ne mô mé bad mébɛ ne béláán
226 people	mbwɔ́kɛl é bad ébɛ ne mô mé bad mébɛ ne ntóób
1000 people	ékɔ́lé é mod ehɔ́g *or* bad ekɔ́lé ehɔ́g
1001 people	ékɔ́lé é mod ehɔ́g ne (mod) nhɔ́g
1002 people	ékɔ́lé é mod ehɔ́g ne (bad) bébɛ
1009 people	ékɔ́lé é mod ehɔ́g ne (bad) abog
1010 people	ékɔ́lé é mod ehɔ́g ne (bad) dyôm
1017 people	ékɔ́lé é mod ehɔ́g ne (bad) dyôm ne saámbé
1020 people	ékɔ́lé é mod ehɔ́g ne (bad) mô mé bad mébɛ
1021 people	ékɔ́lé é mod ehɔ́g ne (bad) mô mé bad mébɛ ne nhɔ́g
1023 people	ékɔ́lé é mod ehɔ́g ne (bad) mô mé bad mébɛ ne béláán
1029 people	ékɔ́lé é mod ehɔ́g ne (bad) mô mé bad mébɛ ne abog
1100 people	ékɔ́lé é mod ehɔ́g ne mbwɔ́kɛl pɔ́g
1101 people	ékɔ́lé é mod ehɔ́g ne mbwɔ́kɛl pɔ́g ne nhɔ́g
1102 people	ékɔ́lé é mod ehɔ́g ne mbwɔ́kɛl pɔ́g ne bébɛ
1107 people	ékɔ́lé é mod ehɔ́g ne mbwɔ́kɛl pɔ́g ne saámbé
1978 people	ékɔ́lé é mod ehɔ́g ne abog mô mé (bad) saámbé ne waam

456.789.123 francs   mbwɔ́kɛl é'dun éniin mô métáan ne ntóób, mbwɔ́kɛl e'kɔ́lé saámbé mô mé waam ne abog, mbwɔ́kɛl pɔ́g ne mô mébɛ ne frânke éláán

A.2. Ideophones

báayy 'noise of gunshot'
bamm 'completely'
báŋgélé' bəngɛlɛ' 'noise of rattles'
bóngóló ŋ 'sound of falling tree or person'
booy 'slowly'
bɔɔ́mm 'quietness'
bungudungudu 'sound of falling tree'
búrú buru 'stubbornly'
bwáŋbwaŋ 'unsteadily, recklessly'
byɔɔd 'slowly'
byɔsɔŋ 'suddenly'
chô chô chô 'movement of monkeys in a tree'
chodchod 'look frighteningly, closely'
chodchod 'step forward'
chóŋŋ 'thoughtfully'
chóo 'noise of jumping quickly'
chórɔd chórɔd chórɔd 'noise of shoes moving'
dímdim 'recklessly, foolishly'
dyôŋdyôŋ 'sound of movement'
epátepém 'suddenly, urgently'
esámsám 'suddenly, immediately'
hɔ́ɔ́ŋ 'open place'
holom 'greedily, very fast'
hólóm 'empty'
hó' hóo' 'noise of hunting'
hɔɔd 'be full to the top'
hɔ́ɔ́ɔ́' 'noise of a shout'
hɔ́ɔ́téd hɔɔted 'weak'
hududu 'running'
húdututu 'noise of pulling a rope'
húum 'start to suddenly run'
huumm 'noise of falling into a hole'
huuu huuu 'noise of vehicle approaching'

húú' 'movement of flies'
hwáb 'finish'
hwăb 'quickly'
hwɛéd 'sound of breakables smashing'
kandaam 'fearful, unprepared'
kéntén kentɛn 'meandering'
kə́géd 'properly'
kírib kírib kírib 'movement of shoes'
kôm kôm 'noise of door opening or any movement in the house'
kóm kóm kóm 'noise of beating a gong'
komm komm 'noise of hammering, knocking'
kɔ kɔ kɔ kɔ 'noise of hen'
kúdudu 'running'
kulékulɛ 'really, ready'
kúlonto kúlonto 'noise of drumming signalling danger'
kúrutu kúrutu 'noise for horse running or grinding of teeth'
kútúd 'noise of cutting wood or clearing'
kwa kwa kwa 'movement'
kwă kwă kwa 'noise of cutting or knocking at door to enter'
kwab 'dart suddenly'
kwáŋ kwáŋ 'noise of door knocking'
kwáred kwáred 'gradually, crafty'
kweb 'be firm'
kwemm 'noise of hand catching hold of'
kwɛéd 'noise of smashing nuts'
kwǒ kwǒ 'noise of hammering, knocking'
kwóngóló ŋ 'noise of something falling down'

Lexical Notes and Special Word Forms

kwóŋ 'noise of something being thrown down and landing'
kwórórórɔ 'noise of whistle or insect'
kwôy kwôy 'movement of shoes'
lambéé 'upright'
maaá' 'noise of a goat'
ḿm ḿm 'noise of a cry'
mógéd mógéd 'close together'
mpwédépwéd 'kick of a horse'
mwǎ kwab 'dart suddenly'
mwǎ peee' 'breeze'
mwed mwed 'hesitatingly'
ndindóɔndɔg 'no response'
nyoŋnyoŋ 'intenseness'
nyoŋnyoó 'buzzing'
nyɔméɛ 'slowly, quietly, privately'
'óɔmm 'óɔmm 'noise of monkeys'
paaa' paaa' 'sound of wings'
pád 'abrupt, unexpected'
pédéb 'very white'
peep 'breeze'
pídípídí 'very early'
píim 'be full to the top'
pîm 'jumping'
ponténponten 'unsteady, hurriedly,
pooy 'jumping'
posomm 'jumping on trees, appear suddenly, big'
potomm 'come suddenly'
puúb 'noise of spearing something'
puutéd puuted 'roughly, unsteadily'
pwoo 'flapping of hen's wings when held'
pworob pworob 'jumping on trees, swimming action'
pyɔɔd 'blessing of peace'

saasaa 'sparingly'
sɔndómm 'falling in water'
sss sss 'be quiet'
swáŋŋ 'far, noise of broom'
táámm 'tight'
tám tám tám 'noise of fastening firmly'
temm 'noise of falling down'
tɛléd 'suddenly, unawares'
təléd 'unawares'
tíim 'noise of falling down'
tóbó tóbó 'special'
toób 'waiting for a long time'
tóomm 'slap'
tumm 'noise of gun-shot'
tumm tumm 'noise of gun-shot or falling down'
túumm 'sound of slap'
vûb 'sound of fire catching'
wagalag 'noise of something loose'
wagél 'suddenly'
wǎŋ wǎŋ 'noise of dog in pain'
wogél 'movement'
wogléd wogled 'roughly'
wógólóŋ 'noise of dog's hunting bells'
wɔléɛɛ 'moving with difficulty like a sick person'
wɔóɔ 'noise of pain'
wudɛtɛɛ 'rain falling, moving very slowly'
wúdudu 'rain falling, movement slowly'
wulululu 'abundant flow of water'
wuuŋŋ 'glittering'
yaa 'surprise'
yɛréd yɛréd 'noise of grinding on a stone'
yiríd yiríd 'noise of grinding on a stone'

A.3. Exclamations

ákan 'expression of surprise'
alâ 'thank you!'
álobó 'friend'
anê 'surprise'
e'e 'surprise'
oô 'surprise'
óó' 'surprise'
o'ó 'alright, OK'
ɔɔɔ́ɔɔ 'surprise'

ɔ́' ɔ́' 'surprise'
ɔ'ɔ 'surprise'
wa 'surprise'
wáá' wáá' 'surprise'
wá' 'surprise'
wɛ́ɛ 'surprise'
wɛ́ɛ 'surprise'
wɛ́ɛ́' 'surprise'
wówó' 'surprise'

A.4. Loanwords

The following is a list of loanwords taken from our dictionary database. As can be seen from the list, the languages from which the words have been borrowed are as follows in descending order of importance as donor languages: English, Douala, German, Portugese, Efik and French. Not all the words have been borrowed directly from these languages. Some of the words must have come via other languages as intermediaries.

From English

ángɛl n 9/10 'angel'
ányɔ́se n 5/6 'onion'
bénze n 9/10 'bench'
blɔ̂g n 14/6 'brick, block'
blúu n 14 'bluing (<blue), bleach for washing clothes'
brêd n 14/6 'bread'
byɛ́ɛ n 1/2 'beer'
díne n 5 'dinner'
díse n 5/6 'dish'
dɔ́gtɛɛ n 1/2 'doctor, nurse, medical personnel'
dɔ́gtɛɛ n 1/2 'hospital'
elísa n 7/8 'razor blade'
esukúle n 7/8 'school'
fâm n 9/10 'farm'
frɛnsé, flɛnsé n 9 'French language'

gáádɛn n 9 'garden'
gɔ̂m n 9 'glue'
-gɔ́m v 'to stick'
háwa n 9/10 'o'clock'
-héd v 'head (a ball)'
hóbin n 9/10 'cocoa drying place, oven'
hóse n 9/10 'horse'
înke n 'ink'
kábîd n 9/10 'cabbage'
kâd n 9/10 'playing cards'
kân n 9 'kind, type'
kánsɛl n 9 'council'
kápe n 9/10 'coin (<copper)'
kápíntɛɛ n 1/2 'carpenter'
kɔ̂ŋ n 9/10 'chief, king'
kílo n 9/10 'scales, seesaw'
kísim n 9/10 'kitchen'
kóte n 9/10 'court'

Lexical Notes and Special Word Forms 251

kɔ́b n 9/10 'cup'
kɔ́bɔ̂d n 9/10 'cupboard'
kɔfí n 10 'coffee'
kɔ́led n 9/10 'college'
kɔ́tin n 9? 'cotton'
krĭstɛn n ? 'Christian'
lánroba n 9/10 'Landrover'
léta n 13/6 'letter'
-mág v 'mark, stitch'
máka n ? 'marks, embroidery'
mâl n 6 'mile'
menúte n 6 'minute'
mesíke n 6 'music, band'
mesîn n 6 'machine, train (engine), sewing machine'
metráse n 6/6 'mattress'
miítim n 6 'meeting, service'
mŏto n 6 'vehicle, car'
mɔ́nde n 9 'Monday'
mɔné n 3 'money'
ngɔ́mnaa n 1/2 'Governor, Government, D.O.'
ɔ́fîd n 9/10 'office'
pân n 9/10 'pan'
pên n 9/10 'pen'
-pɔ́m v 'spray, inflate a ball'
pulsɛ n 9/10 'police'
rádio n 9/10 'radio'
-sán v 'shine, sign'
sápe n 9/10 'shop'
sátedɛ n 1/2 'Saturday'
sílǝŋ n 9/10 'shilling'
símɛnte n 9/10 'cement'
sɔ́bele n 1/2 'spade'
-sɔ́mɛn v 'put to court (summon)'
sɔ̂ndé n 9/10 'Sunday, week'
sɔ́pe n 9/10 'soap'
sɔ́te n 9/10 'shirt'
taaku n 9/10 'tobacco, snuff'
tááse n 9/10 'tax, starch'
-táb v 'type, tap'

táblɛɛ n 1/2 'towel'
taplêd n 'tray'
téblɛ n 9/10 'table'
télɛɛ n 1/2 'tailor'
tíi n 9/10 'tea'
tomáto n 9/10 'tomato'
tɔ́mbēlē n 1/2 'glass, tumbler'
tɔɔsíd n 9/10 'trousers'
tɔ́slām n 9/10 'torch'
wínde n 9/10 'window'

From Douala

bwǎam adv 'well, good'
demute n 5 'crowd'
dyálabé n 5 'answer'
ebanban n 7/8 'trailer, carriage of train'
ebánja conj 'because'
ebómén n 7 'woe, bad luck'
edémo n 7 'fashion'
ekwále n 7/8 'confession'
elímbé n 7/8 'box'
esáó n 7 'pen'
eséngwɛn n 7 'sieve, filter'
etɔ́ɔ n 7/8 'creosote'
ewɔlɛɛ n 1/2 'greens, general word'
kaapónde prep 'as'
mbonja n 9/10 'flower'
metúdú n 6/2 'elder'
miango n 3 'story'
mumbwan n 3 'harvest'
ngande mbúú n 9/10 'Christmas'
ngǝse n 9/10 'dirge, song, melody, sad chanting'

From German

dûm n ? 'stupidity < dumm'
é'sɛl n 14/? 'donkey < Esel'
káásɛɛ n 1/2 'Caesar < Kaiser'

From Efik

akwalɛɛ n 1/2 'prostitute < ?'

From French

aviôn n 5/6 'aeroplane < avion'
frânke n 9/10 'franc'

From Portuguese

mángəle n 6 'mango, bush mango < mangueira'

etrúúkáŋ n 7/8 'lamp < etulukaŋ ?'

A.5. Seasons

There are four or five terms for different seasons in the yearly cycle. There is some disagreement as to the beginning and end of each, as well as whether there are four or five. This needs further clarification.

		Ndando Nelson (p.c.)	Haaren (1988)	Others
eseb	'dry season'	December–March	January–March	October–Febr.
nchoŋ	'showers'	March–May	April–June	March–May
mekol	'interim rains'	May–July	----	August–October
nkóg	'rainy season'	July–November	July–September	June–August
nkwog méseb	'beginning of dry season'	----	October–December	October–Nov.

A.6. Kinship terms

There are three terms which are used to refer to different size kinship units.

mbyaa	'tribe, ancestry'
túmbé	'extended family'
abum á ndáb	'immediate family'

The term *mbyaa* is used to refer to large groups like a whole tribe or nation. However, this seems not strongly established—probably because the larger groups are more abstract and because there were no political groupings at a higher level in the past.

There appears to be no general term for clan. Specific clans are simply referred to by their clan names, many of which are compounds of *mwă* plus the name of the founding ancestor, for example *Mwĕtug* from *mwă Etuge*. *Mwă* may be derived from *mwăn* 'child, offspring'.

Lexical Notes and Special Word Forms 253

The term *túmbé* is used for exogamous local descent groups. Names for such family units are frequently compounds consisting of *ndáb* plus a name, e.g. *Ndáb e Ntɔ́gɛ*.

The term *abum á ndáb* is used for a family group descended from the same father, usually living in the same compound.

Akɔɔse has three terms to refer to various generations of in-laws from the mother's side, or "maternal uncles". They are defined as follows (Levin 1976). See also Ejedepang-Koge (1986:249–253).

nláá, beláá 'in-law(s), mother's brother's lineage'
ekəgél, e'- 'in-law(s), lit. "shoulder", mother's mother's brother's lineage'
kúb e píndé 'in-law(s), lit. "black fowl", mother's mother's mother's brother's lineage'
nkúl, bekúl (pl) is another term that refers to the women from the husband's family.

Below are the terms for 'father' and 'mother'. Note that there are four forms for each. The ones ending in a velar nasal *ŋ* belong to class 9 and take class 9 agreement, the others belong to class 1 and take class 1 agreement. The class 1 forms are due to the addition of the personifier suffix *-é* to the class 9 forms, thus making them change membership to class 1 (see section 3.4.3).

The first two in each row are used for first and third persons, i.e. my and his/her father or mother; the last two for second person, i.e. your father or mother. They can be pluralised by adding the class 2 prefix *be-*.

class	9	1	9	1
	my/his	my/his	your	your
father	**sáŋ**	**sáá**	**sóŋ**	**sóó**
mother	**nyaŋ**	**nyaá**	**nyoŋ**	**nyoó**

There is a parallel to the possessive pronouns (see section 3.3.3) in that forms for the second-person singular end with the "suffix" *-oŋ*. The same "suffix" is also found in the pair of words *mwǎnyaŋ/mwǎnyoŋ* 'brother/sister'.

Another set of terms for friendship relationships is the following.

	sg.		pl.	
1sg	wěd	'my friend'	běd	'our friends'
2sg	wěn	'your friend'	běn	'your friends'
3sg	wăb	'his friend'	băb	'their friends'

These belong to noun class gender 1/2. The "root" is identical to the plural possessive pronoun stems (see section 3.3.3).

A.7. Colour terms

Akɔɔse has three basic colour terms, all verbal in structure.

-yəg	'to be red'
-hín	'to be black'
-púb	'to be white'

From these are derived a certain number of nominal forms:

e'púb	'whiteness'
púbāgē	'white cocoyam'
epûb	'something white'
e'hín	'blackness'
ehínde	'blackness'
ehíntén	'darkness'
ahín	'bush, forest'
hínāgē	'black cocoyam'
píndé asáá	'black plum'
ahínɛɛ kém	'black monkey'
e'yəg	'redness'
n-yəgtéd	'ripeness'

To express colours other than those typically associated with the three basic colours, other expressions are used, for example, mŏlmóle abad 'a yellow cloth'. Mŏl is the word for oil and it is quite clear that 'yellow' is derived from this noun by reduplication.

There is another word for red which basically means 'ripe': -tán 'to be red, ripe'.

There are other terms that are often used to describe an object e.g., speckled, shiny, etc. which do not, strictly speaking, refer to colour.

Appendix B
Swadesh 100 Comparative Wordlists

The words in the following lists are transcribed with symbols from the International Phonetic Alphabet (IPA). The symbol "j" following a consonant represents palatalization.

256   Appendix B

Village: Clan:	Nyasoso— Mwetug	Eboko Bajo— Mbwogmut	Ngonmin— Mwetan	Nkack— Ninong	Nkikoh— Elung	Elambeng— Bajoh
1. I	mɛ	mə	mə	mə	mɛ	mɛ
2. you (sg.)	wɛ	wɛ	wɛ	wɛ	wɛ	we
3. we	sɛ́	sɛ́	sɛ́	sɛ́	sɛ́	sɛ́
4. this	ane (cl.1)		anɛ́n	étʃɛ́n (cl.10)	anɛ̂	ane
5. that	anɛ́n (cl.1)		aníní	étʃíní (cl.10)	aníní	anɛ́n
6. who	nzɛ́	nzɛ́	nzɛ́	nzɛ́:	nzɛ́:	nzɛ́:
7. what	tʃɛ̌		tʃɛ̌	tʃʃɛ̌:	dʒɛ̌	tʃǐ:
	sakɛ́		sakɛ́			sɛ̌:
8. not						
9. all	-syə̀l	-ʃjɛ̀l	-sjə̀l	-sjɛ̀n	-sǐ:n	-sǐ: / -ʃǐ:
10. many	hî:n	mbwele	hîn	jí:n	ɲáɓeí	mbwele
11. one	-hɔ́kˀ	-hɔ́kˀ	-hɔ́kˀ	-hɔ́:ʔ	-hɔ́ʔ	-hɔ́ʔ
12. two	-ɓɛ	-ɓɛ	-ɓɛ	-ɓɛ	-ɓɛ	-ɓɛ
13. big	-kəl / mbá: (n.)	-kəl	-kəl	mbá:	-kɤl	mbɛ́:
14. long	-tʃapˀ	-tʃapˀ	-tʃapˀ	-tʃapˀ	-dʒɛ̌:	-tʃǎ:
15. small	mwǎti:tˀ	mwǎti:tˀ	mwǎti:tˀ	mwǎti:tˀ	môti:d	mwǎti:tˀ
16. woman	mmwǎ:tˀ	mmwǎ:tˀ	mmwǎ:tˀ	mmwɛ̌:tˀ	mmwɛ̌ʔ	mmwǎ:t
17. man	mwendʒóm	mwentʃóm	mwentʃóm	mo:ntʃóm	mwendʒó	mwɛ̌ntʃóm
18. person	mɤtˀ	mɤtˀ	mot	mokˀ	mɔ	motˀ
19. fish	sǔ:	sǔ:	sǔ:	sǔ:	sú	Sǔ:
20. bird	eʔnɔn	eʔnɔn	ɛʔnɔn	aʔnɛn	mónɔʔ	nɔn
21. dog	mbwɛ́	mbwɛ́	mbwɛ́	mbwɛ́	mbwɛ́	mbwɛ́
22. louse	titˀ	tetˀ	tetˀ	tikˀ	ted	tɛʔ

Village:	Nyasoso—	Eboko Bajo—	Ngommin—	Nkack—	Nkikoh—	Elambeng—
Clan:	Mwetug	Mbwogmut	Mwetan	Ninong	Elung	Bajoh
23. tree	bwɛl	bwɛl	bwɛl	bjɛl	bwɛl	bwɛl
24. seed	mbum / mbə́l	mbum	mbə́l	mbə́lebŭ	mbɔ́l	mbum
25. leaf	tʃjǎː	tʃjěː	tʃjǎ	tʃjæ̌ː	dʒjěː	dʒjɛ̌
26. root	ŋkaŋ	ŋkaŋ	ŋkaŋ	ŋkaŋ	ŋkã	ŋkaŋ
27. bark	ekokˈ	ekokˈ	ekokˈ	ekwɔm	ekog	ekuʔ
28. skin	ŋgɤpˈ / ekɤpˈ	ŋgɤpˈ	ŋgopˈ	ŋgɤpˈ	ŋgɤʔ	ŋgɤʔ
29. flesh	ɲam	ɲam	ɲam	ɲæm	ɲæ	ɲæ
30. blood	mekǐː	mekǐː	mekǐː	mekǐː	okǐː	mekǐː
31. bone	ehitˈ	ehɛtˈ	ehɛtˈ	ehiʔ	ehɛg	ehɛʔ
32. grease	ahóŋ	ahóŋ	ahóŋ	ahóŋ	ohɔ̃́	ahóŋ
33. egg	akiː	akiː	akiː	akiː	akiː	aki
34. horn	asépˈ	asípˈ	asípˈ	asípˈ	aséʔ	asíʔ
35. tail	ŋkɤ́n	ŋkɤn	ŋkun	ŋkɪn	ŋkɤ	ŋkɤn
36. feather	etɔkˈ	atɔkˈ	etɔkˈ	etɔʔ	etɔg	etɔʔ
37. hair	esitˈ	ɲoŋ	esetˈ	ɲaŋ	ɲoŋ	ngeŋ
38. head	nló	nló	nló	llé	ĩlé	nló
39. ear	etûː	etûː	etûː	etûː	etûː	etû
40. eye	ditˈ	dĕtˈ	dĕtˈ	diʔ	dég	déʔ
41. nose	dûː	dûː	dûː	dûː	dûː	dû
42. mouth	nsəl	nsəl	nsəl	nsəl	nsɤ	nsje
43. tooth	asoŋ	asoŋ	asoŋ	asoŋ	asoŋ	asoŋ
44. tongue	etʃém	etʃim	etʃém	etʃim	edʒí	adʒĩ́

Village: Clan:	Nyasoso— Mwetug	Eboko Bajo— Mbwogmut	Ngonmin— Mwetan	Nkack— Ninong	Nkikoh— Elung	Elambeng— Bajoh
45. claw	ɲǎn	ɲǎn	ɲǎn	ɲǎn	ɲǎn	ɲǽ
46. foot	eku:	əku:	eku:	eku:	eku:	eku:
47. knee	abúbóŋ	abúbóŋ	abúbóŋ	abúbúŋ	abɔ́:	abṍŋ
48. hand	ekǎ:	ekɛ́:	ekǎ:	ekǽ:	ekɛ́	ekɛ́
49. belly	abúm	abum	abum	abum	abum	abum
50. neck	ŋkə́ŋ / abɔl	abɔl	ŋkə́ŋ	ŋkáŋ	abɔr	abɔʔ
51. breast	abî:	abî:	abî:	abî:	abî:	abî:
52. heart	nlém	nlím	nlém	llém	llé	nlé
53. liver	aba	abə	ebɛ	abæ	abə	abe:
54. drink	-mwɛ́ / -mwák⁻	-mwɛ́ / -mwák⁻	-mwɛ́ / -mwák⁻	-mwɛ́ / -mwák⁻	-mwɛ́ / -mwág	-mwɛ́ / -mwá
55. eat	-djɛ́ / -djǎk⁻	-djɛ́ / -djǎk⁻	-djɛ́ / -djǎk⁻	-djɛ́ / -djǎk⁻	-djɛ́ / -djǎg	-djɛ́ / -djá
56. bite	-kwagɛ́l	-kwǎl	-kwǎ:l	-kwǎ:l	-kwǎl	-kwǎ:
57. see	-ɲén / -nɔ̀n	-ɲén	-nɔ̀n	-nɔ̀n	-ɲî	-nɔ̀n
58. hear	-wók⁻	-wók⁻	-wó:ʔ	-wɔ́ʔ	-wɔ́g	-wúʔ
59. know	-bí:	-bí:	-bí:	-bí:	-bí:	-bí:
60. sleep	-kún	-kún	-kún	-kwán	-kɔ́n	-kɔ́n
61. die	-wɛ́	-wɛ́	-wɛ́	-wɛ́	-wɛ́	-wɛ́
62. kill	-wú:	-wú:	-wú:	-hú:	-wú:	-wú:
63. swim	-ɲǎl	-ɲǎl	-ɲǎl	-ɲǽl	-ɲǽl	-ɲǎl
64. fly	-pumé	-kán	-pumé	-pumə́	-pummwɛ́	-pumɛ́ʔ
65. walk	-kǎk⁻	-kǎk⁻	-kǎk⁻	-kə̌	-kə̌ʔ	-kə̌ʔ
66. come	-hjǎk⁻	-hjǎk⁻	-jǎk⁻	-jǎ:ʔ	-hjǎʔ	-hjǎʔ

Swadesh 100 Comparative Wordlists

Village: Clan:	Nyasoso—Mwetug	Eboko Bajo—Mbwogmut	Ngonmin—Mwetan	Nkack—Ninong	Nkikoh—Elung	Elambeng—Bajoh
67. lie	-nǎː	-nǎː	-nǎː	-nǎ̰	-nǎ̰	-nǎ̰
68. sit	-djɛ̌	-djɛ̌	-djɛ̌	-djɛ̌	-djɛ̌	-diː
69. stand	-tjɛ́m	-tímɛ́	-tjɛ́m	-tjɛ́m	-tíbɔ́	-tjɛ̃́
70. give	-bɛ̌ / -bǎk˥	-bǎʔ	-bɔ̃̌	-bɔ̃̌	-bɔ̃̌	-bǎʔ
71. say	-hɔ́p˥	-hɔ́p˥	-hɔ́p˥	-hɔ́p˥	-hwáʔ	-hɔ́ʔ
72. sun	ɛɲɛn / etɤndɛː	ɛɲɛn	ɛɲɛn	ɛɲɛŋ / etɤndɛː	ɛɲɛ	ɛɲɛ
73. moon	ŋgɔn	ŋgɔn	ŋgɔn	ŋgɔn	ŋgwɔ	ŋgɔn
74. star	tintinɛ	tɛntɛn	tintinɛ	tintinɛ	ɲɛlɛ́ʔ	tɛntɛ̃
75. water	mendíp˥	mendép˥	mendép˥	mendə́p˥	orúb	mendíp˥
76. rain	mbúː	mbúː	mbúː	mbúː	mbwí	mbúː
77. stone	aláː	aléː	aláː	alɛ̃́ː	aléː	aléː
78. sand	nsí	nsí	nsí	nsí	nsí	nsí / bwǎ̰ʔ
79. earth	ndɔːp˥	ndɔːp˥	ndɔːp˥	ndɔːp˥	ndɔ́ʔ	ndɔːʔ
80. cloud	mbak˥	mbə̌mbaːk˥	mbəmbak˥	mbəmbak˥	mbɔ́ʔ	mbambaʔ
81. smoke	mwɛ̃ntut˥	mŭntit˥	mŏntut˥	mɔ́átət˥	mborag	ndúʔ
82. fire	múː	múː	múː	múː	múː	múː
83. ash	mbúmbú	mbúmbú	mbúmbú	mbúmbu	mbúmmwí	mbúmbɔ̃́ / mbúɲ̆mbú
84. burn	-hjǎːt˥		-hjáːt˥	-jǎːʔ	-hjǎːʔ	-hjǎ̰ːʔ
85. path	nzíː	nzíː	nzíː	nzíː	nzíː	nzíː
86. mountain	ekɤnɛ / eláː	ekɔnɛ	ekonɛ	ekonɛ	ekɤd	eleːɛ́ː
87. red	-jɤ̃k˥	-jĭk˥	-jɤ̃k˥	-júɛ́ʔ	-sɔːː	-jɤ̃ː
88. green						

Appendix B

Village: Clan:	Nyasoso— Mwetug	Eboko Bajo— Mbwogmut	Ngonmin— Mwetan	Nkack— Ninong	Nkikoh— Elung	Elambeng— Bajoh
89. yellow						
90. white	-púpˈ	-púpˈ	-púpˈ	-púpˈ	-púpˈ	-pú:
91. black	-hín	-hén	-hén	-hén	-lám	-hán
92. night	ŋku:	ŋku:	ŋku:	ŋku:	ŋku:	ŋku:
93. hot	-hjέ / -hjákˈ	-hjέ	-hjέ	-wanέ	-hɔnjέ	-honέ
94. cold	-hɔ́: / ahépˈ (n)	ahépˈ	-hɔ́:	ahépˈ	ahêbˈ / -hwɛ̂ʔ	ahépˈ / hɣ̂
95. full	-lɣ́n	-lɣ́n	-lón	-lɣ́n	-lɣ́d	-lɣ́n
96. new	ekɔ́:lέ	ekɔ́:lέ	ekɔ́:lέ	ekɔ́:lέ	kwɔ́lɔ́	ekɔ́lέ:
97. good	-bóŋ	-bóŋ	kóse	mbóŋ (n)	-bɔ̃:	-bɔ̃̃:
98. round	kɔ̂:lɘŋgɛ̂:	ahjɔmnέdέ	kɔ́lɛŋgɛ̂	kɔ̂lɔ̀ɘŋgɛ̂:		jɛŋgɛ̀lɛŋ
99. dry	-kín	-kɛ̂:	-kɔ́n	-kín	-kɛ̀ŋ	-kɔ̃̂
100. name	dín	dέn	dέn	díŋ	dɔ̀ŋ	dɛ̌:i

Appendix C

Text

Introduction

The following text is a folk tale about Tortoise and Dog. It was spoken on tape in 1975 by Mr. Martin Mesumbe Ebage of Nyasoso and transcribed by Mr. Godfred Elong Roggy Metuge, also of Nyasoso.

Line 1 gives the text written orthographically.
Line 2 gives the morphemes for the words in line one.
Line 3 gives the glosses for the corresponding morphemes.
Line 4 gives the grammatical category to which the word/morpheme belongs.

Each numbered block of lines is followed by a free translation.
For abbreviations used see the list at the front of the book.

Tortoise and Dog 001

Asón		á	kûl	ne	mbwé.
a-	són	á	kûl	ne	mbwé
5-	friendship	5.of	9.tortoise	and	9.dog
NP-	N5/6	AM	N9/10	CONJ	N9/10

'The friendship of Tortoise and Dog.'

Tortoise and Dog 002

Kûl	ne	mbwé	bé-	bédé		asón.
kûl	ne	mbwé	bé-	bé	-édé	a- són
9.tortoise	and	9.dog	2-	be	-PERF	5- friendship
N9/10	CONJ	N9/10	SM-	V	-ASP	NP- N5/6

'Tortoise and Dog were friends.'

Tortoise and Dog 003

Ábê	besón		bébɛ		bé-	ncháa.
ábê	be- són	bé-	bɛ	bé-	n-	cháa
2.those	2- friend	2-	two	2-	PAST-	give.birth
DEM	NP- N1/2	CP-	NUM	SM-	TNS-	V

'Those two friends bore children.'

Tortoise and Dog 004

Kûl	e-	cháa,	mbwé='ɛ		e-	cháa.
kûl	e-	cháa	mbwé	='ɛ	e-	cháa
9.tortoise	9-	give.birth	9.dog	=ADD	9-	give.birth
N9/10	SM-	V	N9/10	=CLIT	SM-	V

'Tortoise bore children. Dog too bore children.'

Tortoise and Dog 005

Áyɔ́le	ntɔgén	ḿ	bán-nɔ̄,			ndíítéd
áyɔ́le	ntɔgén	ḿ	b- ǎn		='ɔ̄	ndíítéd
because	3.maintenance	3.of	2- child		=DEV	3.food
CONJ	N3	AM	NP- N1/2		=CLIT	N3

	ń-	hédnáá		híin.	
	ḿ-	hédɛn	-áá	híin	
	3-	be.needed	-IMPF.PAST	much	
	SM-	V	-ASP.TNS	ADV	

'Because of the maintenance of children a lot of food was required.'

Tortoise and Dog 006

Hέ	dɔ́ǝ	kúlɛ	á-	kíí	áhîn		tê,
hê	dɔ́ǝ	kûl	-ɛ á-	kɛ -é	á-	a- hín	tê
there	5.TOP	9.tortoise	-PERS O.1-	go -PERF	LOC-	5- bush	inside
ADV	PAR	N9/10	-SFX SM-	V -ASP	PFX-	NP- N5/6	ADV

baŋ	á-	dibé		epŭm		bwɛl.	
baŋ	á-	dib	-é	e-	pum é	bw-	ɛl
then	1.CONS-	find	-CONS	7-	fruit 7	14-	tree
CONJ	SM-	V	-SFX	NP-	N7/8 AM	NP-	N14/6

'So then Tortoise went to the bush and found a fruit tree.'

Tortoise and Dog 007

Échê	epŭm		bwɛl		é-	bédé-'ɛ		nhɔ́g.
échê	e-	pum é	bw-	ɛl	é-	bɛ́ -édé	='ɛ	n- hɔ́g
7.that	7-	fruit 7.of	14-	tree	7-	be -PERF	=ADD	3- (fruit)
DEM	NP-	N7/8 AM	NP-	N14/6	SM-	V -ASP	=CLIT	NP- N3/4

'That fruit was the *nheg* fruit.'

Tortoise and Dog 008

A-	húɛ́náá		ábé	bwĕm-'ɔ̄,		á-	kɛ
a-	húɛn	-áá	ábê	bw- ŏm	='ɔ̄	á-	kɛ
1-	return.with	-IMPF.PAST	8.those	8- things	=DEV	1.NEUT-	go
SM-	V	-ASP.TNS	DEM	NP- N7/8	=CLIT	SM-	V

á-	tɔgnáán		bán.		
á-	tɔgnɛn	-ɛ́'	b-	ăn	
1.CONS-	maintain	-IMPF	2-	child	
SM-	V	-ASP	NP-	N1/2	

'He was bringing those things back and was feeding the children.'

Tortoise and Dog 009

Epun		ehɔ́g-kɔ̄		mbwé	e-	hyedé		wê
e-	pun	e- hɔ́g	='ɔ́	mbwé	e-	hyɛ	-édé	wê
7-	day	7- one	=DEV	9.dog	9-	come	-PERF	to
NP-	N7/8	CP- NUM	=CLIT	N9/10	SM-	V	-ASP	PREP

kúlɛ,		baŋkên	á-	nyēnē		nɛ́ɛ	bǎn		ábe
kûl	-ɛ	baŋkên	á-	nyén	-é	nɛ́ɛ	b-	ăn	ábe
9.tortoise	-PERS	then	1.CONS-	see	-CONS	how	2-	child	2.of
N9/10	-SFX	CONJ	SM-	V	-SFX	CONJ	NP-	N1/2	POSS

kúlɛ		bé- bóó		yɔ̌l,	bé-	kwoge-'ɛ		
kûl	-ɛ	bé- boŋ	-é	yɔ̌l	bé-	kwog	-ɛ'	='ɛ
9.tortoise	-PERS	2- be.good	-PERF	body	2-	grow	-IMPF	=ADD
N9/10	-SFX	SM- V	-ASP	N9/10	SM-	V	-ASP	=CLIT

264   Appendix C

bwǎam,	ê-	díí	nén	bán	ábī-'ɛ		bé-	dé	nkóŋtéd
bwǎam	ê-	díí	nén	bán	ábi	='ɛ	bé-	dé	n- kóŋtéd
well	7-	be.DEP	COMP	2.RP	2.his	=ADD	2-	be	3- skinny
ADV	SM-	V	CONJ	PAR	POSS	=CLIT	SM-	V	NP- N3

ne	nkóŋtéd.
ne	n- kóŋtéd
and	3- skinny
CONJ	NP- N3

'One day, Dog came to Tortoise and saw how the children of Tortoise were very healthy and grew very well, while his own were very skinny.'

Tortoise and Dog 010

Nzɔm	e-	bédé		nén,	ndyééd	eché	bâbe
nzɔm	e-	bé	-édé	nén	ndyééd	eché	bâbe
9.reason	9-	be	-PERF	COMP	9.food	9.which	they.3+3
N9	SM-	V	-ASP	CONJ	N9	REL	PRO

bǎn-nɛ			bé-	dyágáá		e-	nkê-
b-	ǎn	='ɛ	bé-	dyé	-áá	e-	nkê-
2-	child	=ADD	2-	eat	-IMPF.PAST	9-	NEG-
NP-	N1/2	=CLIT	SM-	V	-ASP.TNS	SM-	NEG-

nchognédté		bɔ́.	
n-	chogned	='ɛ́	bɔ́
PAST-	be.sufficient	=SF	2.them
TNS-	V	=SFX	PRO

'The reason was that the food which he and the children were eating was not sufficient for them.'

Tortoise and Dog 011

Hé	dɔ́ə	á-	sɛtɛɛ́			kúlɛ		epun	
hê	dɔ́ə	á-	sɛded	-ɛ'	-'ɛ́	kûl	-ɛ	e-	pun
there	5.TOP	O.1-	ask	-IMPF	-SF	9.tortoise	-PERS	7-	day
ADV	PAR	SM-	V	-ASP	-SFX	N9/10	-SFX	NP-	N7/8

ehɔ́g	aá,		"A	mwéē,	héé	wɛ	wě-	kudɛɛ́	
e-	hɔ́g	aá	a	mwé	héé	wɛ	wě-	kud-ɛ'	-'ɛ́
7-	one	RP.3SG	VOC	7.friend	where	2SG	2SG.NEG-	get -PERF	-SF
CP-	NUM	PAR	PAR	N1	LOC	PRO	SM-	V -ASP	-SFX

échén	ebɔ́l		é	ndyéd	éche	é-			
échén	e-	bɔ́l	é	ndyééd	éche	é-			
7.this	7-	special	7.of	9.food	7.which	7-			
DEM	NP-	N7/8	AM	N9	REL	SM-			

bôŋnaaté			áboŋ	bǎn		nén?"		
boŋned	-ɛ'	-'έ	áboŋ	b-	ǎn	nén		
good.for	-IMPF	-SF	2.your	2-	child	like.this		
V	-ASP	-SFX	POSS	NP-	N1/2	ADV		

'So he asked Tortoise one day, "Friend, where do you get this special food which is so good for your children?"'

Tortoise and Dog 012

Héɛ	kúlɛ		á-	lángé	mɔ́	aá,	"A	mwéɛ̄,
hê	kûl	-ɛ	á-	láa´	-é	mɔ́	aá	a	mwé
there	9.tortoise	-PERS	O.1-	say	-PERF	1.him	RP.3SG	VOC	1.friend
ADV	N9/10	-SFX	SM-	V	-ASP	PRO	PAR	PAR	N1
n-	nyéné	ḿmê	nhɔ́g	áhìn		tê	wê	aá,
n-	nyén	-é	ḿmê	n-	hɔ́g	á-	a-	hín	tê	wê	aá
1SG-	see	-PERF	3.that	3-	(fruit)	LOC-	5-	bush	inside	there	RP.3SG
SM-	V	-ASP	DEM	NP-	N3/4	PFX-	NP-	N5/6	ADV	ADV	PAR
áwed	-ɛέ	ń-	kaké.
áwed	=ɛέ	ń-	kɛ	-ɛ'	-'έ
there	=TOP	O.1SG-	go	-IMPF	-SF
adv	=clit	sm-	v	-asp	-sfx

'Then Tortoise replied, "Friend, I saw that fruit in the bush there, it is there that I am going.'

Tortoise and Dog 013

Aá	kénê	é-	díí	bán,	saké	mɔ́	mɔ́-	wōō	mɔ́,
aá	kénê	é-	díí	bán	saké	mɔ́	mɔ́-	wóŋ	mɔ́
RP.3SG	even.though	O.7-be.DEP		2.RP	not	1.he	LOG-	have	4.it
PAR	CONJ	SM- V		PAR	PAR	PRO	SM-	V	PRO
aá	nwóŋ	aá	a-	dé.					
aá	nwóŋ	aá	a-	dé					
RP.3SG	owner	RP.3SG	1-	be					
PAR	N3	RP	SM-	V					

'Although it is the case that I don't own them, there is an owner.'

Tortoise and Dog 014

Aá	nzé	mɔ́-	kag-kɔɔ́		áwed aá,	mɔ́-	bɛlé		mɔ́-
aá	nzé	mɔ́-	kɛ	-ɛ'	='ɔ̃ áwed aá	mɔ́-	bɛl	-é	mɔ́-
RP.3SG	when	LOG-	go	-IMPF	=DEV there RP.3SG	LOG-	always	-CONS	LOG-
PAR	CONJ	SM-	V	-ASP	=CLIT ADV PAR	SM-	V	-ASP	SM-

pɔ̃l	akɛ.
pɔ́l	a- kɛ
be.early	INF- go
V	PFX- V

'So, when I go there, I always go very early.'

Tortoise and Dog 015

Aá	mɔ́-	hɛd,	mɔ́-	hɛd,	mɔ́-	hɛd.
aá	mɔ́-	hɛd	mɔ́-	hɛd	mɔ́-	hɛd
RP.3SG	LOG-	search	LOG-	search	LOG-	search
PAR	SM-	V	SM-	V S	M-	V

'I search and search and search.'

Tortoise and Dog 016

Aá	boŋ	mɔ́-	báa		wɛ	awále		áwed,	ngáne
aá	boŋ	mɔ́-	báŋ	-ɛ'	wɛ	a-	wále	áwed	ngáne
RP.3SG	but	LOG-	fear	-IMPF	2SG	INF-	take.along	there	as
PAR	CONJ	SM-	V	-ASP	PRO	PFX-	V	ADV	CONJ

wě-	saá	wɛ	edibned,	wě-		kwɛntáán-naá			weé
we-	saá	wɛ	edibned	wě-		kwɛntɛn	-ɛ'	='ɔ̃	weé
2SG-	is.not	you	key?	2SG.FUT.NEG-		accept	-IMPF	=DEV	RP.3SG
SM-	V	PRO	N7/8	SM-		V	-ASP	=CLIT	PAR

chŏm	é-	siitɛn wɛ,	e-	hɛle		e-	bón	esaád,	ɛ́ɛ	mɔ̂
chŏm	é-	siitɛn wɛ	e-	hɛl	-ɛ'	e-	bón	esaád	áde	mɔ̂
7.thing	7-	touch you	2SG-	can	-IMPF	2SG-	shout	7.shout	as	1.he.TOP
N7/8	SM-	V PRO	SM-	V	-ASP	SM-	V	N7/8	CONJ	PRO

mɔ̂-		wóngé	ḿmé	mekuu	mé	mehélé.
mɔ̂-		wóŋ -'ɛ́	ḿmé	me- kuu	mé	me- hélé
LOG.FUT.NEG-		have -SF	6.those	6- foot	6.of	6- race
SM-		V -SFX	DEM	NP- N7/6	AM	NP- N6

'But I am afraid to take you along there, because there is no solution(?), for you will not accept that if something hits you you might shout, and because I don't have those legs for running.'

Tortoise and Dog 017

Ane	mod	a-	hɛle	á-	hyɛ	a-	tán	mɔ́	ásē	wê.
ane	m-	od	a-	hɛl -ɛ'	á-	hyɛ	a-	tán	mɔ́	ásē	wê
1.that	1-	person	1-	can -IMPF	1.NEUT-	come	1-	meet	1.him	down	there
DEM	NP-	N1/2	SM-	V -ASP	SM-	V	SM-	V	PRO	ADV	ADV

'That man may come and meet me down there.'

Tortoise and Dog 018

Chǎn	é-	piinéd	mɔ́	mbɔ́lɔ́n?"
chǎn	é-	piinéd	mɔ́	mbɔ́lɔ́n
tomorrow	2SG.NEUT-	bring	1.him	loss
ADV	SM-	V	PRO	N?

'Tomorrow you bring me loss?"'

Tortoise and Dog 019

"Aáy!"	Mbwé	aá,	"Kám,	aá	a	mwéē	chán
aáy	mbwé	aá	kám	aá	a	mwé	chán
no	9.dog	RP.3SG	no	RP.3SG	VOC	friend	how
PAR	N9/10	PAR	PAR	PAR	PAR	N1	QADV

	é-	hɔ́bɛé		nê.
	é-	hɔ́b -ɛ'	-'ɛ́	nê
	O.2SG-	talk -IMPF	-SF	like.that
	SM-	V -ASP	-SFX	ADV

' "No!" Dog said, "No, Friend, how are you talking like that.'

Tortoise and Dog 020

Aá	ken	nɛ́ɛ	bǎn	bé-	tagɛé			me	nén,
aá	ken	nɛ́ɛ	b- ǎn	bé-	tag -ɛ'	-'ɛ́		me	nén
RP.3SG	Q	as	2- child	2-	suffer -IMPF	-SF		me	like.this
PAR	PAR	CONJ	NP- N1/2	SM-	V -ASP	-SFX		PRO	ADV

baŋ	é-	nyéné-'aá		ene	ndín	e	ndyé	eché
baŋ	é-	nyén -é	='aá	ene	ndín	e	ndyé	eché
then	O.2SG- see	-PERF	=DEV	9.that	9.kind	9.of	9.food?	9.which
CONJ	SM- V	-ASP	=CLIT	DEM	N9/10	AM	N9/10	REL

ě-	bɛ̌	ábem	bǎn		ntɔgén,	boŋ	maa	ḿ-
ě-	bɛ	ábem	b- ǎn		ntɔgén	boŋ	maa	ḿ-
9.NEG-	give	2.my	2- child		maintenance	then	I.too	1SG.CONS-
SM-	V	POSS	NP- N1/2		N3	CONJ	PRO	SM-

bɛlé		échê	ebébtéd		ésyɔ̄ɔ̄syəɔ́l-ɛ?"	
bɛl	-é	échê	e-	bébtéd	ésyɔ̄ɔ̄l	=ɛ
do	-CONS	7.that	7-	evil	all	=Q
V	-SFX	DEM	NP-	N7	ADJ	=CLIT

'When my children suffer like that and you have seen that kind of food which I don't give to my children for maintenance, then I too do all this evil?" '

Tortoise and Dog 021

Kûl	aá,	"O'ó,	aá	né	mɔ́ɔ̄-	wāl̄ē	wɛ."
kûl	aá	o'ó	aá	né	mɔ́ɔ̄-	wále	wɛ
9.tortoise	RP.3SG	ok.	RP.3SG	then	LOG.FUT-	take.along	2SG
N9/10	PAR	EXCL	PAR	CONJ	SM-	V	PRO

'Tortoise said, "OK, I'll take you along then." '

Tortoise and Dog 022

Bɔ̂-'aá		bé-	pɔ́lé		abíd	nê	mbwɛmbwɛ.
bɔ́	='ɔ̆	bé-	pɔ́l	-é	a- bíd	nê	mbwɛmbwɛ
2.they	=DEV	2-	be.early	-PERF	INF- go.out	like.that	morning
PRO	=CLIT	SM-	V	-ASP	PFX- V	ADV	N9

'They then left very early in the morning.'

Tortoise and Dog 023

Nɛ́ɛ	bé-	pédé		á	nhɔ́g	sé	wê	bé-
nɛ́ɛ	bé-	pɛ	-édé	á	n- hɔ́g	sé	wê	bé-
as	2-	arrive	-PERF	LOC	3- (fruit)	under	there	2-
CONJ	SM-	V	-ASP	PFX	NP- N3/4	ADV	ADV	SM-
bóótédé		ahɛd,		bé- hɛdé',		bé- ladé',		bé-
bóóted	-é	a- hɛd		bé- hɛd	-é'	bé- lad	-é'	bé-
begin	-PERF	INF- search		2- search	-CONS	2- gather	-CONS	2-
V	-ASP	PFX- V		SM- V	-SFX	SM- V	-SFX	SM-
hɛdé',		bé-	ladé'		áte.			
hɛd	-é'	bé-	lad	-é'	áte			
search	-CONS	2-	gather	-CONS	into			
v	-sfx	sm-	v	-sfx	adv			

'As they arrived under the nheg tree, they began to search. They searched, they picked up fruit. They searched, they picked up fruit.'

Tortoise and Dog 024

Dɔ́-'aá		nhɔ́g	ḿ-	bídé		ámīn,	baŋ	ḿ-
dɔ́ə	='ɔ̆	n-	hɔ́g	ḿ- bíd	-é	ámín	baŋ	ḿ-
then	=DEV	3-	one	3- come.out	-PERF	up	then	3-
CONJ	=CLIT	CP-	NUM	SM- V	-ASP	ADV	CONJ	SM-
bɔmé		**kúlɛ**		**á**	**mbíd**	**te**	**toóy.**	
bɔm	-é	kûl	-ɛ	á	mbíd	te	toóy	
knock	-PERF	9.tortoise	-PERS	LOC	9.back	in	boom	
V	-ASP	N9/10	-SFX	PFX	N9/10	ADV	IDEO	

'Then one came down and hit Tortoise on the back, boom.'

Tortoise and Dog 025

Kúlɛ		a-	nəgné		áte	aá,	"Mepɔke	mé
kûl	-ɛ	a-	nəgɛn	-é	áte	aá	mepɔke	mé
9.tortoise	-PERS	1-	bend	-PERF	into	RP.3SG	food	6.of
N9/10	-SFX	SM-	V	-ASP	ADV	PAR	N6	AM
mod		**ambáá**		**mê."**				
m-	od	a-	mbáá	mê				
1-	person	1-	big	1.that				
NP-	N1/2	CP-	ADJ	DEM				

'Tortoise squirmed saying, "This is food for a rich man." '

Tortoise and Dog 026

A-	nkaŋ	nlém		ábum,		
a-	n-	kaŋ	nlém	á-	a-	bum
1-	PAST-	be.angry	3.heart	LOC-	5-	stomach
SM-	TNS-	V	N3/4	PFX-	NP-	N5/6
e-	**hɔ́bɛé**					
e-	hɔ́b	-é	-'ɛ́			
1.NEG-	talk	-PERF	-SF			
SM-	V	-ASP	-SFX			

'He was angry, but didn't say anything.'

Tortoise and Dog 027

Bé-	mbé	bé-		hɛdɛ',		bé-	hɛdɛ',		dɔ́ə
bé-	m-	bɛ́	bé-	hɛd	-ɛ'	bé-	hɛd	-ɛ'	dɔ́ə
2-	PAST-	still	2-	search	-IMPF	2-	search	-IMPF	then
SM-	TNS-	V	SM-	V	-ASP	SM-	V	-ASP	CONJ

nhɔ́g	mémpée	ń-	húú	ámīn	ḿ-	bɔmé	mbwɛ́.
n- hɔ́g	mé- mpée	ḿ-	húu	ámín	ḿ-	bɔm -é	mbwɛ́
3- (fruit)	3- other	3-	return	up	3-	knock -CONS	9.dog
NP- N3/4	CP-	ADJ	SM- V	ADV	SM-	V -SFX	N9/10

'They were still looking, they were looking, then another fruit came down and hit Dog.'

Tortoise and Dog 028

Mbwɛ́	aá,	"Wáŋ wáŋ	wáŋ!"
mbwɛ́	aa	wáŋ wáŋ	wáŋ
9.dog	RP.3SG	ow ow	ow
N9/10	PAR	IDEO IDEO	IDEO

'Dog, "Ow, ow, ow!" '

Tortoise and Dog 029

Kúlɛ		á	nlêm	te	aá	ken
kûl	-ɛ	á	nlém	te	aá	ken
9.tortoise	-PERS	LOC	3.heart	in	RP.3SG	Q
N9/10	-SFX	PFX	N3/4	ADV	PAR	PAR
mə̂-	wédɛɛ́			-yɛ̄ɛ̄?		
mə̂-	wɛ́	-édé	-'ɛ́	=yɛ̄ɛ̄		
LOG.NEG-	die	-PERF	-SF	=Q		
SM-	V	-SFX	-SFX	=CLIT		

'Tortoise asked himself in the heart, "Have I not died?" '

Tortoise and Dog 030

Mbwɛ́-'ə́	ngáne	á-	bíí	ḿmé	mehélé	a-	kidé-
Mbwɛ́ ='ə	ngáne	á-	bíí	ḿmé	me- hélé	a-	kidé-
9.dog =DEV	as	o.1-	know.PERF	6.that	6- race	1-	PRIOR-
N9/10 =CLIT	CONJ	SM-	V	DEM	NP- N6	SM-	ASP-
kĕ-'ɛ	mə́	se	etûn.				
kɛ ='ɛ	mə́	se	e- tûn				
go =ADD	1.he	right	7- far				
V =CLIT	PRO	PAR	NP- N7				

'Dog, as he knows how to run, he had disappeared long ago.'

Tortoise and Dog 031

Kúlɛ		a-	wogédé		yǎl,	ě-		hɛlɛé	
kûl	-ɛ	a-	wogled	-é	yǎl	ě-	hɛl	-é	-'ɛ́
9.tortoise	-PERS	1-	struggle	-PERF	9.body	1.NEG-	can	-PERF	-SF
N9/10	-SFX	SM-	V	-ASP	N9/10	SM-	V	-ASP	-SFX

akɛ,	dɔ́ -'aá		á-	típé		mɔ́	á	nkɔg	ḿ
a-	kɛ	dɔ́ə = 'ɔ̆	á-	tíbe	-é	mɔ́	á	n-	kɔg	ḿ
INF-	go then	=DEV	o.1-	go.under	-PERF	1.him	LOC	3-	log	3.of
PFX-	V CONJ	=CLIT	SM-	V	-ASP	PRO	PFX	NP-	N3/4	AM

bwɛl	sé.
bw- ɛl	sé
14- tree	under
NP- N14/6	ADV

'Tortoise struggled to get away, he was not able to walk, so he went under a log.'

Tortoise and Dog 032

Esámsám	ane	mod		á-	pédé,		a-	nɔnɛ',	a-
esámsám	ane	m-	od	á-	pɛ	-édé	a-	nɔn	-ɛ'	a-
suddenly	1.that	1-	person	o.1-	reach	-PERF	1-	look	-IMPF	1-
ADV	DEM	NP-	N1/2	SM-	V	-ASP	SM-	V	-ASP	SM-

nɔnɛ'	aá	ken,	"Benzéé	bé-	chíbe		me	nhɔ́g?"
nɔn -ɛ'	aá	ken	benzéé	bé-	chíb	-ɛ'	me n-	hɔ́g
look -IMPF	RP.3SG	Q	2.who	2-	steal	-IMPF	1SG 3-	(fruit)
V -ASP	PAR	PAR	QPRO	SM-	V	-ASP	PRO NP-	N3/4

'Suddenly the man came, looked and looked and asked, "Who is stealing my fruit?"'

Tortoise and Dog 033

Kuné		mwǎ		e'nɔn		awě	a-	bédé	á
kuné		mw- ǎ		e'- nɔn		awě	a-	bé -édé	á
not.knowing		1- small		14- bird		1.which	1-	be -PERF	LOC
PAR		NP- N1/2		NP- N14/6		REL	SM-	V -ASP	PFX

nkɔg	ń	hóm,	mɔ́-'ɛ		a-	nyéné		ngáne
n- kɔg	ḿ	hǒm	mɔ́	='ɛ	a-	nyén	-é	ngáne
3- side	3.of	place	1.him	=ADD	1-	see	-PERF	as
NP- N3	AM	N5	PRO	=CLIT	SM-	V -	ASP	CONJ

kúlɛ		á-	típé		á	nkɔg	sé.
kûl	-ɛ	á-	tíbe	-é	á	n- kɔg	sé
9.tortoise	-PERS	O.1-	go.under	-PERF	LOC	3- log	under
N9/10	-SFX	SM-	V	-ASP	PFX	NP- N3/4	ADV

'Unknown, a little bird which was nearby had seen Tortoise go under the log.'

Tortoise and Dog 034

A-	bootédé		nkə́ngé	akɔ́n		aá,	"Ówásā
a-	booted	-é	n- kə́ngé	a-	kɔ́n	aá	Ówásā -[1]
1-	begin	-IMPF	3- song	INF-	sing	RP.3SG	
SM-	V -	ASP	NP- N3	PFX-	V	PAR	-

fyăndéé	chəŋ,	ówásā	mukɔkɔ́ɔ́	chəŋ	Ówásā	fyăndéé
fyăndéé	chəŋ	Ówásā	mukɔkɔ́ɔ́	chəŋ	Ówásā	fyăndéé
-	-	-	-	-	-	-
-	-	-	-	-	-	-

chəŋ,	ówásā	mukɔkɔ́ɔ́	chəŋ."
chəŋ	Ówásā	mukɔkɔ́ɔ́	chəŋ
-	-	-	-
-	-	-	-

'It began to sing a song, "Look under the tree, look under the log. Look under the tree, look under the log." '

Tortoise and Dog 035

Ane	mod-tɛ		ě-	chemɛé			m̀mê	nkə́ngé.
ane	m- od	='ɛ	ě-	chem	-é	-'ɛ	m̀mé	n- kə́nge
1.that	1- person	=ADD	1.NEG-	recognise	-PERF	-SF	3.that	3- song
DEM	NP- N1/2	=CLIT	SM-	V	-ASP	-SFX	DEM	NP- N3

'The man did not recognise the song.'

Tortoise and Dog 036

Échê	epun	a-	súú		e-	sôŋtɛnɛé		
échê	e- pun	a-	sú	-é	e-	sóŋtɛn	-é	-'ɛ
7.that	7- day	1-	return	-PERF	1.NEG-	understand	-PERF	-SF
DEM	NP- N7/8	SM-	V	-ASP	SM-	V	-ASP	-SFX

aá,	mwă		e'nɔn	ne	a-	kɔ́ne		nê,
aá	mw-	ă	e'- nɔn	ne	a-	kɔ́n	-ɛ'	nê
RP.3SG	1-	small	14- bird	1.that	1-	sing	-IMPF	like.hat
PAR	NP-	N1/2	NP- N	DEM	SM-	V	-ASP	ADV

---

[1]This song has no translation. It must be from another undetermined language.

Text

álūmed	wê	kúlɛ		á-	sɔɔmɛé.		
á-	lúmed	wê	kûl	-ɛ	á-	sɔɔm	-ɛ'	-'ɛ́
INF-	show	where	9.tortoise	-PERS	O.1-	hide	-IMPF	-SF
PFX-	V	ADV	N9/10	-SFX	SM-	V	-ASP	-SFX

'That day he went home, not understanding that the little bird sang like that to show where Tortoise was hiding.'

Tortoise and Dog 037

Á	mbíd	e	póndé	dɔ́ə,	kúlɛ		á-	syɔ́ngé,	
á	mbíd	e	póndé	dɔ́ə	kûl -	ɛ	á-	syəə	-é
LOC	9.behind	9.of	9.time	5.TOP	9.tortoise	-PERS	O.1-	leave	-PERF
PFX	N9/10	AM	N9	PAR	N9/10	-SFX	SM-	V	-ASP

bán	nɛ́ɛ	á-	pédé		á	ndáb,	á-	tânnɛé		
bán	nɛ́ɛ	á-	pɛ	-édé	á	ndáb	á-	tánen	-ɛ'	-'ɛ́
2.RP	as	O.1-	reach	-PERF	LOC	9.house	O.1-	meet.with	-IMPF	-SF
PAR	CONJ	SM-	V	-ASP	PFX	N9/10	SM-	V	-ASP	-SFX

waáb	debémbém,	á-	sɛtɛé		mɔ́	aá,	"A	
w-	aáb	debémbém	á-	sɛded	-ɛ'	-'ɛ́	mɔ́	aá	a
1-	friend	??	O.1-	ask	-IMPF	-SF	1.him	RP.3SG	VOC
NP-	N1/2	??	SM-	V	-ASP	-SFX	PRO	PAR	PAR

mwéē,	me-	lângɛé			wɛ	ádén	akan	chii,
mwé	me-	láá	-é	-'ɛ́	wɛ	ádén	a- kan	chii
friend	1SG.NEG-	say	-PERF	-SF	2SG	5.this	5- matter	today
N1	SM-	V	-ASP	-SFX	PRO	DEM	NP- N5/6	ADV

mɔ́ɔ̄	we	mbáá	wě-	paléd		mod-ɛ?	
mɔ́ɔ̄	we	mbáá	wě-	paled	m- od	=ɛ	
RP.LOG	2SG	frequently	2SG.FUT-	give.away	1- person	=Q	
PAR	PRO	PAR	SM-	V	NP- N1/2	=CLIT	

'After a while Tortoise left. As he reached home he met his friend. He said to him, "Friend, didn't I tell you this thing today? You always give people away.'

Tortoise and Dog 038

Mɔ́ɔ̄	wě-	saá	edibned-ɛ?	
mɔ́ɔ̄	wě-	saá	edibned	=ɛ
RP.LOG	2SG.FUT.NEG-	is.not	7.key?	=Q
PAR	SM-	V	N7/8	=CLIT

'You can't keep quiet.'

Tortoise and Dog 039

Wě-	bɛnteé			me	ádén	ámpē	chii-yéɛ́?
wě-	bɛled	-é	-'ɛ́	me	ádén	ámpē	chii = yēɛ̄
2SG.NEG-	treat	-PERF	-SF	1SG	5.this	again	today = Q
SM-	V	-ASP	-SFX	PRO	DEM	ADV	ADV = CLIT

'Didn't you treat me like this again today?'

Tortoise and Dog 040

Mɔ́	me-	lângeɛ́			wɛ	ábwed	meé
mɔ́	me-	láá	-é	-'ɛ́	wɛ	ábwed	meé
??	1SG.NEG-	say	-PERF	-SF	2SG	before	RP.1SG
??	sm-	v	-asp	-sfx	pro	adv	par

wé-	hɛnlé		nwɛsɛn-ɛɛ́?"	
wé-	hɛle	-é	nwɛsɛn	= ɛɛ́
2SG.NEG-	can	-PERF	perseverance	= Q
SM-	V	-ASP	N3	= CLIT

'Didn't I tell you that you can't persevere?"'

Tortoise and Dog 041

Yɔ̌l	e-	kɔ́mé	mbwé	áte, chom-ɛ́ɛ		á-	hɛleɛ́		
yɔ̌l	e-	kɔ́m	-é	mbwé	áte chǒm	= ɛ́ɛ	á-	hɛl -ɛ'	-'ɛ́
9.body	9-	tire	-PERF	9.dog	into 7.thing	= which	o.1-can	-IMPF	-SF
N9/10	SM-	V	-ASP	N9/10	ADV N7/8	= CLIT	SM-	V	-ASP-SFX

aláá	waáb	é-	bēdɛɛ́.		
a-	láa	w-	aáb	é-	bɛ́ -édé -'ɛ́
INF-	tell	1-	friend	7.NEG-	be -PERF -SF
PFX-	V	NP-	N1/2	SM-	V -ASP -SFX

'Dog was surprised. He didn't know what to tell his friend.'

Tortoise and Dog 042

Hɛ́ɛ	mwěn	á-	kɛɛnɛɛ́			mechángé	ámpē	aá,
hê	mwěn	á-	kɛɛn	-é	-'ɛ́	mechángé	ámpē	aá
there	himself	o.1-	go.with	-PERF	-SF	pleadings	again	RP.3SG
ADV	PRO	SM-	V	-ASP	-SFX	N6	ADV	PAR

"A	mwɛ́ɛ̄, sôn	sôn	aá,	mɔ́-	belé	ádê	akan	ámpē.
a	mwé sôn	sôn	aá	mɔ́-	bɛle	ádê	a- kan	ámpē
VOC	friend please	please	RP.3SG	LOG.NEG-	do.to	5.that	5- matter	again
PAR	N1 PAR	PAR	PAR	SM-	V	DEM	NP- N5/6	ADV

'Then he pleaded with him, "Friend, please, please, I won't do that thing again.'

Text 275

Tortoise and Dog 043

Aá,	ádê	akan	á-	kɔ́mté		me	yɘ̌l	áte	-yōō?
aá	ádê	a-	kan	á-	kɔ́med -é	me	yɘ̌l	áte	=yoó
RP.3SG	5.that	5-	matter	5-	surprise -PERF	1SG	9.body	into	=Q
PAR	DEM	NP-	N5/6	SM-	V -ASP	PRO	N9/10	ADV	=CLIT

'That thing took me by surprise.'

Tortoise and Dog 044

Aá,	mɔ́	mwěn	mɔ́-	pedé		á	ndáb	ámpē	aá	mɔ́-
aá	mɔ́	mwěn	mɔ́-	pɛ	-édé	á	ndáb	ámpē	aá	mɔ́-
RP.3SG	1.he	himself	LOG-	arrive	-PERF	LOC	9.house	again	RP.3SG	LOG-
PAR	PRO	PRO	SM-	V	-ASP	PFX	N9/10	ADV	PAR	SM-

nɔné		áte,	mɔ́ɔ̄	mɔ́-	bɛlé		awusé.
nɔn	-é	áte	mɔ́ɔ̄	mɔ́-	bɛl	-é	a- wusé
look	-PERF	into	RP.LOG	3-	do	-PERF	5- mistake
V	-ASP	ADV	PAR	SM-	V	-ASP	NP- N5/6

'I myself reached the house and looked into it thinking, I made a mistake.'

Tortoise and Dog 045

Aá	sôn,	e-	bɛlé		é-	kɛ̄ɛ̄n	mɔ́	ámpē.
aá	sôn	e-	bɛl	-é	é-	kɛɛn	mɔ́	ámpē
RP.3SG	please	2SG-	always	-PERF	2SG.NEUT-	go.with	1.him	again
PAR	PAR	SM-	V	-ASP	SM-	V	PRO	ADV

'Please, still take me along again.'

Tortoise and Dog 046

Aá	ken,	chán	băn		bé-	tagɛɛ́			mɔ́	á
aá	ken	chán	b-	ăn	bé-	tag	-ɛ'	-'ɛ	mɔ́	á
RP.3SG	Q	how	2-	child	2-	suffer	-IMPF	-SF	1.him	LOC
PAR	PAR	QADV	NP-	N1/2	sm-	V	-asp	-sfx	pro	pfx

ndáb,	boŋ	mə̂-	kóbé		nlém.
ndáb	boŋ	mə̂-	kób	-é	nlém
9.house	but	LOG-	catch	-PERF	3.heart
N9/10	CONJ	SM-	V	-ASP	N3/4

'How my children are suffering in the house, so I must be courageous.'

Tortoise and Dog 047

Aá	kəg	é-	wále	mɔ́	ámpē."
aá	kɜ̌g	é-	wále	mɔ́	ámpē
RP.3SG	try.IMP	2SG.HORT-	take.along	1.him	again
PAR	V	SM-	V	PRO	ADV

'Try and take me along again."'

Tortoise and Dog 048

Kúlɛ		aá,	"A	mwéē	aá	mɜ̂-	dúpɛɛ́		
kûl	-ɛ	aá	a	mwé	aá	mɜ̂-	dúbe	-é	-'ɛ́
9.tortoise	-PERS	RP.3SG	VOC	friend	RP.3SG	LOG.NEG-	think	-PERF	-SF
N9/10	-SFX	PAR	PAR	N1	PAR	SM-	V	-ASP	-SFX
mɔ́ɔ̄	mɔ́ɔ̄-	hĕl	wɛ	awále."					
mɔ́ɔ̄	mɔ́ɔ̄-	hɛl	wɛ	a-	wále				
RP.LOG	LOG.FUT-	can	2SG	INF-	take.along				
par	sm-	v	pro	pfx-	v				

'Tortoise said, "Friend, I don't think I can take you along."'

Tortoise and Dog 049

Nɛ́ɛ	á-	cháa'ɛ́			kɜ́ŋ	ne	kɜ́ŋ,	boŋ
nɛ́ɛ	á-	cháŋ	-ɛ'	-'ɛ́	kɜ́ŋ	ne	kɜ́ŋ	boŋ
as	o.1-	beg	-IMPF	-SF	until	and	until	then
CONJ	SM-	V	-ASP-	SFX	PREP	CONJ	PREP	CONJ
kúlɛ		**á-**	**suté**		**nlém.**			
kûl	-ɛ	á-	sude	-é	nlém			
9.tortoise	-PERS	1.CONS-	lower	-CONS	3.heart			
n9/10	-sfx	sm-	v	-sfx	n3/4			

'As he kept on begging for long, then Tortoise relented.'

Tortoise and Dog 050

Ngɔl	é-	kennéd	mɔ́	aá,	"O'ó	né	mɔ́ɔ̄-
ngɔl	é-	kenned	mɔ́	aá	o'ó	né	mɔ́ɔ̄-
sympathy	9.CONS-	spread	1.him	RP.3SG	ok.	then	LOG.FUT-
n9	sm-	v	pro	par	excl	conj	sm-
wālē		**wɛ."**					
wále		wɛ					
take.along		2SG					
v		pro					

'Pity overcame him. So he said, "OK, I'll take you then."'

Tortoise and Dog 051

Échíníí	epun		bé-	sɔ́lé		ámpē.
échíníí	e-	pun	bé-	sɔ́l	-é	ámpē
that	7-	day	2-	set.out	-PERF	again
DEM	NP-	N7/8	SM-	V	-ASP	ADV

'Another day they set out again.'

Tortoise and Dog 052

Nέɛ	bé-	sɔ́lé		áhīn	te,	bé-	pédé		á
nέɛ	bé-	sɔ́l	-é	á- a- hín	te	bé-	pɛ	-édé	á
as	2-	enter	-PERF	LOC- 5- bush	in	2-	arrive	-PERF	LOC
CONJ	SM-	V	-ASP	PFX- NP- N5/6	ADV	SM-	V	-ASP	PFX

nhɔ́g	sē	wê.
n- hɔ́g	sé	wê
3- (fruit)	under	there
NP- N3/4	ADV	ADV

'As they entered the bush they arrived under the nheg tree.'

Tortoise and Dog 053

Bé-	bóótédé		ahɛd		ámpē.
bé-	booted	-é	a-	hɛd	ámpē
2-	begin	-PERF	INF-	search	again
SM-	V	-ASP	PFX-	V	ADV

'They started seaching again.'

Tortoise and Dog 054

Nέɛ	sánkala	nhɔ́g		ne	mwěn	á-	húú		ámīn,
nέɛ	sánkala	n-	hɔ́g	ne	mwěn	á-	húu	-é	ámín
as	big	3-	(fruit)	1.that	itself	o.1-	return	-PERF	up
CONJ	N1	NP-	N3/4	DEM	PRO	SM-	V	-ASP	ADV

a-	bɔmé		kúlɛ		á	mbíd	te	toóy.
a-	bɔm	-é	kûl	-ɛ	á	mbíd	te	toóy
1-	knock	-PERF	9.tortoise	-PERS	LOC	9.back	in	boom
SM-	V	-ASP	N9/10	-SFX	PFX	N9/10	ADV	IDEO

'As a huge *nheg* fruit came down, it knocked Tortoise on the back, boom.'

Tortoise and Dog 055

Kúlɛ		á-	nɔ̄gēn	áte	tim,	aá,	"Mepɔke	mé
kûl	-ɛ	á-	nəgɛn	áte	tim	aá	mepɔke	mé
9.tortoise	-PERS	1.CONS-	bend	into	???	RP.3SG	6.food	6.of
N9/10	-SFX	SM-	V	ADV	IDEO	PAR	N6	AM
mod			ambáá	mê."				
m-	od		a- mbáá	mê				
1-	person		1- big	1.that				
NP-	N1/2		CP- ADJ	DEM				

'Tortoise squirmed saying, "This is fine food for a big man." '

Tortoise and Dog 056

Bé-	bé	bé-	hɛdɛ',	bé-	hɛdɛ',	bé-	hɛdɛ'.	
bé-	bé	bé-	hɛd -ɛ'	bé-	hɛd -ɛ'	bé-	hɛd	-ɛ'
2-	still	2-	search -IMPF	2-	search -IMPF	2-	search	-IMPF
SM-	V	SM-	V -ASP	SM-	V -ASP	SM-	V	-ASP

'They kept on searching and searching and searching.'

Tortoise and Dog 057

Héɛ	nhɔ́g	mémpée	ḿ-	páté		ámīn,	ḿ-
hê	n- hɔ́g	mé- mpée	ḿ-	páde	-é	ámín	ḿ-
there	3- (fruit)	3- other	3-	get.cut	-PERF	up	3-
ADV	NP- N3/4	CP- ADJ	SM-	V	-ASP	ADV	SM-
bɔ́mé		mbwé,	boŋkên	á-	lēpē		esaád, boŋ
bɔm	-é	mbwé	baŋkên	á-	lébe	-é	esaád boŋ
knock	-PERF	9.dog	then	1.CONS-	shout	-CONS	7.shout then
V	-ASP	N9/10	CONJ	SM-	V	-SFX	N7/8 CONJ
ekíde	é-	sɛ̌nlé		áte.			
ekíde	é-	sɛlen	-é	áte			
7.place	7.CONS-	run.off	-CONS	into			
N7/8	SM-	V	-SFX	ADV			

'Then another fruit fell down and hit the dog. He let out a scream and ran off.'

Tortoise and Dog 058

Kúlɛ		aá,	mɔ́-	wēdē-'ɔ̄.		
kûl	-ɛ	aá	mɔ́-	wé	-édé	='ɔ̄
9.tortoise	-PERS	RP.3SG	LOG-	die	-PERF	=DEV
N9/10	-SFX	PAR	SM-	V	-ASP	=CLIT

'Tortoise thought, I have died.'

Tortoise and Dog 059

Mbwέ	chɔ́	mbáá	e-	maá	chɔ́	akɛ	se	etûn.
mbwέ	chɔ́	mbáá	e-	maá	chɔ́	a- kɛ	se	e- tûn
9.dog	9.it	frequently	9-	finish.PERF	9.it	INF- go	right	7- far
N9/10	PRO	PAR	SM-	V	PRO	PFX- V	PAR	NP- N7

'Dog, as always, he had already gone very far.'

Tortoise and Dog 060

Kúlɛ	a-	haglédé,	boŋkên	ngáne	nkɔg	ḿ
kûl -ɛ	a-	hagled -é	baŋkên	ngáne	n- kɔg	ḿ
9.tortoise -PERS	1-	struggle -PERF	then	as	3- log	3.of
N9/10 -SFX	SM-	V -ASP	CONJ	CONJ	NP- N3/4	AM

bwɛl	ḿ- bédé	áhed, dɔ́ə	á- típé	áwed ásē.
bw-ɛl	ḿ- bé -édé	áhed dɔ́ə	á- tíbe -é	áwed ásē
14- tree	3- be -PERF	there then	o.1-go.under -PERF	there down
NP- N14/6	SM- V -ASP	ADV CONJ	SM- V -ASP	ADV ADV

'Tortoise struggled to get away. Then, as there was a log nearby, he went under it.'

Tortoise and Dog 061

A-	mbíí	nɛ́n	aá	nzé	mɔ́-	hɔ̄bē	mɔ́ɔ̄	mɔ́-
a-	m- bíí	nɛ́n	aá	nzé	mɔ́-	hɔ́b -é	mɔ́ɔ̄	mɔ́-
1-	PAST- know	COMP	RP.3SG	if	LOG-	talk -PERF	RP.LOG	LOG-
SM-	TNS- V	CONJ	PAR	CONJ	SM-	V -ASP	PAR	SM-

nəgtɛ'	aá,	né	ane	mod	ă-	kōb	mɔ́.
nəged -ɛ'	aá	né	ane	m- od	ă- kób	mɔ́
run -IMPF	RP.3SG	then	1.that	1- person	1.FUT- catch	1.him
V -ASP	PAR	CONJ	DEM	NP- N1/2	SM- V	PRO

'He knew if he said that he would run, then the man would catch him.'

Tortoise and Dog 062

Esámékɔ̄mtēnē	ane	mod	a-	maá-'ɛ
Esámékɔ̄mtēnē	ane	m- od	a-	maá = 'ɛ
immediately	1.that	1- person	1-	finish-PERF = ADD
ADV	DEM	NP- N1/2	SM-	V = CLIT

apɛ,	a-	bootédé	ekíde	anɔn.
a- pɛ	a-	booted -é	ekíde	a- nɔn
INF- arrive	1-	begin -PERF	7.place	INF- look
PFX- V	SM-	V -ASP	N7/8	PFX- V

'Immediately that man arrived and began to look around the place.'

Tortoise and Dog 063

Aá	ken,	"Héé		bad		ábe	bé-	bɛle	ḿmê		mbɛntéd
aá	ken	héé	b-	od		ábe	bé-	bɛle	ḿmé	m-	bɛntéd
RP.3SG	Q	where	2-	person	2.who		2-	do.to	3.that	3-	deeds
PAR	PAR	QADV	NP-	N1/2	REL		SM-	V	DEM	NP-	N3

ńsyɔ̄ɔ̄l			bé-	díí,	ábe	mɔ́-		nyēnēē."		
ḿ-		syəɔ́l	bé-	díí	ábe	mɔ́-		nyén	-ɛ'	-'ɛ́
3-		all	2-	be.DEP	2.who	LOG.NEG-		see	-IMPF	-SF
CP-		ADJ	SM-	V	REL	SM-		V	-ASP	-SFX

'He asked, "Where are the people who do all those things, and who he doesn't see?" '

Tortoise and Dog 064

Mwǎ		e'nɔn		mbáá		a-	boótédé		akɔ́n		á
mw-	ǎ	e'-	nɔn	mbáá		a-	booted	-é	a-	kɔ́n	á
1-	small	14-	bird	frequently		1-	begin	-PERF	INF-	sing	LOC
NP-	N1/2	NP-	N14/6	PAR		SM-	V	-ASP	PFX-	V	PFX

bwɛl		mîn	ámpē.	
bw-	ɛl	mîn	ámpē	
14-	tree	on	also	
NP-	N14/6	ADV	ADV	

'The little bird, as always, began to sing on the tree again.'

Tortoise and Dog 065

"Ówásā	fyǎndéé	chəŋ,	ówásā	mukɔkɔ́ɔ́	chəŋ	Ówásā
Ówásā	fyǎndéé	chəŋ	Ówásā	mukɔkɔ́ɔ́	chəŋ	Ówásā
-	-	-	-	-	-	-
-	-	-	-	-	-	-

	fyǎndéé	chəŋ,	ówásā	mukɔkɔ́ɔ́	chəŋ."
	fyǎndéé	chəŋ	Ówásā	mukɔkɔ́ɔ́	chəŋ
	-	-	-	-	-
	-	-	-	-	-

' "Look under the tree, look under the log. Look under the tree, look under the log." '

Tortoise and Dog 066

Ane	mod	a-	dulé	áte	chóŋŋ	aá,
ane	m- od	a-	dul -é	áte	chóŋŋ	aá
1.that	1- person	1-	think -PERF	into	thoughtfully	RP.3SG
DEM	NP- N1/2	SM-	V -ASP	ADV	IDEO	PAR

"Mbwé-ē		esaád	é-	bídé		á	nhɔ́g
m- bwé	=ɛ́ɛ	esaád	é-	bíd	-é	á	n- hɔ́g
3- day	=which	7.shout	o.7-	come-out	-PERF	LOC	3- (fruit)
NP- N3/4	=clit	N7/8	sm-	v	-asp	pfx	np- n3/4

sé	wén,	néne	e'nɔn	bén	bé-	nkɔ́nné		ámpē.
sé	wén	nén-e	e'- nɔn	bén	bé- n-		kɔ́n -'ɛ́	ámpē
under	there	then?	14- bird	14.this	14- PAST-		sing -SF	again
ADV	ADV	????	NP- N14/6	DEM	SM- TNS-		V -SFX	ADV

'The man reflected, "The day when a shout came from under the *nheg* tree there this bird also sang.'

Tortoise and Dog 067

Chii-'ɛ		ámpē	a-	kɔ́né.
chii	='ɛ	ámpē	a-	kɔ́n -é
today	=ADD	again	1-	sing -PERF
ADV	=CLIT	ADV	SM-	V -ASP

'Today too it sang.'

Tortoise and Dog 068

Aá	dyam-ɛɛ́		mwǎ		e'nɔn	nén	á-
aá	dy- am	=ɛɛ́	mw- ǎ		e'- nɔn	nén	á-
RP.3SG	5- thing	=TOP	1- small		14- bird	1.this	o.1-
PAR	NP- N5/6	=CLIT	NP- N1/2		NP- N14/6	DEM	SM-

lângeɛ́			mɔ́	nén."
láá	-ɛ'	-'ɛ́	mɔ́	nén
tell	-IMPF	-SF	1.him	like.this
V	-ASP	-SFX	PRO	ADV

'It is something this little bird is telling me like that." '

Tortoise and Dog 069

A-	wógé	mwǎ		e'nɔn	a-	kɔ́ne	ámpē.
a-	wóg -é	mw- ǎ		e'- nɔn	a-	kɔ́n -ɛ'	ámpē
1-	hear -PERF	1- small		14- bird	1-	sing -IMPF	again
SM-	V -ASP	NP- N1/2		NP- N14/6	SM-	V -ASP	ADV

'He listened to the little bird again.'

Tortoise and Dog 070

"Ówásā	fyăndéé	chəŋ,	ówásā	mukɔkɔ́ɔ́	chəŋ	Ówásā
Ówásā	fyăndéé	chəŋ	Ówásā	mukɔkɔ́ɔ́	chəŋ	Ówásā
-	-	-	-	-	-	-
-	-	-	-	-	-	-

	fyăndéé	chəŋ,	ówásā	mukɔkɔ́ɔ́	chəŋ."
	fyăndéé	chəŋ	Ówásā	mukɔkɔ́ɔ́	chəŋ
	-	-	-	-	-
	-	-	-	-	-

' "Look under the tree, look under the log. Look under the tree, look under the log." '

Tortoise and Dog 071

Háā	á-	dúlé	debyéé	áte,	bɔŋkên	á-	bootéd-tɛ
hɛ́ɛ	á-	dul	-é	debyéé	áte	bəŋkên	á-	booted	='ɛ
then	o.1-	think	-PERF	wisdom	into	then	1.CONS-	begin	=ADD
CONJ	SM-	V	-ASP	N5	ADV	CONJ	SM-	V	=CLIT

nkɔg	ḿme	ḿ-	bédé	áhed	ńsyɔ̄ɔ̄l	anɔn	ásē.
n-	kɔg	ḿme	ḿ-	bé	-édé	áhed	ń-	syəɔ́l	a-	nɔn	ásē
4-	log	4.which	4-	be	-PERF	there	4-	all	INF-	look	down
NP-	N3/4	REL	SM-	V	-ASP	ADV	CP-	ADJ	PFX-	V	ADV

'Then he reflected and began to look under all the logs which were nearby.'

Tortoise and Dog 072

Dɔ́ə	á-	táné	kúlɛ		a-	dyĕ	hê	chóŋŋ.
dɔ́ə	á-	tán	-é	kûl	-ɛ	a-	dyɛ	hê	chóŋŋ
then	o.1-	meet	-PERF	9.tortoise	-PERS	1-	stay	there	quietly
CONJ	SM-	V	-ASP	N9/10	-SFX	SM-	V	ADV	IDEO

'Then he met Tortoise sitting there quietly.'

Tortoise and Dog 073

"Oóo	wĕ	e-	madé	me e'pum	é'	mɛl	ásē	wén?
Oóo	wĕ	e-	mad	-é	me e'- pum	é'	m- ɛl	ásē	wén
Yeow	you	2SG-	finish	-PERF	1SG 8- fruit	8.of	6- tree	down	there
excl	pro	sm-	v	-asp	pro np- n7/8	am	np- n14/6	adv	adv

' "Yeow, you finished all my tree fruits under there?'

Tortoise and Dog 074

Aá	ken,	Chán	-e	mɔ́-	bɛlɛé		wɛ	bɔɔb?
aá	ken	chán	-e	mɔ́-	bɛl	-ɛ' -'ɛ́	wɛ	bɔɔb
RP.3SG	Q	how	-??	LOG-	do	-IMPF -SF	2SG	now
PAR	PAR	QADV	-??	SM-	V	-ASP -SFX	PRO	ADV

'What shall I do with you now?'

Tortoise and Dog 075

Aá	á	mekuu		e-	bɛlé	mɔ́-ēē'."
aá	á	me-	kuu	e-	bɛl -é	mɔ́ =ɛ
RP.3SG	LOC	6-	foot	2SG-	do -PERF	1.him =Q
PAR	PFX	NP-	N7/6	SM-	V -ASP	PRO =CLIT

'Your legs have been your downfall."'

Tortoise and Dog 076

Hɛ́ɛ	á-	tédé		lo	kúlɛ,		boŋ	a-	hé	mɔ́
hê	á-	téd	-é	lo	kûl	-ɛ	boŋ	a-	hé	mɔ́
there	O.1-	take	-PERF	Mr.	9.tortoise	-PERS	then	1-	put	1.him
ADV	SM-	V	-ASP	TIT	N9/10	-SFX	CONJ	SM-	V	PRO

	ékwɛ		tê.
á-	e-	kwɛ	tê
LOC-	7-	bag	inside
PFX-	NP-	N7/8	ADV

'Then he took Mr. Tortoise and put him in a bag.'

Tortoise and Dog 077

A-	kɛɛne		kúlɛ,		kúlɛ-'ɛ			a-
a-	kɛɛn	-ɛ'	kûl	-ɛ	kûl	-ɛ	='ɛ	a-
1-	go.with	-IMPF	9.tortoise	-PERS	9.tortoise	-PERS	=ADD	1-
SM-	V	-ASP	N9/10	-SFX	N9/10	-SFX	=CLIT	SM-

nyag	abúú			ékwɛ	tê	wê.
nyɛ	a-	búú	á-	e- kwɛ	tê	wê
defecate	5-	excrement	LOC-	7- bag	inside	there
V	NP-	N5/6	PFX-	NP- N7/8	ADV	ADV

'He took him along, and Tortoise excreted into the bag.'

Tortoise and Dog 078

Apɛɛn	áde	á-	pééné	kúlɛ		á	ndáb	te,
a-	pɛɛn	áde	á-	pɛɛn -é	kûl -ɛ	á	ndáb	te
INF-	bring	5.which	O.1-	bring -PERF	9.tortoise -PERS	LOC	9.house	in
PFX-	V	REL	SM-	V -ASP	N9/10 -SFX	PFX	N9/10	ADV

a- bwémé	mɔ́	ásē	néngāne	mod		a-	hɔ́bé	
a- bwém -é	mɔ́	ásē	ngáne	m-	od	a-	hɔ́b	-é
1- throw -PERF	1.him	down	as	1-	person	1-	talk	-PERF
SM- V -ASP	PRO	ADV	CONJ	NP-	N1/2	SM-	V	-ASP

nέn	aá,	mɔ́-	wūū	nyam	eché	e-	maá		awé.
nέn	aá	mɔ́-	wúu	nyam	eché	e-	maá	a-	wé
COMP	RP.3SG	LOG-	kill	9.animal	9.which	9-	finish.PERF	INF-	die
CONJ	PAR	SM-	V	N9/10	REL	SM-	V	PFX-	V

'Bringing him into the house he threw him down like when somebody says, I have killed an animal, it is already dead.'

Tortoise and Dog 079

Mwěn-nɛ	a-	bídé		mɔ́.
mwěn -'ɛ	a-	bíd	-é	mɔ́
himself -ADD	1-	come.out	-PERF	1.he
PRO -CLIT	SM-	V	-ASP	PRO

'He himself went out.'

Tortoise and Dog 080

Nɛ́ɛ	kúlɛ		á-	nɔ́né	ekíde	nέn,	e-	
nɛ́ɛ	kûl	-ɛ	á-	nɔn -é	ekíde	nέn	e-	
as	9.tortoise	-PERS	O.1-	look -PERF	7.place	like.this	1.NEG-	
CONJ	N9/10	-SFX	SM-	V -ASP	N7/8	ADV	SM-	

nyénɛé		modmod,	a-	bíté		mekáá,		a-
nyén -é	-'ɛ	modmod	a-	bíde	-é	me-	káá	a-
see -PERF	-SF	nobody	1-	go.out	-PERF	6-	hand	1-
V -ASP	-SFX	N1	SM-	V	-ASP	NP-	N7/6	SM-

wéd-tɛ		mwǎ		yɔ̌l	áte.
wéd	='ɛ	mw-	ǎ	yɔ̌l	áte
gather.strength	=ADD	1-	small	9.body	into
V	=CLIT	NP-	N1/2	N9/10	ADV

'As Tortoise looked around the place he saw nobody, he put out his hands and stretched himself.'

Text

Tortoise and Dog 081

Kúrúd	kúrúd	kúrúd,	a-	bídé-'aá			á	pīpīī.
kúrúd	kúrúd	kúrúd	a-	bíd	-é	-'ɔ̌	á	pípíí
-	-	-	1-	come.out	-PERF	-DEV	LOC	behind
IDEO	IDEO	IDEO	SM-	V	-ASP	-CLIT	PFX	N

'He went out behind (the house).'

Tortoise and Dog 082

Nɛ́ɛ	á-	wóglɛ́né		nɛ́n	á-	sɔ̄ɔ̄m-mɛ.	
nɛ́ɛ	á-	woglɛn	-é	nɛ́n	á-	sɔɔm	='ɛ
as	o.1-	listen	-PERF	like.this	1.NEUT-	hide	=ADD
CONJ	SM-	V	-ASP	ADV	SM-	V	=CLIT

'As he listened like that he also hid.'

Tortoise and Dog 083

Póndé-ɛ		ane	mod	á-	sɔ́lé		á	ndáb	te,
póndé	=ɛ́ɛ	ane	m- od	á-	sɔ́l	-é	á	ndáb	te
time	=which	1.that	1- person	o.1-	enter	-PERF	LOC	9.house	in
N9	=CLIT	DEM	NP- N1/2	SM-	V	-ASP	PFX	N9/10	ADV

aá	mɔ́ɔ̄-	nyěn ekwɛ	ásē,	a-	wóge		nɛ́ɛ ekwɛ	
aá	mɔ́ɔ̄-	nyen e- kwɛ	ásē	a-	wóg	-ɛ'	nɛ́ɛ e-	kwɛ
RP.3SG	LOG.FUT-	lift 7- bag	down	1-	feel	-IMPF	as 7-	bag
PAR	SM-	V NP- N7/8	ADV	SM-	V	-ASP	CONJ NP-	N7/8

é-	délé	áte,	a-	se-	bíi	nɛ́n	aá	mebúú	
é-	del	-é	áte	a-	se-	bíí	nɛ́n	aá	me- búú
o.7-heavy		-PERF	into	1-	NEG	know	COMP	RP.3SG	6- excrement
SM- V		-ASP	ADV	SM-	PFX-	V	CONJ	PAR	NP- N5/6

ḿme	kúle		á-	tímé.
ḿme	kûl	-ɛ	á-	tim	-é
6.which	9.tortoise	-PERS	o.1-	return	-PERF
REL	N9/10	-SFX	SM-	V	-ASP

'When the man entered the house intending to lift the bag, he felt that the bag was heavy, he didn't know it had become the excrements of Tortoise.'

Tortoise and Dog 084

Lo	kúlɛ		a-	mmǎd	akɛ,	á-	pɛ̄
lo	kûl	-ɛ	a-	m- mad	a- kɛ	á-	pɛ
Mr.	9.tortoise	-PERS	1-	PAST- finish	INF- go	1.NEUT-	arrive
TIT	N9/10	-SFX	SM-	TNS- V	PFX- V	SM-	V

.

áwi   ndáb   te.
áwi   ndáb   te
LOC.his   9.house   in
POSS   N9/10   ADV

'Mr. Tortoise had already gone and arrived in his house.'

Tortoise and Dog 085

Boŋ	**epun**		**ehɔ́g**		**nɛ́ɛ**	**bɔ́**	**mbwé**	**bé-**	**nyénné**	
boŋ	e-	pun	e-	hɔ́g	nɛ́ɛ	bɔ́	mbwé	bé-	nyénɛn	-é
then	7-	day	7-	one	as	2.they	9.dog	2-	see.REFL	-PERF
CONJ	NP-	N7/8	CP-	NUM	CONJ	PRO	N9/10	SM-	V	-ASP

ámpē,	**boŋ**	**á-**	**lāngē**		**mɔ́**	**aá,**	**a**	**mwɛ́ɛ̄,**	**haá**
ámpē	boŋ	á-	láŋ	-é	mɔ́	aá	a	mwé	haá
again	then	1.CONS-	say	-CONS	1.him	RP.3SG	VOC	friend	is.it.not
ADV	CONJ	SM-	V	-SFX	PRO	PAR	PAR	N1	PAR

chii	**mɔ́-**	**paké**		**á**	**ndáb**	**nén-ɛ̄ɛ̄?**	
chii	mɔ́-	pag	-'é	á	ndáb	nén	=ɛɛ́
today	LOG-	arrive	-SF	LOC	9.house	like.this	=Q
ADV	SM-	V	-SFX	PFX	N9/10	ADV	=CLIT

'Then one day as he and Dog saw each other again, he said to him, "Friend, is it not today that I am reaching the house."

Tortoise and Dog 086

Wě-	**kudted-áa**		**mɔ́**	**mbɔ́lɔ́n**	**nɛ́ɛ̄?"**
wě-	kudted	=áa	mɔ́	mbɔ́lɔ́n	nɛ́ɛ̄
2SG.NEG-	make.get	=DEV?	1.him	loss	like.that
SM-	V	=CLIT	PRO	N	ADV

'Didn't you cause me to get that loss (delay) like that?"'

Tortoise and Dog 087

Hɛ́ɛ	**echoŋ**	**éche**	**mbwé**	**ne**	**kûl**	**é-**	**tímé**	
hê	echoŋ	éche	mbwé	ne	kûl	é-	tim	-é
there	friendship	7.which	9.dog	and	9.tortoise	O.7-	at.last	-PERF
ADV	N7	REL	N9/10	CONJ	N9/10	SM-	V	-ASP

amaa.	
a-	maa
INF-	finish
PFX-	V

'There the friendship of Dog and Tortoise ended at last.'

Bibliography

General works

Alobwede d'Epie, Charles. 1982. The language of traditional medicine in Bakossi. Ph.D. dissertation, Yaoundé University.
Angenot, Jean Pierre, Ulunga Mukubi Wamunshiya, and Jacques L. Vincke. 1973. Introduction to a theory of marking and transposition. A transpositional anti-grammar of the Koose language of Cameroon. *Culture au Zaïre et en Afrique, Révue Zaïroise des Sciences de l'homme,* ONRD 2:33–83.
Apuge, Michael Etuge. 1997. On Wh-operator extraction in Akosse Syntax. M.A. thesis, University of Buea, Cameroon.
Clarke, John. 1848. *Specimens of dialects: Short vocabularies of languages and notes of countries and customs in Africa.* Berwick-upon-Tweed: Daniel Cameron.
Dorsch, Heinrich. 1910/11. Grammatik der Nkosi-Sprache. *Zeitschrift für Kolonialsprachen* 1:241–283.
Dorsch, Heinrich. 1911/13. Vocabularium der Nkosi-Sprache (Kamerun). Nkosi-Deutsch. *Zeitschrift für Kolonialsprachen* 2:16–193, 324–330; 3:34–62.
Dorsch, Heinrich. 1915. Vocabularium der Nkosi-Sprache (Kamerun). Deutsch-Nkosi. *Jahrbuch der Hamburgischen Wissenschaftlichen Anstalten* XXXII. 1914. (5. Beiheft: Mitteilungen, veröffentlicht

vom Seminar für Kolonialsprachen. Hamburg: Otto Meissner Verlag.)

Ebong, Mesumbe. 1999. Tense: A contrastive morphosyntactic study of Akoose. DIPES II dissertation, Ecole Normale Supérieur, Universtiy of Yaoundé.

Ejedepang-Koge, Samuel Ngome. 1986. *The tradition of a people: Bakossi. A historico-socio-anthropological study of one of Cameroon's Bantu peoples*. Revised edition. Published by the author.

Ekanjume, Beatrice. 1998. A sketch outline of tones in Akoose. M.A. thesis, University of Yaounde 1.

Ekanjume, Beatrice. 2006. The phrasal phonology of tones in Akɔ́ɔ́se: Evidence form naturally occurring code-switching data. Ph.D. thesis, University of Yaounde 1.

Enang Ajang Aloysius. n.d. The classification of Akosse nouns. ms.

Enang Ajang Aloysius. 1994. Some observations on Bakossi names. In Hedinger and Hedinger (comps.). *Mĭn mé Akɔɔse—Bakossi Names*, 10–13.

Friesen, Lisa. 2002. Valence change and Oroko verb morphology (Mbonge dialect). M.A. thesis, University of North Dakota.

Gordon, Raymond G. Jr., ed. 2005. *Ethnologue: Languages of the world*, fifteenth edition, Dallas: SIL International. http://www.ethnologue.com

Guthrie, Malcolm. 1953. *The Bantu languages of Western Equatorial Africa*. London: Oxford University Press.

Guthrie, Malcolm. 1967–1971. *Comparative Bantu: An introduction to the comparative linguistics and prehistory of the Bantu languages*. Farnborough: Gregg International Publisher.

Haaren, Wim van. 1988. *Nyandong: een dorp van cacaoverbouwers in Zuidwest Kameroen. Een cultureel antropologisch onderzoek naar de integratie van een cash crop-economie in de Bakossi-samenleving*. Leiden, Rijksuniversiteit te Leiden: Instituut voor Culturele Antropologie en Sociologie der Niet-Westerse Samenlevingen (ICA).

Hatfield, Deborah, Janneke Vanderkooy, and Marcia Bleeker. 1991. A sociolinguistic survey among the Bakossi.Yaoundé: SIL. ms. Published in 2003 as SIL Electronic Survey Report 2003–007. <http://www.sil.org/silesr/abstract.asp?ref=2003-007>. Accessed on 31 October 2007.

Hedinger, Robert. 1980. The noun classes of Akɔɔse (Bakossi). In Larry M. Hyman (ed.), *Noun classes in the Grassfields Bantu borderland*. Southern California Occasional Papers in Linguistics 8:1–26.

Hedinger, Robert. 1981. Pronouns in Akɔɔse. Studies in African Linguistics 12:277–290.

Hedinger, Robert. 1983. Locatives in Akɔɔse (Bakossi). *Journal of West African Languages* 13.2:7–22.
Hedinger, Robert. 1984. Reported speech in Akɔɔse. *Journal of West African Languages* 14.1:81–102.
Hedinger, Robert. 1985a. The verb in Akɔɔse. *Studies in African Lingustics* 16:1–55.
Hedinger, Robert. 1985b. Double reflexes of PB stops and the lenis/ non-lenis distinction, evidence from Proto-Manenguba and Akɔɔse. Paper read at the 16th WALS Congress, Yaoundé, Cameroon. March 25–29, 1985.
Hedinger, Robert. 1985c. Some issues in the establishment of an orthography for Akɔɔse. ms.
Hedinger, Robert. 1986. A preliminary analysis of the verb phrase and auxiliaries in Akɔɔse. Paper presented to the 17th West African Languages Congress, Ibadan, Nigeria. March 17–22, 1986.
Hedinger, Robert. 1987. *The Manenguba languages (Bantu A.15, Mbo cluster) of Cameroon.* London: School of Oriental and African Studies.
Hedinger, Robert. 1992. Verbal extensions in Akɔɔse: Their form, meaning and valency changes. *Afrika und Übersee* 75:227–251.
Hedinger, Robert. 1993. Bakossi alphabet and orthography statement. ms.
Hedinger, Robert. 2001. Akɔɔse-English dictionary. Lexical database of approx. 4500 entries.
Hedinger, Robert, and Sylvia Hedinger. 1977. *Phonology of Akɔɔse (Bakossi).* Yaoundé: SIL.
Heine, Bernd. 1976. *A typology of African Languages.* Berlin: Dietrich Reimer.
Ittmann, Johannes. 1930. Aus dem Rätselschatz der Kosi. *Zeitschrift für Eingeborenensprachen.* 21:25–54.
Ittmann, Johannes. 1936. Sprichwörter der Kosi. *Mitteilungen des Seminars für Orientalische Sprachen* 39:111–176.
Jacquot, A., and I. Richardson. 1956. Part I. Report of the western team. Atlantic coast to Oubangui. *Linguistic survey of the Northern Bantu borderland,* I:9–62. London: Oxford University Press.
Kilham, Hannah. 1828. *Specimens of African languages, spoken in the colony of Sierra Leone.* London: Society of Friends for Promoting African Instruction.
Koelle, Sigismund Wilhelm. 1854. *Polyglotta Africana, or a comparative vocabulary of nearly three hundred words and phrases in more than one hundred distinct African lanugages.* London: Church Missionary

House. Reprinted 1963, Graz: Akad. Druck und Verlagsanstalt.
Levin, Michael David. 1976. Family structure in Bakosi: Social change in an African society. Ph.D. dissertation, Princeton University.
Longacre, Robert E. 1976. *An anatomy of speech notions.* Lisse: Peter deRidder Press.
Maho, Jouni. 2003. A classification of the Bantu languages: An update of Guthrie's referential system. In Derek Nurse and Gérard Philippson (eds.), *The Bantu languages.* London and New York: Routledge.
Meeussen, A. E. 1967. Bantu grammatical reconstructions. *Africana linguistica* III:79–121.
Ngome, Manasse. nd. Akose orthography. ms.
Palle, Angela Diengu. 2000. The lexical phonology of Akoose nouns. M.A. thesis, University of Buea, Cameroon.
Richardson, Irvine. 1957. *Linguistic survey of the Northern Bantu borderland,* 2. London: Oxford University Press.
Schadeberg, Thilo C. 1982. Les suffixes verbaux séparatifs en bantou. *Sprache und Geschichte in Afrika* 4:55–66.
Wamunshiya, Ilunga M. 1973. Quelques aspects de la grammaire générative et transformationelle de la langue Koose (langue bantoue du Cameroun). Mémoire de Licence, Université Nationale du Zaïre, Lubumbashi.
Welmers, William E. 1973. *African language structures.* Berkeley: University of California Press.

Works written in Akɔɔse

Kwééd ne mpuu ḿme Yésuɛ. 1995.
Echyáa é Yésu. 1996.
Ngan e ńdyɔŋ ḿ mbód ḿme mé bɔ́ɔ. 1996.
Ngan echě mwăn awĕ ambɔ́ɔ. 1996.
Ngan echě bad bébɛ ábe bé nkĕ akáne. 1996.
Nkalaŋ ḿ bwáam ḿme Yésuɛ ngáne Lúkasɛ á télé. 1998.
Nkalaŋ ḿme Rûtɛ. 2000. Yaoundé: CABTAL.
Kálag e nkáŋge e BAPRESCA. The BAPRESCA Song Book. 2002 Tombel: Bakossi Bible Translation Project.
Nkalâŋ ḿ bwáam ḿme Yésuɛ. The four Gospels in Akɔɔse. Trial edition for reading in the churches. 2006. Tombel. Bakossi Bible Translation Project.

Bakossi Language Committee. 1993. *E'kii bé Akɔɔse. The Bakossi Alphabet.* Yaoundé: Bakossi Language Committee.

BAPRESCA. 1998. Mendíb mé achóm. Volume 2. (Tape of 15 songs in Akɔ́ɔsé composed by Paul Epie Mesumbe and Njume Ray Etone).
BAPRESCA. 1998. Mboŋ ne mbéb bé wanɛ. Volume 3. (Tape of 15 songs in Akɔ́ɔsé composed by Paul Epie Mesumbe and Njume Ray Etone)
Ekinde, Epwene Ntube. 2000. N yɔ́ke Akɔ́ɔ̄sē (I am learning Akɔɔse). Tombel: Akɔɔse Language Committee (ALACOM).
Hedinger, Robert, Sylvia Hedinger, and G.E.R Metuge. 1977. *Friendship stories in Akɔɔse.* Yaoundé: SIL.
Hedinger, Robert, Sylvia Hedinger, and G.E.R Metuge. 1977. *Dé tel, dé lâŋgɛ Akɔɔse (Let's Read and Write Akɔɔse).* Yaoundé: SIL.
Hedinger, Robert, Sylvia Hedinger and G.E.R Metuge. 1992. *Dé tel, dé lâŋ-'ɛ Akɔɔse. Let's Read and Write Bakossi.* Yaoundé: SIL.
Hedinger, Robert, Sylvia Hedinger, and G.E.R. Metuge. 2001. *Dé tel, dé lâŋgɛ Akɔɔse (Let's Read and Write Bakossi).* Yaoundé: SIL. Revision.
Hedinger, Robert, and Sylvia Hedinger (comps.). 1994. *Mǐn mé Akɔ́ɔ́sé. Bakossi Names.* Yaoundé: Bakossi Language Committee.
Metuge, G.E.R. 1976. Echáa Ékɔɔsé. (Birth in Bakossi.) Yaoundé: S.I.L. Experimental edition.
Metuge, G.E.R (trans.). 1998. *Kálag e mesoŋgé e'só.* Yaoundé: SIL. PROPELCA Series No. 67. DALL, FLSS, University of Yaoundé.
The Participants at the Akɔɔse Literacy Teacher Training Program. 1998. Menyâ mé Akɔ́ɔsé (Stories in Akɔ́ɔsé). Duplicated.

Index

A

ability 159, 160
abstract quality 170
accompaniment 77, 167, 176, 177, 204, 206
active clauses 172
additive 5
addressee(s) 215, 218–220, 222
adjectival 46
adjective(s) 16, 33, 34, 44–46, 60, 62
adjunct(s) 77, 106, 144, 165, 167, 175–177, 204
adverbial(s) 62, 141, 142, 152, 153, 157, 161, 169, 208, 213, 232
adverb(s) 41, 75, 154, 155, 158, 166, 177, 179, 181, 182, 184, 206–208, 211, 214, 244
affirmative 101–106, 109–112, 124, 168, 189, 190, 241, 242
aforementioned 34, 35, 39
afterthought 198
agentive nouns 23
agent-object 67
agent(s) 67, 77, 90, 97, 99
agglutinative 83
agreement 2, 11, 16–19, 24, 26, 34, 38, 42, 45, 47, 54, 55, 64, 65, 80, 85, 152, 167, 183, 193, 200, 207, 223, 232, 253
allophone 4
Alobwede d'Epie 2
analytic causatives 213
anaphoric demonstrative 38, 39
and-coordination 225
Angenot 2
answer 198, 210, 251
antecedent 16, 17
applicative 87, 91, 93, 94, 99
apposition(s) 59, 205, 222
Apuge 2
argument(s) 28, 45, 214

article 51, 91
aspect(s) 2, 5, 7, 47, 84–86, 100, 101, 103, 134, 137, 151, 152, 169, 241
aspectual(s) 152, 153, 158, 159
assertion 166, 167
assimilation 6
associative 8, 16–18, 25, 29, 30, 32, 33, 45, 46, 53, 55, 57, 58, 60, 62–66, 69, 70, 76, 77, 155, 156, 194, 197
associative (marker) 8, 16, 17, 32, 45, 53, 57, 60, 62, 63, 70, 76, 77, 155, 156, 194
associative noun phrase(s) 18, 30, 33, 46, 57, 62, 64, 65, 69, 76
attributive 165
attributively 44
auxiliaries 158, 159, 162
auxiliary 79, 138, 151–153, 156–162

B

Bakosi/Bakossi 1–3, 15, 20, 79, 201, 222
Bangem 1
Bantu 2, 11, 16, 19, 21, 43, 83, 88, 183
Basedow 2
benefactive 96, 167, 186
beneficiary 99
but-coordination 226

C

Cameroon 1
cardinal numerals 50
causative(s) 87, 89, 94, 97, 174, 213, 233
causative verb(s) 174, 213

circumstantial 235
Clarke 2
class(es) 2, 3, 5, 11–24, 26, 28, 29, 32–45, 50–58, 60–64, 67, 70, 72, 76, 77, 80, 81, 84–86, 109, 112, 116, 124, 126, 128, 152, 153, 156–159, 166, 169, 178, 179, 183, 193, 196, 200, 203, 204, 207, 208, 215, 223, 232, 253, 254
class/gender 22, 26
classification 21, 158, 159
clause combination(s) 213, 225
clause constituent(s) 165, 190, 199, 201, 204
clause(s) 16–18, 24, 33, 34, 47, 48, 56, 57, 59, 77, 79, 85, 96, 102, 104–106, 134, 141–144, 151–156, 158, 165, 167, 168, 170–176, 178, 182–184, 186, 189–191, 193–195, 198, 199, 201–208, 210, 211, 213–218, 222–238, 241, 243, 244
clitic 58, 80, 191, 198, 200
coalescence 26
cognate 173, 202, 209, 210
cognitive(s) 160
colour terms 47, 254
comitative 77, 87, 90, 93–95, 98, 204, 206
comparative clauses 238
comparative(s) 48, 49, 72, 79, 198, 225, 238, 255
comparison(s) 19, 48, 79, 162, 170, 184
complementiser(s) 175, 214, 215, 221, 222, 224, 225
complement(s) 45, 89, 96, 106, 144, 151–157, 165–167, 169, 170, 171, 175, 180, 204, 224
complex prepositions 76

complex sentences 213
compound noun(s) 30, 65, 66
compound pronouns 80, 81, 220
concessive 234
concord(s) 2, 16, 17, 19, 21, 26, 29, 35, 44, 83, 84, 109, 120, 136, 179, 207, 220, 241
conditional 105, 122, 236
condition(s) 64, 122, 237
conjunction(s) 53, 70–74, 78, 79, 106, 182, 194, 213, 225–228, 231, 235, 238, 244
connectives 238
consecutive 137
consonant(s) 3–6, 8, 9, 20, 22, 51, 86, 88, 178, 192, 255
constituent(s) 33, 34, 105, 151, 165, 189, 190, 193–196, 198, 199, 201, 203, 204, 206, 207, 210, 241
construction(s) 17, 25, 29, 45, 55, 60, 62, 65, 69, 70, 71, 138, 156, 157, 171, 189, 190, 194, 209, 210
container-contents 68
content clauses 222, 223
content questions 191, 193
contra-expectation 235
coordinate noun phrase 33, 70
copular 47, 167–169, 171, 194
copular verb 47, 167–169, 171

D

demonstrative(s) 16, 33–39, 41, 61, 72, 165–167, 178, 182, 200, 243
dependent clause(s) 102, 104–106, 168
dependent form(s) 100, 102–104, 231, 242
dependent subject 132
dependent verb form(s) 102, 104, 205
derivational 56, 86, 92
derivational affixes 86
desiderative 146
desire 159, 160
determiner(s) 45, 61
dialectal 78, 243
dialect(s) 3, 20, 21, 39, 44, 45, 101, 122, 193
diminutive 29
directional(s) 155, 158, 159, 161
direct object 97–99, 153, 165, 167, 174, 189, 203–205, 214, 222
direct speech 214, 218–221
discourse 16, 51, 109, 118, 122, 134, 137, 167, 168, 171, 176, 182, 209, 217, 225
distal 34, 35, 37, 166, 200
distributional subclasses 158
ditransitive 97, 174
Dorsch 2, 19
double-class gender(s) 12, 13
downstep 6–8, 45, 46, 64, 67, 118, 134
downstepped 7, 8, 37, 138
downstepped-high 7
Duala 3
dual pronouns 81, 82

E

Ebage 1, 28, 261
Ebong 2
echo verb(s) 143, 144, 151, 152, 157, 168
Efik 250, 252
Ejedepang-Koge 1, 253
Ekanjume 2

elide(s) 6, 64, 114
elision 6, 8, 26, 29, 32
Elong 1, 261
Elung 2, 3, 256–260
emphasis 186, 192, 218
emphatic 39–41, 46, 59, 60, 72, 78, 80, 81, 111, 157, 168, 179
Enang 2, 211
English 3, 194, 243, 245, 250
Epang 1
Epie 2
exclamations 250
exclusive 41, 82
existence 25, 166, 169, 171
exogamous 253
extention 97
extraposition 168

F

far-distal 34, 35, 166
finite verb 85, 138
folk tale(s) 26, 261
formal suffix 89, 91, 92
French 250, 252
Friesen 88
fronting 189, 195, 210
future 85, 100–104, 126–133, 141–143, 227
future imperfective 100–104, 130–133
future imperfective negative 132, 133
future negative(s) 128, 129, 132

G

gap 203–205
gapping 204, 206
gender(s) 12–16, 20, 22, 23, 26, 52, 64, 254

generic 52, 68, 196, 243
glide(s) 6
glottal 5, 6, 96, 102
Gordon 2
Guthrie 2

H

Haaren 252
habitual 114, 159
Hatfield 3
headless relative clause(s) 207, 208
head-modifier 66
hearer 182
Hedinger 2, 3, 11, 27, 51, 83, 84, 89, 102, 211, 241
homorganic nasal(s) 63, 85, 101, 118
hortative imperfective 146–148
hortative perfective 146, 147
human/non-human 13, 18, 26, 71, 75, 167, 193, 222

I

ideophone(s) 4, 184, 185, 244, 248
immediate future 141–143
immediate past 109, 141, 142
imperative and hortative negative 148, 149
imperative imperfective 146
imperative perfective 145
imperfective 25, 88, 100–104, 114–117, 122–125, 130–133, 137, 145–148, 241
inanimate 98, 167, 177
inceptive 159
inclusive 82
incompletive 159

indefinite 51
independent 25, 104, 108, 112–114, 116, 118, 120, 122, 124, 126, 128, 130, 132, 134, 138, 139, 168, 190, 191
indirect object(s) 77, 96, 97, 99, 165, 167, 169, 174, 175, 201, 203–205, 210, 214, 215, 221, 222
indirect questions 199, 224
indirect speech 214, 218, 219, 220, 221
infinitival 71
infinitive(s) 24, 155, 156, 202, 209, 229
information questions 193
in situ 195–197, 204, 210
instrument 77, 89, 96, 98, 151, 167, 175, 176, 201, 203–205
instrument/accompaniment 167
instrumental 25, 87, 89, 93–96, 98, 165, 205, 206
intensification 157
intensifier(s) 60
intent 159, 160
intention 146, 160, 214, 224
intransitive 97, 99, 168, 170, 172, 173
intransitive clause(s) 168, 170, 172
Ittmann 2

J

jussive 146

K

Kilham 2
kinship terms 18, 70, 252

Koelle 2
Kosi, Kɔssi 2

L

leading questions 198
Levin 253
lexical negation 243
loan word(s) 194, 231
locational phrase(s) 18, 19, 167, 180, 181, 183, 204
location(s) 18, 43, 74–76, 165, 167, 169, 176, 181–183, 193, 195, 201–208, 210, 225
locative preposition 79, 181
locative(s) 11, 18, 25, 43, 44, 73, 75, 76, 79, 96, 151, 155, 179, 181, 183, 184, 206–208
logophoric 85, 215, 216, 219, 220, 224
Londo 88
Longacre 158
Lundu-Balong 2

M

Maho 2
Manenguba 2
manner 151, 165, 167, 176, 184–186, 193, 197, 201, 203, 204
manner adverbs 184
manner particle 186
manner phrase(s) 184, 186, 201, 203
means 54, 77, 218, 229, 233, 245, 254
Meeussen 83
mental activities 160
mental states 160
Mesumbe 1, 261
Metuge 1, 261

modal auxiliary 160
modal(s) 152, 153, 159, 160
modifier-head 66
modifier(s) 11, 16, 18, 33, 34, 44, 45, 50, 55, 57, 58, 61, 66, 178, 179, 182, 183, 196
Mwanenguba 1

N

names 2, 14, 26, 27, 30, 70, 72, 211, 235, 252, 253
Ndando 1, 252
Ndom 1
necessity 159, 160
negation 7, 61, 100, 101–103, 151, 191, 241, 243
negative conditions 237
negative prohibitive 149, 150, 242
negative(s) 28, 30, 61, 73, 79, 85, 101–106, 109, 112, 113, 116, 117, 120, 121, 124, 125, 128, 129, 132, 133, 136, 141, 145, 148–150, 153, 154, 159–161, 166, 168, 189–191, 193, 198, 235, 237, 241–244
neutral 84, 134–136, 151–153, 242, 244
neutralisation 110
neutral negative 136, 242, 244
Ngalame 1
Ngemengoe 3
Ngoe 1, 2
Ngole 1
Ngome 2, 15
nickname(s) 31, 59, 235
Nkōssi, Nkosi 2
Nkwelle 1
Nninong, Ninong 2, 3, 20, 224, 226, 256–260

non-count 15
non-subject 104, 106, 168, 189, 203, 209
non-verbal clause(s) 165, 241
noun modifiers 16, 34, 44, 45, 50, 55, 57, 61
noun phrase(s) 2, 11, 16–18, 30, 33, 34, 46, 55, 57, 59, 61, 62, 64, 65, 69, 70, 73, 74, 76, 80, 96, 98, 99, 165, 173, 193, 202, 245, 246
noun prefixes 11, 19, 20, 22
nouns, abstract 24
noun, structure 22, 29
number(s) 2, 8, 11, 21, 33, 50, 53–56, 80, 81, 83, 86–88, 91, 93, 96, 101, 109, 134, 146, 152, 158, 193, 215, 223, 225, 227, 254
numeral(s) 16, 28, 34, 50–57, 61, 71, 245, 246
Nyandong 3

O

object(s) 8, 11, 17, 29, 32, 61, 67–69, 75, 77, 81, 83, 96–99, 153, 156, 165, 167–169, 172–175, 177, 181, 186, 189, 193, 195–197, 201–206, 209, 210, 214, 215, 221, 222, 224, 225, 254
obligation 159, 160
oblique phrase(s) 77, 176, 186
or-coordination 225, 226
ordinal numeral(s) 50, 56, 57
Oroko 88
orthography 3, 5, 7, 100
O-type 108, 112–114, 116, 118, 120, 122, 124, 126, 128, 130, 132, 134, 138, 139

P

paired 11
pairings 13
Palle 2
paradigm(s) 93, 109, 136, 145, 146, 168, 169, 198
participant(s) 16, 26, 38, 77, 99, 171, 218, 220
particle(s) 25, 59, 61, 75, 78, 94, 153–155, 158, 181, 186, 192, 193, 198, 199, 210, 214–217, 219, 221, 224, 225, 243, 244
part-whole 66
past 16, 19, 87, 88, 100–104, 109, 118–125, 138–142, 152, 155, 156, 163, 175, 178, 179, 181, 183, 185, 192, 195, 197–201, 203, 208, 210, 223–226, 229–236, 242, 252, 262–264, 269, 279, 281, 285
past imperfective 100–104, 122–125
past imperfective negative 124, 125
past negative 120, 121
peak 210
Peng 207
perfect 79, 100, 101, 104, 109–113, 124, 241
perfect affirmative 110, 111
perfective 100–104, 142, 145–148, 242
perfective/imperfective 100
perfect negative 79, 112, 113, 124
performative(s) 158–160
person 12, 18, 25, 27, 30, 31, 39–43, 47–49, 51, 55–57, 59–61, 65, 68, 72, 73, 76, 80–82, 84, 85, 97, 98, 101, 109, 111–113, 115–117, 119, 121, 123–125, 127–129, 131, 133–141, 143, 145–150, 152–155, 171, 172, 176, 179, 181, 191, 192, 194, 196, 200, 205, 206, 208, 209, 211, 214, 215, 218–220, 222–226, 229, 231, 233, 236, 241, 243, 245, 246, 248, 249, 253, 256, 267, 269, 271–273, 278–280, 284, 285
person/class 84, 152
person/concord 84, 136, 241
personifier suffix 26, 72, 253
phasals 158, 159
phoneme(s) 4, 8
phrasal verb(s) 48, 94, 154, 155
phrase(s) 2, 11, 16–19, 30, 33, 34, 46, 48, 49, 55, 57, 59, 61, 62, 64–66, 69, 70, 73–78, 80, 85, 96, 98, 99, 151–153, 155, 156, 158, 162, 165, 167, 170, 173, 176–181, 183, 184, 186, 191, 193, 194, 196, 197, 200–206, 217, 225, 245, 246
Pidgin 3
plural(s) 11–15, 19, 21–24, 28, 32, 40–43, 50–55, 64, 67, 72, 73, 80–82, 85, 99, 110, 112, 114, 116, 118, 120, 122, 124, 126, 128, 130, 132, 134, 141, 142, 147, 149, 172, 215, 216, 220, 222, 223, 254
polarisation 27
polarity 225
polar questions 191–193, 224
politeness adverb(s) 211
portmanteau 73
Portugese 250
positive 73, 198, 242
positive/negative 73
possessed 43, 70
possession 42, 70, 169, 171

possessive noun phrase 33, 70
possessive(s) 16, 18, 19, 33, 34,
    42–44, 58, 61, 70, 253, 254
possessor(s) 70, 175, 204
pragmatic 168, 176
pre-complement 152, 153
predicate 175, 202
predicative(ly) 44, 47, 165
prefixes, double 23
prefixless 63
pre-nasalisation 23
pre-nominal 35–38
prepositional phrase(s) 33, 48,
    49, 55, 74–78, 170, 177, 179,
    184
preposition(s) 48, 49, 71, 72,
    74–79, 170, 175–177, 180, 181,
    184, 186, 198, 204, 225, 244
presentative 165
present imperfective 100, 104,
    114–117, 241
present imperfective negative
    116, 117
prior action 227, 228
prior past 138, 139
pro-drop 167
product-material 69
pro-form 224
prohibitive 149, 150, 242
pronoun, emphatic 39–41
pronoun(s) 16, 17, 37–44, 57,
    58, 70, 72, 73, 80–82, 167,
    168, 178, 183, 186, 187, 189,
    203–205, 207, 208, 214, 218,
    220, 243, 253, 254
pronoun(s), personal 44, 80
property concepts 33, 44, 46, 47
proto-Bantu 43
proximal 34, 35, 166
purpose 24, 33, 69, 81, 85, 155,
    156, 229, 230

Q

qualifier 64
qualifier-head 64
quantification 67
quantifier 60
quantity 64, 67, 162
question phrase(s) 80, 193, 194,
    196, 197
question(s) 45, 46, 52, 79, 80,
    102, 105, 106, 189–199, 210,
    216, 224, 243
question word(s) 52, 80, 189,
    191, 193–197

R

reason 30, 37, 79, 178, 186, 194,
    197, 198, 231, 232, 264
reason and cause 231
reciprocal(s) 72, 87, 90, 95, 99,
    172, 206
reconstruction 241
reduplicated 29, 30, 46, 184, 243
reduplication 28–30, 241, 243,
    254
referential 186, 189
referent(s) 18, 71, 98, 167, 168,
    222
reflexive(s) 39, 41, 173
relative clause(s) 18, 24, 33,
    34, 47, 56, 57, 59, 102, 105,
    106, 178, 182, 189–191, 194,
    202–208, 213, 233
relative pronoun(s) 16, 44, 57, 58,
    70, 178, 183, 189, 203–205,
    207, 208
relativisation 204, 209
relativised 105, 106, 203–207,
    209, 213
repetition 71, 186

repetitive 159
reported speech 85, 213, 214, 218, 224
reporting particle 214–217, 219, 221, 224
restrictive 202
result clause(s) 232
resumptive 24
root-initial 4
root(s) 4, 22, 23, 25, 29–32, 37, 84, 86–89, 92, 96, 99, 107–110, 122, 134, 138, 141, 168, 254, 257
root tone(s) 86, 110, 122, 134, 138

S

Schadeberg 91
season(s) 252
semantic subclasses 158
semidirect speech 214, 218–220
semivowels 6, 108
sentence-final 191, 193
sentence-initial 16, 211
sentence pro-form 224
sentence(s) 16, 18, 19, 73, 79, 122, 134, 157, 186, 189–191, 193, 203, 205, 209–211, 213, 217, 218, 222, 224, 225, 230
separative 91, 92
serial 151–153, 156, 158, 162
single-class gender(s) 12, 13, 15
singular(s) 11–16, 19, 21–24, 28, 30, 40, 42, 43, 50, 51, 54, 55, 60, 64, 65, 67, 73, 80–82, 85, 109–143, 145–150, 153, 215, 216, 219, 223, 253
SOV 165
spatial relation 37, 78

speaker(s) 1, 2, 4, 37, 45, 85, 182, 207, 215–220
specific-generic 68
speech margin(s) 214–217, 219, 221, 223, 224
statement 47, 191, 198, 243
stem-final 27, 65
stem(s) 8, 20, 22–27, 29, 35, 37, 42, 43, 45, 46, 51, 58, 63–67, 69, 83, 84, 86–89, 91–96, 99, 100, 103, 107, 109, 114, 116, 118, 120, 122, 126, 128, 134, 136, 138, 141, 143, 145, 146, 149, 154, 157, 168, 211, 242, 254
story 46, 80, 109, 134, 186, 210, 223, 225, 228, 251
S-type 108, 112–114, 116, 118, 120, 122, 124, 126, 128, 130, 132
subject marker(s) 18, 62, 80, 84, 85, 100, 101, 102, 128, 132, 136, 137, 140, 141, 148, 149, 152, 153, 214–216, 219, 220
subject repetition 186
subject(s) 2, 16, 18, 19, 39, 47, 61, 62, 77, 80, 84, 85, 96, 97, 99–101, 104–106, 120, 126, 128, 132, 136, 137, 140, 141, 148, 149, 151–153, 155, 165, 167–169, 172, 177, 186, 187, 189–191, 195, 196, 201, 203–205, 209, 210, 213–220, 223, 225, 229, 230, 232
subject-verb 2, 165, 167
subordinate 106, 165
subsequent past 140
superlative(s) 49, 79
SVO 2, 165
syllable(s) 4–8, 22, 86

T

tag questions 198
temporal(s) 75, 161, 166, 167, 204, 214, 218, 225, 227
temporal sequence(s) 227
tense/aspect 7, 84–86, 100, 101, 103, 151, 152, 169
tense/aspect markers 100
tense/aspect/mood 84, 85, 103, 151, 152, 169
tense/aspect/mood/negation 151
tense(s) 7, 84–86, 100, 101, 103, 109, 112, 114, 118, 122, 126, 134, 138–140, 142, 143, 151, 152, 169, 196, 214, 227, 241
terminative 159
terms of address 26, 211
thought 214, 221, 223, 224, 278
time 1, 5, 15, 17, 38, 44, 58, 68, 71, 78, 99, 151, 161, 165–167, 171, 176–180, 194, 197, 201, 203, 204, 207, 208, 218, 227, 229, 233, 238, 249, 273, 285
time phrase(s) 177, 203, 204
time words 178
titles 26, 27
Tombel 1, 3, 177
tonal(ly) 38, 43, 58, 75, 84, 103, 124, 140, 141, 168, 192, 241
tone classes 35, 85, 86
tone(s) 2, 6–8, 19, 24, 25, 27, 30, 35, 37, 43, 45, 51, 52, 58, 64, 65, 67, 75, 80, 84–87, 100–103, 107–111, 113, 115–119, 121–141, 143–150, 153, 155, 156, 168, 189, 194, 196, 197, 200, 211, 241
topicalisation 81, 189, 199, 202, 210

topicalised 80, 81, 105, 106, 189–191, 200–202, 213
topic (marker) 96, 189, 199–201
trace(s) 1, 11, 43, 204–206
transitive clauses 153, 154, 173
transitivity 168
tritransitive clauses 175

U

undergoer 99
unmarked 34, 35, 85, 111, 202, 209, 232, 235, 237
unreleased 5
upstep 141

V

valency changes 96, 99
valency, valencies 89, 96–99, 151, 165, 167, 180, 221
velar nasal(s) 89, 96, 192, 253
verbal 24, 25, 44, 47, 79, 83, 86, 90, 96, 101, 134, 143, 157, 158, 160, 165, 167, 210, 213, 241, 243, 254
verbal clause(s) 165, 167, 241, 243
verbal extension(s) 25, 83, 86, 96, 134, 167, 213
verbal noun(s) 24
verb moods 145
verb negation 101
verb-object 8, 29, 156, 165
verb phrase(s) 78, 85, 151–153, 155, 158, 162
verb(s) 2, 4, 5, 7, 8, 16–18, 23–25, 27, 29, 31–33, 44, 47–49, 61, 62, 67, 68, 71–73, 75, 77–81, 83–89, 91–94, 96–109, 111, 113–121, 123, 125, 127,

Index 303

    129–131, 133–141, 143–162,
    165, 167–176, 180, 181, 187,
    189–191, 195, 196, 198, 199,
    202–206, 209, 210, 213–217,
    220–222, 224, 225, 227, 228,
    231, 235, 241–244
verbs of speech, perception and
    cognition 221
verbs relativised 209
verb stem(s) 24, 25, 67, 83,
    86–89, 91, 92, 96, 99, 100,
    103, 114, 118, 120, 134, 136,
    143, 145, 146, 149, 154, 157
verb structure 83
verb tense(s) 7, 100, 101, 109,
    134

verb-verb 155, 156
V-initial 22
vocative(s) 26, 27, 189, 211
vowel(s) 3–6, 8, 9, 22, 26, 27, 29,
    60, 79, 82, 83, 85, 87, 108,
    109, 124, 192, 200

W

Wamunshiya 2
Wh-questions 105, 106, 193
wordlists 2, 255

Y

yes/no questions 191

www.ingramcontent.com/pod-product-compliance
Lightning Source LLC
Chambersburg PA
CBHW070749020526
44115CB00032B/1595